EYEWITNESS

THE AMAZON

Yellow poison arrow frog

Fungus beetle

Cinnamon sticks

Hercules beetle

Souvenir mask made from natural rubber

Blue morpho butterfly

Golden tegu

Amazon River

EYEWITNESS
THE
AMAZON

Written by
TOM JACKSON

Paradise tanager

Macaw

Golden lion tamarin

Green-billed
toucan

Green and black poison dart frog

Penguin
Random
House

Vine snake

Consultant John Woodward

DK Delhi
Project editor Bharti Bedi
Editor Priyaneet Singh
Art editor Pooja Pipil
Design team Tanvi Sahu, Nidhi Rastogi, Nishesh Batnagar
DTP designers Nityanand Kumar, Pawan Kumar
Picture researcher Aditya Katyal
Jacket designer Suhita Dharamjit
Managing jackets editor Saloni Talwar
Pre-production manager Balwant Singh
Production manager Pankaj Sharma
Managing editor Kingshuk Ghoshal
Managing art editor Govind Mittal

DK London
Senior editor Chris Hawkes
Senior art editor Spencer Holbrook
US senior editor Margaret Parrish
Jacket editor Claire Gell
Jacket designer Laura Brim
Jacket design development manager Sophia MTT
Producer, pre-production Luca Frassinetti
Producer Gemma Sharpe
Managing editor Linda Esposito
Managing art editor Philip Letsu
Publisher Andrew Macintyre
Publishing director Jonathan Metcalf
Associate publishing director Liz Wheeler
Design director Stuart Jackman

First American Edition, 2015

Published in the United States by DK Publishing
345 Hudson Street, New York, New York 10014

A Penguin Random House Company

15 16 17 18 19 10 9 8 7 6 5 4 3 2 1
001—280097—June/15

Published in Great Britain by Dorling Kindersley Limited.

A catalog record for this book is available from the
Library of Congress.

ISBN 978-1-4654-3566-8 (Paperback)
ISBN 978-1-4654-3567-5 (ALB)

DK books are available at special discounts when
purchased in bulk for sales promotions, premiums,
fund-raising, or educational use. For details, contact:
DK Publishing Special Markets, 345 Hudson Street,
New York, New York 10014 or SpecialSales@dk.com.

Printed by South China Printing Co. Ltd., China

A WORLD OF IDEAS:
SEE ALL THERE IS TO KNOW
www.dk.com

Ocelot

Pineapple

Passion
fruit

Palm oil
and fruits

Amazonian
children on
a traditional
canoe

Contents

Gold mask from Colombia

The Amazon

The Amazon is the site of the world's largest rain forest and its biggest river system. The Amazon rain forest contains some large cities, and ancient settlements also exist deeper in the jungle. The amazing wildlife and geography and a wealth of culture—ancient and modern—make the region one of Earth's greatest treasures.

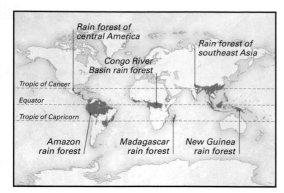

Rain forest of central America

Rain forest of southeast Asia

Congo River Basin rain forest

Tropic of Cancer

Equator

Tropic of Capricorn

Amazon rain forest

Madagascar rain forest

New Guinea rain forest

Rain forest climate

The Amazon, like all rain forests around the world, is in a region called the tropics—the land that lies between the Tropics of Cancer and Capricorn. In the tropics, it is hot all year round, and it rains a lot. Parts of the Amazon rain forest get just over 8 ft (2.5 m) of rain every year. All this heat and water make it possible for dense jungles to grow.

A sight to see

Tourists visit the Amazon rain forest to see its wildlife and amazing scenery. Tourism is one of the most important industries in this rain forest. It is a good way for the local people to make money without having to clear the forest to make way for farms and factories.

Toco toucan

Black caiman

Blue morpho butterfly

Agouti

Modern cities

The Amazon rain forest contains several big cities. Iquitos, in Peru, is one of the largest. It is home to 420,000 people, and it is just like any modern city—with parks, movie theaters, and a sports stadium. The main difference is that the city is surrounded by the rain forest and there are no highways linking it to the next town. The things people need to live arrive in ships sailing up the Amazon River.

Scarlet macaw

Tree crown

Blue and yellow macaw

It's a jungle out there
The Amazon rain forest is one of the most diverse habitats on Earth. One in 10 of the world's animal and plant species lives in its forests and rivers. Some animals, such as monkeys, seldom leave the tangle of branches, while plenty more live beside the shallow rivers. Others spend their entire lives on the forest floor.

Howler monkey

Three-toed sloth

Emerald tree boa

Giant otter

Capybara

Giant lily pad

Green iguana

Jaguar

The Amazon Basin

The Amazon rain forest exists because of South America's unique climate and geography. Storms from the Atlantic Ocean travel inland to produce rain on a vast, bowl-shaped area known as the Amazon Basin. Like a sink, or basin, in a bathroom, it collects the rain that falls into it. Some of that water feeds the rain forest; the rest gushes into rivers that join to form the Amazon River.

Ridge of mountain peaks surrounds the Amazon Basin

Expansive region
The Amazon Basin covers 40 percent of South America. The basin is surrounded by a wall of hills and mountains. Every drop of rain that falls inside this wall enters the Amazon River system.

ATLANTIC OCEAN

Kaieteur Falls= △ Mount Roraima

Angel Falls= △ Auyen Tepui

Llanos

Rio Negro

Amazon

Rio Purus

Rio Madeira

Rio Japura

Amazon

Rio Putumayo

Rio Jurua

Iquitos

Rio Ucayali

Volcan Sangay △

△ Volcan Cotopaxi

Yerupaja △

A N D E S

PACIFIC OCEAN

At the mouth
The Amazon has the largest mouth of any river—about a fifth of all the river water in the world enters the Atlantic Ocean through it. This water carries immense amounts of sediment, which eventually settles at the bottom of the ocean. That forms an area of seabed called the Amazon Cone, which reaches about 435 miles (700 km) from the coast.

Rainfall
The Amazon Basin receives an average of 7½ ft (2.3 m) of rainfall every year. However, this rain is not spread evenly. Most of it falls between November and May.

Chart: AVERAGE RAINFALL (MM) by MONTH

Month	Average Rainfall (mm)
JANUARY	265
FEBRUARY	295
MARCH	320
APRIL	305
MAY	260
JUNE	95
JULY	80
AUGUST	50
SEPTEMBER	75
OCTOBER	115
NOVEMBER	180
DECEMBER	220

Kaieteur Falls

Most of the Amazon Basin is very flat, so waterfalls and rapids are rare. The biggest waterfall inside the Basin is the Kaieteur Falls in the Guiana Highlands. Here, the water drops from a height of 741 ft (226 m), more than four times the height of the Niagara Falls. This waterfall carries a massive 23,400 cu ft per second (663 cu meters per second) of water.

KEY

- Basin boundary
- ● City
- ═ Waterfall
- △ Mountain

Belém
10
7
Rio Tocantins
Rio Araguaia
Rio Xingu
Atlantic Forest
● Rio de Janeiro
● Brasília
● São Paulo
Mato Grosso
Pantanal
Iguazu Falls ═
● Porto Velho
Rio Mamore
Lake Titicaca
● LA PAZ
△ Volcan Tutupaca
Salar de Uyuni
A N D E S
● Machu Picchu
3
Atacama Desert
4

Soil has a reddish tinge because of its iron content

Basin soil

Even though the world's largest rain forest grows out of it, the soil in the Amazon Basin is surprisingly thin and does not contain many nutrients. Most fertile soils are filled with organic material that forms from the remains of dead plants and animals. This is not the case in the Amazon region. Here, fungi and bacteria recycle these substances so quickly that they are absorbed immediately by the roots of living plants.

POINTS OF INTEREST

1 Tidal bore
A wave up to 13 ft (4 m) high that rushes upriver at high tide.

2 Meeting of the waters
The Rio Negro's dark waters meet the muddy Amazon River here.

3 Nevado Mismi
The source of the Amazon River in the Peruvian Andes.

4 Nazca Lines
Ancient patterns cut into the desert by the Nazca people.

5 Lábrea
One end of the Trans-Amazonian Highway (runs through the forest).

6 Rio Negro Bridge
The first major road bridge to cross a river in the region.

7 Carajás Mine
The largest iron ore mine in the world.

8 Kuelap
An ancient fortress built by the Chachapoya people.

9 Marajó island
The largest river island in the world.

10 Tucuruí Dam
A huge power plant built across the Rio Tocantins.

Drought in the basin

These fishermen from Marajó Island, on the Amazon River, have nowhere to paddle their boat. In July and August, the water level around the Amazon River's mouth drops because of less rain farther upstream.

The Amazon River

The Amazon River is the largest river in the world—it is twice as large as its nearest rival, the Congo in Central Africa. The water flows from west to east and eventually divides to form a huge 202-mile- (325-km-) wide estuary near Macapá, Brazil. Here, the river empties enough water into the Atlantic Ocean to fill 5,000 Olympic swimming pools every minute.

A wooden cross marks the Amazon River's source

The source

The Amazon River's source is Nevado Mismi in the mountains of Peru. From here, meltwater flows through the mountains into the Amazon and on to the Atlantic. The Amazon is commonly thought to be 4,049 miles (6,516 km) long, second in length only to the Nile in Africa, although some scientists believe it could be longer.

Meeting of the waters

The Amazon River's largest tributary is the Rio Negro, or black river. Its water is filled with chemicals washed out of soil and plants, which make it very dark. It joins the Amazon near the Brazilian city of Manaus, but the waters of the two rivers do not mix for a few miles, creating a two-tone river.

The river sea

The Amazon contains so much water that it is more like a sea than a river. The main channel is about 165 ft (50 m) deep and can be more than 6 miles (10 km) wide when flooded by heavy rains.

A satellite image of the mouth of the Amazon River

Rio Negro
Amazon
Basin
Amazon River
Rio Ucayali
Rio Madeira
Rio Tapajós
Rio Xingu
Rio Tocantins

Great roar

Top surfers come to ride the Amazon River's tidal bore—a wave created in the river's wide mouth by the ocean tides. Twice a day, water from the Atlantic surges up the river, reversing its flow. When the tide is high and the river level is low, a 13-ft- (4-m-) high wave rushes up the river, traveling up to 500 miles (800 km) upstream. The Brazilian name for the wave is the *pororoca*, or "great roar."

Many branches

The Amazon River flows from Peru to the Atlantic coast of Brazil. Along the way, it is joined by about 1,100 tributaries, many of which are huge rivers. The Madeira, Negro, and Paraná Rivers, for example, each carry more water than any river in Europe or North America. At its mouth, the Amazon again splits into several channels, creating the world's largest river islands; the biggest, Marajó, is roughly the size of Switzerland.

Mixing with the ocean

When it reaches the sea, the Amazon River's muddy freshwater flows 250 miles (400 km) out into the Atlantic. The tucuxi, an Amazon River dolphin, also follows the river out to sea. Some groups of tucuxi have even been found living near Rio de Janeiro, more than 1,500 miles (2,500 km) to the south.

Land of forests

The Amazon Basin contains the world's largest tropical forest—10 times the size of Spain. Most of the basin is covered in lowland rain forest, which gets plenty of rain, so the trees here grow faster and taller than anywhere else in the Amazon rain forest. This region is also home to other types of forest, depending on climate and geography.

Palm

Along the southern edge of the Amazon rain forest, where it is a little drier, the forest is dominated by palm trees. The most common type of palm is the babassu, which local people use both as a building material and as a source of food.

Woody vines

Lianas are thick, woody vines that grow up from the ground using the branches of trees to support them. Once it reaches sunlight, a liana spreads out, running from tree to tree, sprouting leafy branches. A liana forest grows in places in which trees are widely spaced, and the vines can fill the gaps between them. It is most common in the hills to the south of the Amazon River's mouth.

Dry forests

The arid highland areas around the edge of the Amazon rain forest are covered in caatinga, meaning "white forest" in the local language—a reference to the area's dry, sandy soil. Only small trees and thorny shrubs can grow here. Other areas that are too dry for full forests are covered in cerrado, the Brazilian word for savanna.

Underwater roots

After heavy rains, river levels in the Amazon can rise by several yards, leading to flooding in large parts of the rain forest. Roots need air to function well, so trees in a flooded forest do not grow as tall as in other areas, since their roots are submerged.

Seeds in water
The rubber plant times the release of its seeds—which float—for when the water is at its highest. The seeds are a source of food for many fish, but those that are not eaten are washed far and wide and grow into new trees when the water goes down.

Cloud forest
Mountain forests are known as "cloud forests," as they are often shrouded in thick fog. The weather on mountain slopes is different from that in the lowlands: it rains less, and the temperature is lower. The trees there do not grow tall and are often covered in mosses and creepers.

Near the Atlantic
A woolly spider monkey can be seen climbing a vine in the Atlantic Forest on the Brazilian Highlands, near the Atlantic Ocean. A band of hills cuts off this area from the main Amazon Basin. Much of the wildlife found here is unique to this region. The area is also one of the most deforested zones in South America, and many of its animals are endangered.

Around the rain forest

The Amazon Basin is surrounded on three sides by mountains. The Guiana Highlands in the north feature incredible waterfalls. To the south are the Brazilian Highlands, a huge mass of rolling hills. To the west lie the Andes—the world's longest mountain range, dotted with volcanoes.

Wall of mountains

The Andes are about 4,350 miles (7,000 km) long and run from Venezuela in the north to the southern tip of South America. The Central Andes, which run through Ecuador, Peru, and Bolivia, are closest to the Amazon Basin. They contain several high, flat areas on which ancient civilizations, such as the Incas, once thrived.

Floating village

The body of water shown here is Lake Titicaca, South America's largest freshwater lake. Nestled nearly 2.5 miles (4 km) above sea level in the Andes, it is inhabited by the Uru people, who live in floating houses.

Table mountain

Flat summit is covered in rocks and pools of rainwater

Salt flat

Ten cities the size of Paris could fit inside the Salar de Uyuni—the world's largest salt flat. Located in the Bolivian Andes, it was formed when a prehistoric lake dried out, leaving behind a layer of salt. It is also the flattest place on Earth.

Table mountain

At a height of 9,219 ft (2,810 m), Mount Roraima is one of the highest points in the Guiana Highlands. Two billion years old, it is made of a block of sandstone that was left behind after the softer rocks around it were washed away.

Cracked crust covers lower layers of salty slush

Mountain animals

The high slopes of the Andes Mountains can be very cold and dry. Llamas survive there because they have thick wool. Like their relative the camel, they can also survive for long periods without water.

125-ft- (38-m-) tall concrete statue

Crowded coast

Seen here is the statue of Christ the Redeemer looking down on Rio de Janeiro from a forested peak. This city, which is home to about 12 million people, is one of the largest cities in the Brazilian Highlands and is located where the hills meet the Atlantic Ocean.

Long, flexible neck

Anhinga

Wetlands

In addition to the Amazon River, there are also vast wetlands that collect water in the Amazon Basin. To the south is the Pantanal, the planet's biggest swamp; to the north is Los Llanos, a grassland that turns into a huge temporary marshland once a year. These wetlands are fertile and have been important farming regions for centuries. They also contain unique animals, such as the saberfin killifish and the Orinoco crocodile.

Llanos

Pantanal

Waterways

Water flowing from the hills around the Pantanal collects in a wetland, where it becomes trapped in the basin and drains away through the Paraguay River. Los Llanos is fed by the yearly flooding of the Orinoco River that covers the low areas of Venezuela and Colombia for months on end.

Spear fishing

The anhinga is a fish-hunting water bird that lives in the Pantanal. It spears its prey with its long beak and then swallows the prey whole. Its name means "snakebird" in the local language. When it is in the water, only its long neck and head are visible, making it look like a snake rising out of the water.

Powerful jaw muscles

Golden lizard

The golden tegu is one of the largest lizards in South America, growing to a length of 3¼ ft (1 m). It hunts for food on land and in water, and can stay underwater for around 20 minutes at a time. This reptile eats all kinds of food, from fruits to dead animals.

Thick tail

Golden tegu

Pink tree

Unlike most forest trees, which are evergreens, the pink lapacho tree is deciduous—it loses its leaves seasonally. It sheds its leaves in the dry, winter months, and grows its flowers before the leaves return in spring. This makes it look pink and attracts pollinators such as hummingbirds.

Terena

Seen here is an archer at Brazil's Indigenous Games in 2013. He is representing the Terena tribe, who have lived around the Pantanal wetland for thousands of years. Terena warriors used their weapons for real recently, as they took back their traditional lands from farmers who were using it illegally. Despite their ancient customs, they organized the campaign using Facebook.

Cattle country

Huge herds of cattle are raised on the Pantanal and Los Llanos. Most of the wetland areas are flooded for only part of the year, so when the water recedes, lush pastures grow on the fertile soil. Cowboys—known as *Pantaneiros* in the Pantanal and *Llaneros* in Los Llanos—look after the cattle herds in these pastures.

Pantaneiros

Giant lily pads

The Victoria lilies of the Pantanal have pads about 8¼ ft (2.5 m) wide, which makes them the largest leaves in the world. Although they are fragile, the pads can support the weight of small animals, such as frogs and birds, if their weight is spread evenly. The lily's large flowers also float on the surface. They are pollinated by beetles that fly from one bloom to the other.

Plants and fungi

Of the 40,000 species of plant in the Amazon rain forest, only about a third are trees. The rest include plants without roots that collect water from the air, long creepers, and even species that catch insects. This region also teems with fungi, many of which grow in the soil and turn dead leaves into vital nutrients for plants.

Kapok

Growing to roughly 230 ft (70 m) tall and about 10 ft (3 m) around the base, the kapok is one of the largest trees in the rain forest. Its trunk grows large buttress roots, which help support the tree.

Plant ponds

This poison dart frog raises its tadpole in a small pond that has formed in the base of a bromeliad plant. Bromeliads have fleshy leaves that fan out in circles, creating bowl shapes.

Sticky liquid on soft tentacle

Moth stuck to leaf

Eating bugs

Sundews live in swampy regions of the rain forest. Their leaves are covered in soft tentacles that are coated in sticky liquid. When an insect lands on a leaf, it becomes stuck. The leaf then curls around the insect and digests it, extracting useful nutrients.

Symbiosis

Cecropia trees recruit an army of ants to defend them against attack. The small trees have hollow areas in their stems and branches in which the ants make their home. In return, the ants clean fungus off the leaves and attack other insects that venture on to the plant, including those that come to feed on the leaves. As a reward, the plant produces oily nodules, which the ants cut off and eat. The way in which both plant and animal benefit from one another is called symbiosis.

Cecropia ant carrying oily nodule produced by plant _____

Up in the air

About a quarter of rain forest plants do not grow a long stem or trunk to reach sunlight. Instead, they grow on bigger plants above the ground. These plants—called epiphytes—have leaves, flowers, and fruits, but no true roots. They get the water they need from the moisture in the air.

Spores fall out of cap as tiny, cup-shaped mushroom dries out _____

Strangler fig

This network of stems (above) once contained a tree trunk. The stems belong to a strangler fig, a plant that grows from a seed at the top of a tall tree. The roots grow down to the ground to get water and nutrients and end up encircling the tree trunk. Eventually, the tree inside dies under the weight of the fig and rots away.

Forest mushrooms

Fungi are key waste recyclers in the forest. These mushrooms (right) are growing on and inside the dead wood, helping it to rot away and release nutrients into the soil.

Birds of the Amazon

Around 1,500 bird species live in the Amazon rain forest. They range from macaws—the world's biggest parrots—to tiny hummingbirds. Many water birds also live in the region's vast wetlands and along its riverbanks. Forest birds have plenty of places to hide, but the males can use their bright plumage when they want to be seen, especially when they want to attract mates.

Green-billed toucan

Long bill

The toucan's long, chunky bill makes up about a quarter of its body length. However, the bill is light and is made of a spongy bone covered in a coat of keratin, the material found in a human's fingernails. The bill has rough edges that are useful for cracking nuts and peeling fruits. Toucans rarely fly far, preferring to hop from branch to branch.

Hovering to feed

Although it weighs only 0.03 oz (9 g) and is just 6 in (15 cm) long, the swallowtail hummingbird is the largest hummingbird in the Amazon. Living at the mid-level of the rain forest, its wings beat at a rate of 50 times a second, allowing it to hover in front of a flower while sipping the nectar with its long tongue.

High fliers

Brightly colored macaws flying high above the trees are easy to notice. These large birds eat unripe fruits that most forest animals ignore, as the macaw's hooked beak can rip away the tough outer layers of the fruits. They also often gather in large flocks on muddy riverbanks, where they lick the soil to get the salts and nutrients missing in their food.

Laughing falcon

This bird of prey with a high-pitched cackle perches above a clearing and looks for prey on the ground. When it spots a victim, such as a snake, it swoops down and lands on top of it. It kills its victims with a quick bite to the back of the head.

Coral snake

Bright plumage

Tail makes up more than half the bird's length

Hanging nests

These bags of woven grasses and twigs are the nests of oropendolas—songbirds that eat insects and fruits. Each nest cluster is a breeding colony ruled by a single male, who mates with most of the females there. The female lays two eggs at the bottom of the nest, and her chicks learn to fly about a month after hatching.

Adults have a crest of spiked feathers

Stinkbird

The strange hoatzin ferments meals of fruits and leaves in a bloated stomach filled with bacteria. Local people call it the stinkbird, because its digestion produces bad odors. Hoatzin chicks are born with claws on their wings, which they use to climb through branches before learning to fly.

Fishing for food

The boat-billed heron is one of the many water birds that live in the Amazon rain forest. It uses its long legs to wade through shallow water when looking for food. It scoops up food using its wide, shovel-shaped bill, which helps it to feel for prey in the mud and among the weeds. The heron shown here is about to feast on a fish, but this species also eats shellfish, water voles, and birds' eggs.

Colorful songbird

Feeding on insects, paradise tanagers are little songbirds that live in the forest canopy, far above the ground. Although tanagers can be difficult to spot, the males are brightly colored so that they can get noticed by mates. They show off their plumes by performing a bowing dance on a perch. By contrast, the females tend to stay out of sight, building small, cup-shaped nests hidden among the leaves.

Amazon monkeys

Some 130 species of monkey live in the Amazon rain forest, eating leaves, fruits, and insects. The monkeys of the Amazon belong to a group called New World monkeys that descended from African monkeys. Unlike their Old World relatives, Amazon monkeys have flat noses with nostrils that point sideways. Many species also have a flexible tail that can work as a hand or foot to wrap around branches and grip objects.

Adult marmosets are only 5 in (12 cm) long

Agile climber

Named after the way it looks when it hangs from its strong tail, the spider monkey lives at the top of tall trees and almost never comes to the ground. They gather in troops of about 30, and work together to protect a feeding territory, seeking out food such as fruits, leaves, and even birds' eggs.

Mini monkey

The pygmy marmoset is the tiniest monkey in the world. It lives in small bushes that grow along riverbanks and the edge of the forest. Its main food is sap—a sweet, sticky liquid made by plants.

Hair on forehead can be raised

Brown capuchin monkey

Hard nut cracked open with stone

Clever capuchins

There are nine species of capuchin monkey in the Amazon rain forest. They are highly intelligent and are known to use simple tools, such as stones, to crack open nuts and a sponge of mashed-up leaves to soak up fruit juices. The capuchin monkeys were given their name because their brown fur and the dark "cap" on their head reminded early European explorers of Capuchin monks.

Capuchin monk

Loud howler

Howler monkeys are not only the largest and noisiest monkeys in the Amazon rain forest, but also the loudest land animals. Their calls can travel up to 2.5 miles (4 km) through the forest. They use their large, flexible throats to boost their volume when calling from the treetops. Males do most of the calling, to attract females or to warn other males to stay away.

Howler monkeys can grow up to 35 in (90 cm) tall

Dark and hairless face

Nocturnal monkey

The douroucoulis, or owl monkeys, are the only monkey species in the world that is nocturnal, or active at night. Their huge eyes allow them to see well enough in the dark to run and jump through the branches. They move around in small family groups, and if one monkey sees a predator, such as a snake, it will give out a long "wook" call to warn the others.

Large eyes only see in black-and-white

Lion's mane

The flowing mane of a golden lion tamarin resembles the mane of a lion. These brightly colored monkeys live in the dense, hot, and humid jungles of the Atlantic Forest. They are most active in the cool mornings and evenings and take naps during the middle of the day. These tamarins live in groups of about eight. Only the chief male and female breed, while the other group members help them raise their young.

On the forest floor

Not all animals in the Amazon rain forest live in trees—many species, including the giant armadillo and the peccary, also live on the forest floor. The thick covering of trees means very little sunlight reaches the ground. There is not much wind down there either, and the moisture in the air makes it very humid.

Flatworm

Most of the world's flatworms live in water, but it is so humid in the Amazon rain forest that some, such as the Amazonian land planarian (above), slither around on the ground. If it is bitten in half by a predator, a new worm will grow back from each half.

Circles of pale fur around eyes look like eyeglasses

Tough, dark brown shell composed of bony plates

Giant armadillo

The Amazon's giant armadillo— the world's largest species of armadillo—can grow up to 5 ft (1.5 m) long. This forest giant forages at night and digs its way into termite mounds and ant nests using long claws on its forelegs. It licks up the insects inside using a long, sticky tongue.

Spectacled bear

The spectacled bear is the only bear species in the Amazon rain forest. It is not a fierce hunter. During the day, it prefers to sleep in a cave or hollow tree. At night, it climbs through low branches, feeding on fruits, lush leaves, and any insects and rodents it can catch.

Long claws help to grip while climbing

Pack hunters

Bush dogs are related to wolves. They work in packs of around 12 to chase rodents and ground birds through the forest. They make squeaking calls to keep track of each other among the thick undergrowth.

Peccaries

Even though it resembles a wild boar, the white-lipped peccary is only distantly related to pigs. Moving through the forest in herds of more than 100, it uses its flexible snout to find roots, mushrooms, and rotting fruits to eat.

Deadly viper

The lancehead is a venomous viper that lies hidden among fallen leaves and strikes quickly when prey, such as a rodent, walks past. Its venom does not kill straight away. If its prey runs away, the snake tracks its victim using heat-sensitive pits on its snout.

Arrow-shaped head gives the snake its name

Exposed tip of the tail may help lure prey when the viper is hidden on the forest floor

Jungle cat

The ocelot may look like a leopard, but it is not much bigger than a domestic cat. During the day it sleeps on a shady branch, but at night it hunts, mostly on the ground, tracking small prey, such as opossums, mice, and frogs, by their smell. It has excellent night vision.

Long whiskers help the ocelot to feel its way around

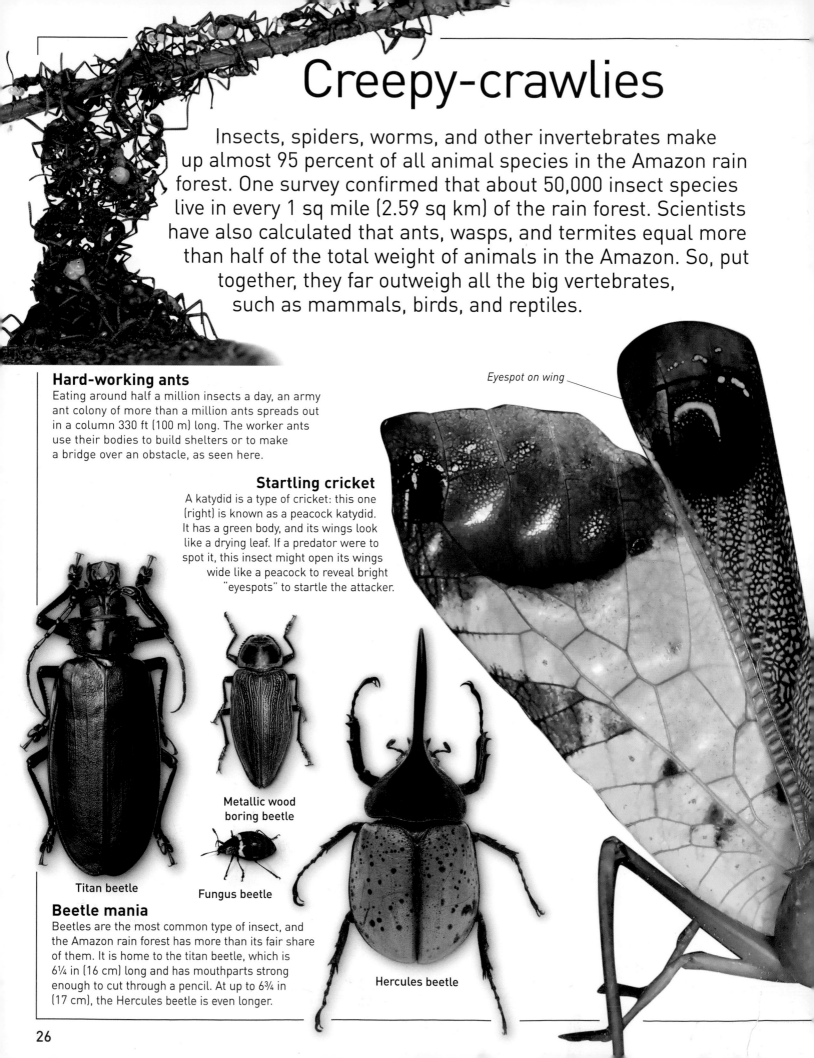

Creepy-crawlies

Insects, spiders, worms, and other invertebrates make up almost 95 percent of all animal species in the Amazon rain forest. One survey confirmed that about 50,000 insect species live in every 1 sq mile (2.59 sq km) of the rain forest. Scientists have also calculated that ants, wasps, and termites equal more than half of the total weight of animals in the Amazon. So, put together, they far outweigh all the big vertebrates, such as mammals, birds, and reptiles.

Hard-working ants

Eating around half a million insects a day, an army ant colony of more than a million ants spreads out in a column 330 ft (100 m) long. The worker ants use their bodies to build shelters or to make a bridge over an obstacle, as seen here.

Startling cricket

A katydid is a type of cricket: this one (right) is known as a peacock katydid. It has a green body, and its wings look like a drying leaf. If a predator were to spot it, this insect might open its wings wide like a peacock to reveal bright "eyespots" to startle the attacker.

Eyespot on wing

Titan beetle

Metallic wood boring beetle

Fungus beetle

Hercules beetle

Beetle mania

Beetles are the most common type of insect, and the Amazon rain forest has more than its fair share of them. It is home to the titan beetle, which is 6¼ in (16 cm) long and has mouthparts strong enough to cut through a pencil. At up to 6¾ in (17 cm), the Hercules beetle is even longer.

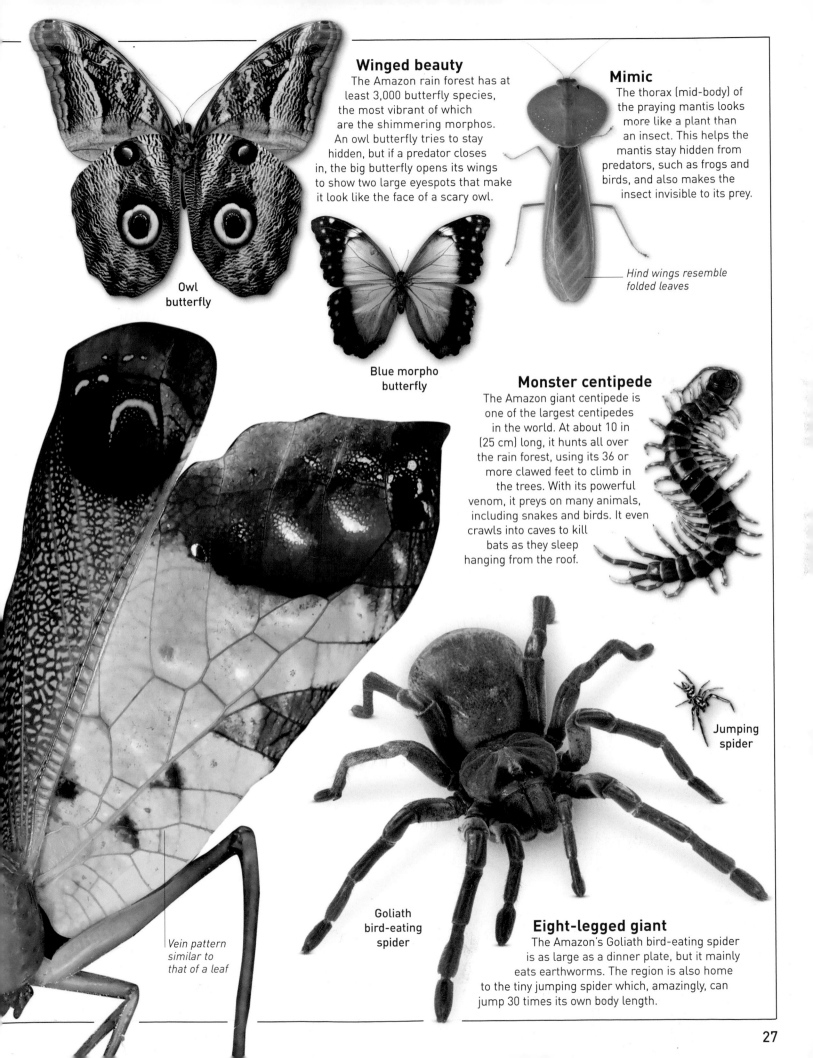

Winged beauty

The Amazon rain forest has at least 3,000 butterfly species, the most vibrant of which are the shimmering morphos. An owl butterfly tries to stay hidden, but if a predator closes in, the big butterfly opens its wings to show two large eyespots that make it look like the face of a scary owl.

Owl butterfly

Blue morpho butterfly

Mimic

The thorax (mid-body) of the praying mantis looks more like a plant than an insect. This helps the mantis stay hidden from predators, such as frogs and birds, and also makes the insect invisible to its prey.

Hind wings resemble folded leaves

Monster centipede

The Amazon giant centipede is one of the largest centipedes in the world. At about 10 in (25 cm) long, it hunts all over the rain forest, using its 36 or more clawed feet to climb in the trees. With its powerful venom, it preys on many animals, including snakes and birds. It even crawls into caves to kill bats as they sleep hanging from the roof.

Jumping spider

Vein pattern similar to that of a leaf

Goliath bird-eating spider

Eight-legged giant

The Amazon's Goliath bird-eating spider is as large as a dinner plate, but it mainly eats earthworms. The region is also home to the tiny jumping spider which, amazingly, can jump 30 times its own body length.

In and around the river

Several animals that are more common in the ocean have made their homes in the rivers of the Amazon Basin. For example, there are dolphins living in the flooded forests of Peru and Ecuador, 1,865 miles (3,000 km) from the ocean. Some unusual animals also live on the riverbanks, including tapirs, which are South America's closest relatives to the horse.

River mermaid
The Amazonian manatee looks like a seal, but it is an aquatic relative of the elephant. Some manatees—although not this species— live in the ocean, and legend has it that lonely sailors mistook them for mermaids.

Flippers help the Amazonian manatee to steer in the water

Giant rodent

The order of animals known as rodents includes small animals such as mice and squirrels. At 4¼ ft (1.3 m) long and weighing as much as an adult human, the capybara is the world's largest rodent. Its sharp front teeth can slice through plant stems. Capybaras live in herds that graze together on lush riverbanks.

Thick fur keeps out water

Eyes on top of the head help the capybara to stay alert even when it is almost completely submerged in water

Barrel-shaped body contains a large gut that is ideal for digesting plants

Feet are partially webbed, which helps when swimming

Flexible snout helps to sniff out food, water, and mates

Rump

Brazilian tapir

At 6½ ft (2 m) long, the tapir (left) is the largest land animal in the Amazon rain forest. During the day, it stays hidden in dense bushes. At night, it comes out to graze on the riverbank and take a swim, wallowing in the shallow water.

River dolphin

The Amazon River dolphin, or boto, spends most of the year in the wide, deep rivers. In the rainy season, the rivers flood parts of the forest, and the dolphins follow the water to feed among the tree trunks.

Wide hooves make it easier to walk on soft mud

Giant otter

Measuring up to 4½ ft (1.4 m) long, the Amazonian giant otter is the largest otter in the world. Large webbed feet and a long flattened tail make it a very powerful swimmer. Because it is not very agile on land, this species seldom ventures far from the riverbank.

Yapok

A relative of Australia's kangaroos and koalas, the yapok is an aquatic marsupial—a mammal that carries its babies in a pouch and that spends much of its time in the water. The yapok's pouch is watertight, so the young do not drown.

Hunting for food

The Amazon rain forest teems with deadly hunters—on the ground, in the water, and in the treetops. They include not only big cats, massive alligators, and giant snakes, but also the world's deadliest spiders, birds big enough to kill monkeys, and a bat that can suck your blood as you sleep.

Front legs raised during attack

Deadly hunter
Although most spiders are harmless to humans, the Brazilian wandering spider is the most dangerous spider on Earth. In the absence of treatment, its venom could kill a person in 30 minutes. This deadly spider chases mice on the forest floor or frogs among the leaves, killing them in seconds with a single bite.

Flat snout used to feel for warm skin

Bloodsucker
Named after Count Dracula, the vampire bat comes out to feed on dark, moonless nights. It lands near sleeping mammals, including humans, and crawls over their bodies searching for a warm patch of skin. It then makes a tiny cut with its pointed fangs and drinks the blood that flows out.

Giant snake
At up to 16½ ft (5 m) long, the green anaconda—the world's largest snake—spends most of its time in shallow water, ready to ambush prey that wanders too close to the water's edge. The anaconda shown here has captured a caiman—another fearsome predator. The snake kills its victim by squeezing it so tightly that it stops breathing. And like all snakes, it swallows its prey headfirst and whole.

Night stalker

The jaguar is the Amazon rain forest's largest predator, and is usually a lone, nocturnal hunter. It leaps on its prey, such as tapirs and caimans, from above, killing them with a skull-crushing bite. By day, the jaguar snoozes on a shaded branch. The fur's pattern helps the jaguar blend in to its environment.

6½-ft- (2-m-) wide wingspan

On the wing

The harpy eagle is the largest bird of prey in the Amazon rain forest. It perches high up in the forest, and when it spots its prey, it swoops down and grabs its victim with its huge talons. This eagle often captures monkeys, killing them with a bite from its hooked beak, and carries them back to its perch. It also dives to the forest floor to grab ground mammals, and chases smaller birds through the trees, plucking them out of the air.

Talons are the longest among all eagles

Head thrown back to swallow small prey whole

Killer caiman

The Amazon rain forest's caiman (a type of alligator) can grow up to 20 ft (6 m) long. They lie in shallow water and when land animals, such as peccaries, come too close, they pull them under the water and drown them. They will also attack fish and birds on the water's surface.

Short, stocky legs are good for swimming and climbing

Of both worlds

Frogs, toads, and salamanders are amphibians—animals that live in water and on land. Yet, most amphibians cannot survive for long without water, which is abundant in the Amazon rain forest. A huge range of amphibians thrive there—from wormlike creatures that burrow through damp soil, to frogs that are poisonous to touch.

Large eyes help to see at night

Salamander
As expert climbers, the Amazon rain forest's salamanders have webbed feet to grip leaves and branches. Most active at night, they catch insects with their long, sticky tongues. They lack lungs and do not breathe air; instead they absorb all the oxygen they need through their moist skin.

Pointed snout pushes through soil

Hornlike projections above the eyes

Limbless
Although it resembles a worm or snake, this creature is a type of caecilian—a limbless amphibian that burrows through soil and eats underground insects. Strangely enough, caecilian babies feed on their mother's skin, pausing occasionally to let it grow back.

Big mouth
One of the Amazon rain forest's largest amphibians, the horned frog can grow up to 8 in (20 cm) long. This frog hides itself in leaves, then uses its huge mouth, measuring half the size of its body, to gulp down mice, lizards, and other frogs.

See-through
The glass frog's upper body looks green, but its belly skin has no color, making its heart, stomach, and bones clearly visible. It sleeps on large leaves, and the transparent skin lets the leaf color show through from underneath, making it hard to spot.

Paradoxical frog
A paradox is something that seems impossible but is true. This Amazonian frog is a paradox because its tadpole, which grows up to 9 in (22 cm) long, gets smaller as it gets older. When it is an adult frog, it is a third of that size.

Yellow poison arrow frog

Red poison dart frog

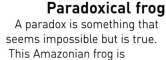

Green and black poison dart frog

Tree-dweller

The red-eyed tree frog (right) has long, slender legs for climbing and jumping, and its fingers and toes have round suction cups for gripping branches. Like other tree frogs, it lays its eggs on leaves overhanging a pool. When the tadpoles hatch, they fall into the water beneath.

Bright coloration startles predators

Suction pads on fingers help frog to climb

Pretty poisonous

Poison dart frogs are named after the Amazonian hunters who use the powerful toxins in the skin of the species to make poisoned darts for killing monkeys. These toxins come from the chemicals in ants and other insects that these frogs eat. The toxic skin is brightly colored, which serves as a warning to predators to stay away.

Unusual toad

The Suriname toad (above) spends its whole life in water. It uses its long, sensitive fingers to find small fish and other prey in the riverbed. During mating, the male loads fertilized eggs onto the female's back, where they are absorbed into the skin. Instead of tadpoles, tiny toadlets hatch from the eggs and burst out of the mother's back.

Blue poison dart frog

Amazon dart frog

Pasco poison dart frog

Imitating poison frog

Forest reptiles

Reptiles have scaly skin and live in the warmer parts of the world. From killer crocodiles to venomous snakes, around 500 reptile species live in the tree tops and on the river beds of the Amazon rain forest. However, there are probably many more that scientists are yet to discover.

Warning flap
This tree-climbing anole lizard has a skin flap on its neck called a dewlap. When a predator comes too close, the lizard unfurls the flap, scaring off the predator. Males have brighter dewlaps than females, and they often flash them in and out to attract mates.

Snorkeling turtle
Like all reptiles, the mata mata turtle (left) breathes air. But instead of coming to the surface to breathe, this little river turtle has a flexible snout with long nostrils, which it uses like a snorkel. To eat, it waits among river plants, then opens its mouth very wide to suck in its prey, such as small fish.

Tiny alligator
Seen here is a baby dwarf caiman (a type of alligator). Among all crocodiles and alligators, dwarf caimans are the world's smallest, growing to little more than 4 ft (1.2 m) in length. They live in small streams and hunt for water snails, crabs, and frogs.

Males have longer spikes than females

Jungle dragon
Also known as a wood lizard, the forest dragon has a ridge of armored spikes along its back and tail. If threatened, it opens its mouth in a wide gape, revealing bright pink gums. The sudden flash of color often startles any attacker and helps the lizard to escape.

Sensing heat
The bright green body of the emerald tree boa helps it to blend in with the leaves. At night it hunts for mice, using heat-sensitive pits on its snout to track prey in the dark. These pits sense body heat given off by other animals.

Heat sensitive pits are located along upper and lower lips

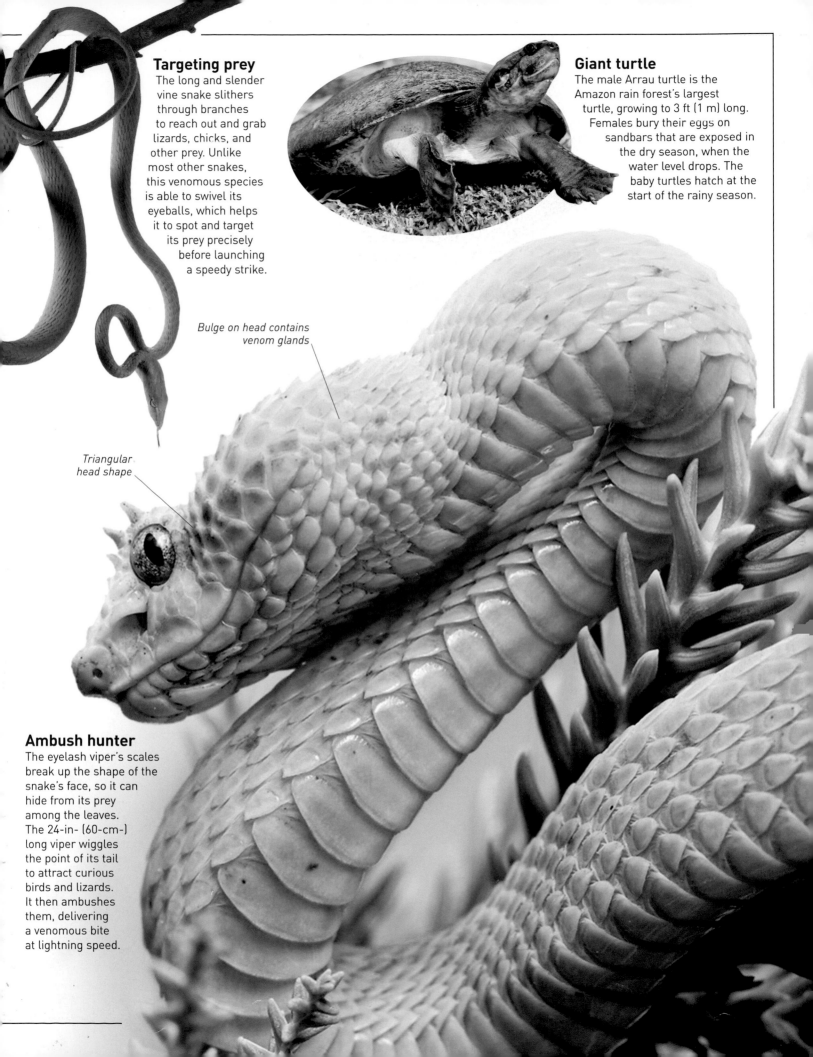

Targeting prey

The long and slender vine snake slithers through branches to reach out and grab lizards, chicks, and other prey. Unlike most other snakes, this venomous species is able to swivel its eyeballs, which helps it to spot and target its prey precisely before launching a speedy strike.

Giant turtle

The male Arrau turtle is the Amazon rain forest's largest turtle, growing to 3 ft (1 m) long. Females bury their eggs on sandbars that are exposed in the dry season, when the water level drops. The baby turtles hatch at the start of the rainy season.

Bulge on head contains venom glands

Triangular head shape

Ambush hunter

The eyelash viper's scales break up the shape of the snake's face, so it can hide from its prey among the leaves. The 24-in- (60-cm-) long viper wiggles the point of its tail to attract curious birds and lizards. It then ambushes them, delivering a venomous bite at lightning speed.

Amazon fish

The many rivers found in the Amazon Basin are home to nearly 5,600 species of fish—15 percent of all the world's fish species. The water in some places does not contain much oxygen, especially when the river levels are low. As a result, even though they all have gills, some Amazon fish are able to breathe air as well.

Feeding frenzy

A piranha only grows to about 8 in (20 cm) long, yet, despite its size, this sharp-toothed, meat-eating fish has a fearsome reputation. It is said that these fish can devour large animals, including cattle and humans, within minutes. However, these attacks are rare, and they only occur when the river level is low and the piranhas are bunched together looking for food.

Venomous sting

Rays, like this stingray, are related to sharks, and the Amazon River is home to more than 20 species of them. Known as the ocellate river stingray, this fish defends itself with a venomous spike in its tail. However, it does not use its tail to catch prey, which includes crustaceans and snails.

Giant fish

The arapaima is the largest freshwater fish in the world, weighing up to 450 lb (200 kg). The longest specimen ever caught was 15 ft (4.25 m) long, but most are about half that length. This giant fish has gills, but it also breathes air using a lunglike organ, taking a gulp of air every 10 minutes or so.

Deadly shark

At 10 ft (3 m) long, the bull shark is one of the largest sharks in the world. Known for its aggressive nature, this predator specializes in hunting in shallow, muddy, coastal water. Bull sharks have been spotted 2,500 miles (4,000 km) upstream on the Amazon River.

Water monkey

The arowana feeds mainly on fish. However, it can also leap up to 6½ ft (2 m) out of the water to snatch birds, bugs, or other prey. Because of this unique behavior, locals refer to this species as the "water monkey."

Distinctive metallic blue and orange stripe

Tetras

Just ¾ in (2 cm) long, neon tetras are bright little freshwater fish found commonly in home aquaria all over the world. However, their natural habitat is in the Amazon River. The first pet tetras were taken from this river in the 1930s. They are bred in captivity today, with nearly 20 million being sold every year in the United States alone.

Ancient civilizations

People have lived in the Amazon region for at least 11,000 years. For a long time, scientists thought the region was an untouched wilderness, but new evidence shows that large settlements existed even in the densest parts of the jungle. The civilizations that grew up around the edge of the rain forest left the greatest mark. They included the mighty Inca Empire of the Andes.

Marajoara pottery
This jar contained the ashes of a person who died about 1,000 years ago and was made by the Marajoara people. They are named after Marajó Island, which, located at the Amazon River's mouth, was the center of their civilization. Much of what is known about them comes from their pottery.

Cliff burial
This 500-year-old mummy was buried in a cave carved into a cliff in the Peruvian Andes. The cold, dry air in the Andean mountains has preserved several mummies. They belonged to a culture known as the Chachapoyans, also called Warriors of the Clouds because they lived in cloud forests in an area located in present-day Peru.

Buildings made from stone blocks

Cloud city

Shown here are the ruins of a walled city called Kuelap, in the cloud forests of Peru, above the Amazon Basin. The Chachapoyans built this city in the 6th century CE, fortifying it to defend against invaders. However, the Inca—from the other side of the Andes—conquered the Chachapoyans in the 15th century. When the Spanish took over the region a century later, Kuelap was eventually abandoned.

Ruins surround a reconstructed house at Kuelap

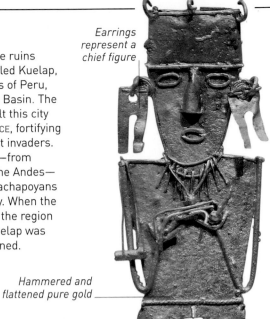

Earrings represent a chief figure

Hammered and flattened pure gold

Made of gold

The Muisca people, who lived in the mountains of Colombia, made this gold figure. In one ritual, a Muisca chief was covered in gold dust, which he washed off in a sacred mountain lake. Priests threw other gold artifacts into the lake as gifts to the goddess who was believed to live there. These rituals would eventually give rise to the myth of *El Dorado*, the legendary kingdom of gold.

The great Inca

Machu Picchu, seen below in ruins, is a city built by the once-powerful Inca Empire in the Andes, about 155 miles (250 km) north of the Amazon River's source. It was built around 1450 as a retreat for the Inca emperor Pachauti.

Ciudad Perdida

The Ciudad Perdida, or "lost city"—located on the northernmost tip of the Andes range in Colombia—lay forgotten until the 1970s. No one knows who built it, but archeologists think it is around 1,400 years old. The city has terraced fields and paved roads. Nearly 5,000 people may have lived there.

Discovery and conquest

In 1494, Spain and Portugal agreed to divide the "new world" in two parts by drawing a vertical line halfway between North America and Europe. Only later did they realize that the line went right through the Amazon Basin. A Spanish army conquered the Inca Empire, creating a territory called Peru. Meanwhile, Portuguese colonists settled at the mouth of the Amazon River, eventually creating the country of Brazil.

Amazons

In 1542, Spanish explorer Francisco de Orellana became the first European to travel all the way down the Amazon River to the ocean. His men were attacked by female warriors—known as Amazons in Greek mythology—and he gave their name to the river.

Remains of Jesuit settlement at Rio Grande do Sul, Brazil

A new religion

The first Europeans who traveled in the Amazon region included Jesuit priests, sent to convert the local people to Christianity. Some of these priests founded churches—later called missions—in the jungle. Many of the region's first modern towns grew around these sites.

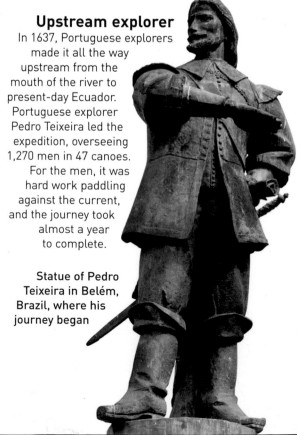

Upstream explorer

In 1637, Portuguese explorers made it all the way upstream from the mouth of the river to present-day Ecuador. Portuguese explorer Pedro Teixeira led the expedition, overseeing 1,270 men in 47 canoes. For the men, it was hard work paddling against the current, and the journey took almost a year to complete.

Statue of Pedro Teixeira in Belém, Brazil, where his journey began

Slave trade

The European colonists brought African slaves to the Amazon region's mines and plantations to replace local workers who were dying in their thousands from disease and overwork. Between 1550 and 1880, nearly four million Africans ended up in Brazil.

Many slaves worked in mines, collecting diamonds from broken rocks

Seeking cinnamon

Early European explorers were looking for spices, which were very valuable in the 16th century. In 1541, Spanish explorer Gonzalo Pizarro heard about a Valley of Cinnamon located to the east of the Andes. He went looking for it, in the hope of becoming wealthy, but returned empty handed.

Rubber boom

In the 1880s, the Amazon region became the world center for rubber production—this period became known as the "Rubber Boom". Businessmen took over large areas of rain forest, and forced local people to work. These rubber barons became very rich; however, the boom only lasted for 30 years, as rubber had begun to be produced in other parts of the world.

Strong beak cracks open nuts

Explorers' species

Many of the Amazon's animals are named after naturalists and scientists who led expeditions into the rain forest. For example, the Amazon river dolphin, *Inia geoffrensis*, was named after the French researcher Étienne Geoffroy Saint-Hilaire; Spix's macaw was named after the German biologist Johann Baptist von Spix.

Long snout grabs slippery fish

Amazon River dolphin

Spix's macaw

Myths

The Amazon rain forest is home to many myths and legends. Some ancient stories revolve around good and evil forest spirits, while other myths arose around the time the first Europeans reached the rain forest. Many European fortune seekers heard stories about lost cities and treasures. They never found anything, but the legends lived on, adding more magic to this incredible region.

Phantom boa

In the rain forest's western parts, many locals believe in the legend of Sachamama, the "spirit mother" of the jungle who looks like a huge snake. People often mistake her body for a fallen tree trunk. Sachamama is considered to be a kind spirit, but will rise up and eat any person who steps on her.

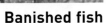

Armored scales on fish

Banished fish

Legend has it that the arapaima (also called pirarucu), the Amazon's biggest fish, is a warrior banished by the gods. The warrior, Pirarucu, was cruel to the villagers, so the gods taught him a lesson. On a stormy fishing trip, Pirarucu was too proud to seek shelter, so was struck by lightning, which turned him into the fish.

Sacred cassava

The cassava root—known as mandioca to the people of the Amazon rain forest—is thought to be a gift from the gods. Legend has it that a chief's unmarried daughter was made pregnant by the gods. She gave birth to a pale-skinned girl named Mani. Sadly, Mani died on her first birthday, and a strange new plant grew from her grave. This plant was the delicious mandioca.

Postage stamp from Brazil showing the mandioca legend

Sorcerer tree

Many Amazon villages regard the largest and oldest lupuna tree in the area as a "sorcerer tree." It is believed that the tree can punish bad people by giving them a terrible stomach ache. Some people leave the clothes and possessions of their enemies at the base of the trunk, in the hope that the tree will make them suffer. The sap of the tree is also used to make poisons.

Young lupuna tree

Quest for gold

Gold was common in the Andes, and the Inca and other native people made many objects from it, like this mask from Colombia. Many European explorers came to the Americas hoping to find *El Dorado*—literally "the golden one"—hidden in the forest. However, no one could find this mythical kingdom.

Owl spirit

The Amazon rain forest's owls are said to embody the spirit of the Moon goddess Chia. According to an ancient myth, the god of farming, Chibchacum, turned Chia into an owl because she made people very lazy and badly behaved.

Velvety wings absorb sound and allow owl to fly silently

Lost city of the Inca

In the 16th century, after the Spanish conquered the Inca Empire, the Inca fled their cities. But a rumor spread that an army moved to a hidden city called Vilcabamba. Many lost Inca towns have been rediscovered since, like Huinay Huayna (below) in 1941. However, no one has identified Vilcabamba, although some archeologists think that a site called Espíritu Pampa is, in fact, the lost city.

Stone walls have survived erosion

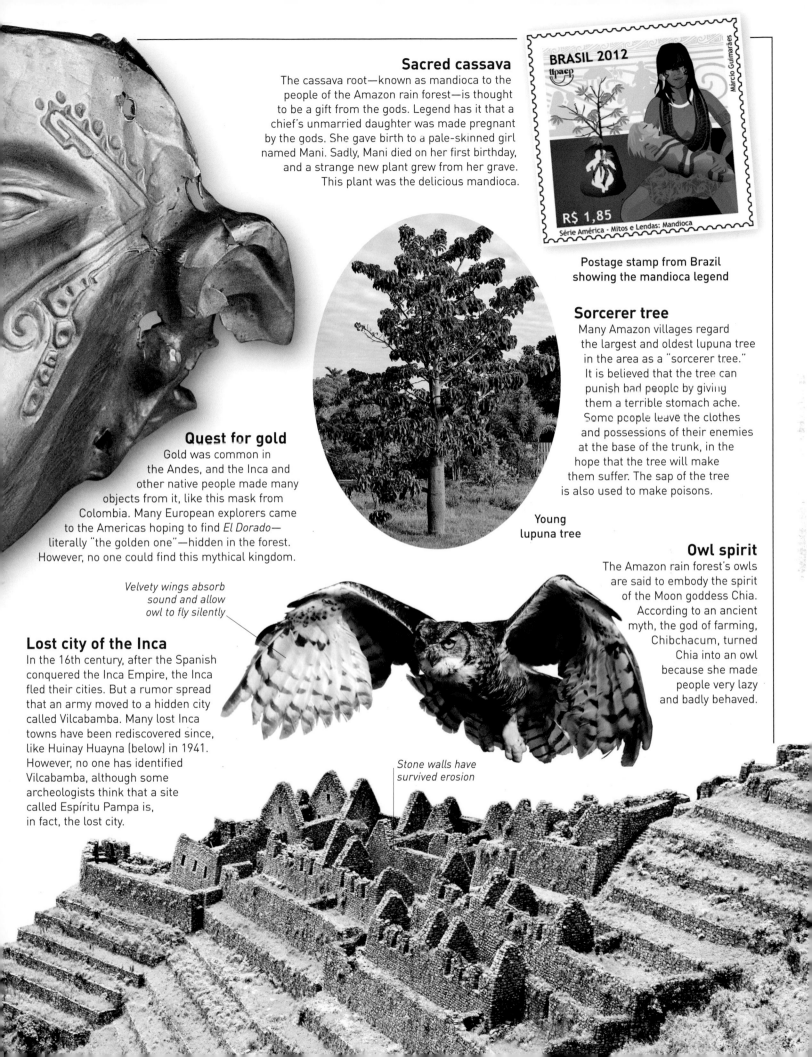

Traditional life

Millions of people lived in the Amazon region before the European conquests of the 16th century. There are about a million indigenous Amazonians left today, although some tribes only have a few hundred members. Many follow the ways of their ancestors, gathering things they need from the forest.

Magic and medicine
Seen here is a shaman from the Kamentsá tribe of Colombia. A shaman is both a priest and a medicine man. Many Amazonians believe in magic, and if someone becomes sick, they are taken to a shaman for herbal medicines made from forest plants and for rituals that are believed to help in healing.

Uncontacted tribes
This man belongs to the Matis tribe, which lives in the far west of the Amazon region. The tribe first made contact with Brazilian government officials in 1978. The Matis had no natural defenses against diseases common in the rest of the world and about 80 percent of them died from viral infections caught from outsiders.

Arrows used to shoot monkeys in trees

Hunting and gathering
These hunters show their skill with long bows made from wood cut from forest trees. The men belong to the Awá tribe, one of the smallest communities living in the Amazon rain forest. There are about 450 Awá living in Brazil's northeastern Amazon region—around 100 are nomadic and avoid contact with outsiders. They move regularly to new camps, where they gather fruits and hunt animals.

Following rituals

Young Amazonian men often participate in ancient ritual dances. Every year, the tribes of the Xingu area, located in the southeastern part of the Amazon region, gather for a festival known as *Quarap*. During the event, the tribes organize dances, rituals, and wrestling matches to honor their dead ancestors.

Chief youth leads the dance

Body painted with natural dyes

Leg bindings strengthen ankles for wrestling

Traditional craft

The Amazon region's indigenous people know how to make everything they need from materials found in the forest. This craftsman from the Yanomami tribe, which lives on the border of Venezuela and Brazil, is making a basket from leaves and vines collected from the forest. Yanomami families live in large shared homes made of logs, dried palm fronds, and other materials.

Basket is lined with thick leaves

River food

The Amazon River and its tributaries are an important source of food for the local people. These fishermen are from the Yawalapiti tribe that lives along the Xingu River. They catch fish by spearing them using bows and arrows. The fish are stored in nets and dried in sunlight so that they can be eaten later.

Cooking meals

It is traditional for the women of the Amazon region to prepare food. Often, enough food is made for the whole village to eat at once. This woman from the Mawé tribe is roasting guarana seeds in a giant clay dish over a wood fire. Guarana is similar to coffee, and Mawé hunters eat the seeds when they go on long expeditions into the jungle. The Mawé tribe now sells guarana products all over the world.

Modern Amazonia

Most people in the Amazon region lead normal lives, from watching sports to going to school. Traditional homes stand next to modern buildings in big cities, such as Manaus, Brazil. Yet even here, you are never more than 6 miles (10 km) from the rain forest, and river boats are often the best way to travel between towns and cities.

Beach resort
The Amazon region has a beach resort 900 miles (1,450 km) away from the ocean. Located at Ponta Negra—on the edge of Manaus, Brazil—bathers take a dip in the Rio Negro, home to Amazon River dolphins and many fish. Lifeguards keep watch over the swimmers, but also look out for caimans.

Medical boat belongs to the Peruvian navy

MARINA DE GUERRA DEL PERÚ

302

Floating hospital
It can take a long time to get to a hospital in remote parts of the Amazon rain forest. Hospital ships, such as the one shown above, make regular visits to isolated villages in the forest so that ill or injured people can see a doctor and receive treatment. In emergencies, faster river ambulances are used to take patients to the nearest city hospital.

Carnival culture
These jaguar dancers are performing at a carnival in Parintins, a Brazilian city located beside the Amazon River. A carnival is a party that can be enjoyed by thousands of people from all around the world over several days. Big cities in Brazil have a strong tradition of carnivals, merging African and European traditions with native American culture.

Amazon communication
Rain forests grow in very sunny places—and these solar panels are using that sunlight to supply electricity for a village in the Amazon rain forest. The electricity powers computers and charges mobile phones. Telecommunication masts on the riverbanks transmit telephone calls and Internet signals.

River village

Most Amazonian villages are built beside the river. Houses are placed high on the riverbank so they do not flood when the water level of the river is high. Seen here is an unusual village called Belén in Iquitos, Peru. The houses—attached to poles driven into the river bed—float on the river itself, rising and falling with the water.

Roof thatched with dried palm leaves

Soccer city

The Arena da Amazônia stadium is a recent addition to the skyline of Manaus. It was built for the 2014 FIFA World Cup. The stadium's design was inspired by the straw baskets woven by people in the region. The climate of Manaus is very hot and humid, so the stadium's ventilation system, shaded areas, and its light-colored structure help to keep the spectators reasonably comfortable.

Schooling

Traditional Amazonian villages do not have schools. Children just play until they are old enough to help their parents with tasks. Without basic literacy skills, they cannot find jobs when they are adults. The Brazilian government is building more schools to help solve this problem.

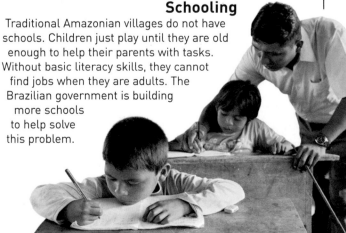

Getting around

The land is heavily forested in the Amazon region, so the long, wide rivers are ideal for traveling long distances. Even though modern highways now cut through the rain forest, and aircraft connect remote villages with the rest of the world, most of the people living in this region get around by boat, just as they have done for thousands of years.

Just walk!
Away from the river, the only way to travel through the jungle is by foot. Even the toughest off-road vehicles cannot make their way through the undergrowth and fallen trees. The tourists seen here are taking a short stroll. For longer journeys, travelers need to have a machete to cut through bushes that block their way.

On the road
In the 1970s, the Brazilian government cut a 3,000-mile (5,000-km) roadway from the Atlantic Coast through the Amazon rain forest to the border with Peru. This Trans-Amazonian Highway is still unfinished, but it has allowed road traffic, and even loggers, right into the heart of the rain forest.

Bridges

The only road bridge in the Amazon river system crosses the Rio Negro near the city of Manaus, Brazil. Opened in 2011 and 11,800 ft (3,595 m) wide, it had to be high enough for ocean-going cargo ships and the Amazon's ferries to travel to Manaus's port—the region's main transportation hub.

Riding on horseback

Sure-footed horses and mules are the best way to travel in the foothills of the Andes. Before horses were brought to the region by 16th-century European explorers, Andean people used llamas to carry cargo. However, llamas are not strong enough to carry humans.

Float allows plane to land on water

Air travel

The calm waters of the Amazon River make a good runway for seaplanes. The largest Amazonian cities, such as Manaus and Iquitos, have full-sized airports, but small aircraft, as shown, can fly to remote communities far from any city. Inland, away from the river, skilled pilots land planes on airstrips cut from the forest.

Going for a paddle

The traditional method of travel on the Amazon Basin's many rivers is to paddle a canoe. They may be carved out from logs, or made from planks of wood, such as balsa. Balsa trees grow across the region, and their wood is lightweight and ideal for canoes and rafts.

Deforestation

The biggest threat to the Amazon rain forest is deforestation, a process in which trees are cleared, leaving nowhere for the wildlife to live. The forest is being cut down for logging, road building, and to make way for farms. If cleared, the rain forest will never grow back in the same way. Today, strict laws limit deforestation in some parts, although other areas continue to be cleared.

2002

2012

Satellite surveillance
About a fifth of the Amazon rain forest has been cut down in the last 40 years. The Brazilian government uses satellite images to monitor the rate at which the rain forest is being cleared. The satellites can see changes in the color of the ground, which indicates where trees have been cut down. The images above track deforestation in a section of the rain forest between 2002 and 2012.

Divisive road
The building of roads is one of the main causes of deforestation. Roads were first cut into the rain forest in the 1970s to help poor people from Brazil's cities to settle in the Amazon region to start a new life. The roads also divide up the forest, making it difficult for many animals to move around as much as they need.

Lumber being transported from the rain forest

Logging
Another major cause of deforestation is logging. The hardwood trees of the Amazon rain forest are used for making furniture that is sold around the world. The loggers cut down a few of the largest trees and then move on to another area.

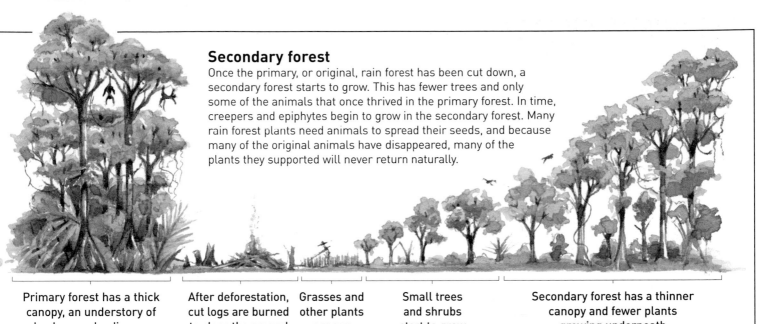

Secondary forest

Once the primary, or original, rain forest has been cut down, a secondary forest starts to grow. This has fewer trees and only some of the animals that once thrived in the primary forest. In time, creepers and epiphytes begin to grow in the secondary forest. Many rain forest plants need animals to spread their seeds, and because many of the original animals have disappeared, many of the plants they supported will never return naturally.

Primary forest has a thick canopy, an understory of bushes, and a diverse animal population

After deforestation, cut logs are burned to clear the ground

Grasses and other plants appear

Small trees and shrubs start to grow

Secondary forest has a thinner canopy and fewer plants growing underneath

Slash and burn

A helicopter carrying environmental officers (right) is flying in to arrest thieves who have cleared trees illegally for farming. The main method of clearing the forest is called slash and burn, a process in which trees are cut up and burned. The ash makes the soil a little more fertile, but only for a few years.

Mining and damming

The Amazon region is home to millions of people and to some of the world's biggest cities. In order to fuel the cities' quick growth, the region's largest rivers have been dammed to generate electricity, and enormous mines have been dug for metals and useful minerals. There is still room for more dams, and the Amazon Basin is thought to contain vast, untapped reserves of minerals. The big question is whether the rain forest is more valuable than the rich resources it holds.

Gold rush

There are gold rushes happening all over the Amazon region, with people clearing the forest to look for gold in the rocks underneath. Miners crush the rocks and wash water through them; if they are lucky, this carries away the dust and sand to reveal grains of shiny gold.

River port

The city of Belém, located near the Amazon River's mouth, has been a very important port in Brazil for hundreds of years. The large market hall, seen on the left, was built beside the port in the 19th century. It sells fish caught from the river, as well as fruits and other products transported downstream from the forest.

Mighty mine

The Carajás Mine in Brazil is the largest iron ore mine in the world. About 3,000 people work there, digging out rock that contains iron and other metals. Once all the ore has been dug out, the mine will be filled and a new rain forest will be planted to cover the bare ground.

Carrying oil

This pipe is carrying crude oil pumped from a well in the rain forests of Ecuador. This valuable resource will be used to make fuel, chemicals, plastic, and medicines. However, pipes and wells can leak, and the spilled oil pollutes the area's rivers, damaging wildlife and causing health problems for those who live in the forests.

Growing fuel

Brazil is the world's leading producer of sugar cane. Raw sugar from the cane is used to make ethanol, a plant-based alternative for non-renewable fuels, such as coal. Biofuels such as ethanol are thought to be environmentally friendly, but creating sugar cane plantations means cutting down forests, or using land that could be used to grow food crops.

Battle for land

Many mines, dams, and oil wells occupy land in the Amazon region that belongs to indigenous tribes. These people sometimes protest, so the government must consider the benefits of industry alongside the interests of the indigenous people, and what is good for the environment.

Damming the river

The Amazon Basin's largest dam—the Tucuruí Dam in Brazil—provides electricity for about 13 million people. However, when it was finished in 1984, it created an enormous reservoir that flooded parts of the rain forest and forced thousands of people to move out of the area. Still, dams such as these also have some environmental benefits, as they help produce electricity without releasing carbon dioxide. Today, nearly all of Brazil's electricity is generated in this manner.

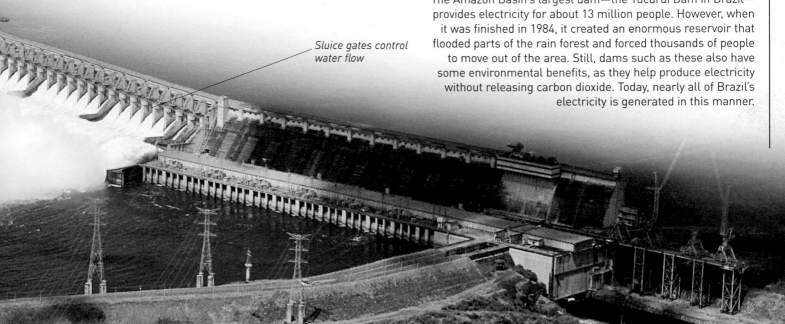

Sluice gates control water flow

Endangered species

Small patches of the Amazon rain forest have remained unchanged for two million years. Today, nearly three million species of plant and animal may be living there. Yet, as human activity continues to damage the rain forest, a number of species are running out of places in which to survive, and many of these species are in danger of becoming extinct.

Pacarana

This shy, leaf-eating animal is the last surviving relative of giant, 10-ft- (3-m-) long rodents that lived in the Amazon region about eight million years ago. Small gangs of three or four pacaranas climb through the trees, using their long whiskers to feel their way. This species is becoming scarce because the forests of the western Amazon in which they live are being cut down by farmers.

Blue birds

The hyacinth macaw is the largest parrot in the Amazon rain forest. It is about 3 ft (1 m) long from its hooked beak to the tip of its long tail feathers. There are now fewer than 6,500 of these birds left in the wild. Its size and bright-blue plumage make this species a tempting target for bird trappers, who sell the parrots as pets.

Termite hill

Maned sloth

Living in the Atlantic Forest, southeast of the main Amazon Basin, the maned sloth moves slowly through the trees, so as not to attract attention. It never cleans its fur, and the algae growing in it lends its hair a green tinge. They are endangered because they are hunted for food, and the trees in which they live are being cut down by loggers.

English monkey

Local people call the uakari monkey the English monkey because it looks like a sunburned tourist. Living in the trees above flooded forests in Peru, they only climb to the ground in search of seeds when the floodwater has drained away. Hunters can spot these monkeys when they are near the water, so their population is now in decline.

Redness of face indicates strength to other monkeys

White-blotched ray

White-blotched rays live on pebbly riverbeds where they hunt for snails and crabs. They live only in the Xingu River in Brazil, which meets the Amazon River near its mouth. A new electricity-generating dam that is being built across the Xingu will make the river deeper. This may reduce feeding areas and could lead the rays on a path to extinction.

Giant anteater

The giant anteater rips open the nests of ants and termites and licks up the insects inside with its sticky tongue. At 24 in (60 cm) long, the tongue is one of the longest in the animal kingdom. However, the anteater is vulnerable to extinction, partly because it is too slow to run away from forest fires, which are becoming more common in the region.

Black-and-white stripes on flank

Long arms help monkey to move from tree to tree

Modern industry

The Amazon Basin provides many Amazonians with jobs. This helps local communities to build homes, schools, and hospitals, so they can lead comfortable lives. The biggest industry in the region is agriculture and other types of food production. In the future, industries may grow around new products the forest holds.

Palm oil and fruits

Palm oils
The fruits of palm trees are a traditional food for some Amazonians, but they are also grown for the oil they contain. The oil is used in products such as salad dressings, washing powder, and even in fuels. If managed correctly, palm oil plantations do not damage natural habitats. However, there have been many cases in which palm oil farms have caused environmental problems in the Amazon region because of widespread deforestation.

Fishing
The Amazon River provides fish for millions of people. The largest fish, the arapaima, is regarded as a delicacy because it has few bones in it and can be cut into thick steaks. But so many wild arapaimas have been taken from the river that the Brazilian government has made it illegal to catch them. Today, arapaimas are raised in fish farms—areas of the river that are surrounded by nets and stocked with fish.

Soybean farming
This huge farm in the cerrado grasslands south of the Amazon rain forest grows only soybeans. Farms like this dot many parts of the Amazon region. Soybeans are used all over the world to make vegetarian foods and to feed cattle, chickens, and other livestock. Brazil is the world's largest producer of soybeans.

Medicinal plants

This researcher is talking to a local shaman, or medicine man, to find out which plants he uses to make traditional medicines. The drug curare was discovered in an Amazonian plant. Tribes in the forest traditionally used it as a poison, but in the 1940s, surgeons began to use it to relax patients' muscles during surgery.

Cattle ranches

There are about 10 million cattle in the Amazon region and many millions more in the surrounding hills. Cattle ranches—which include land for growing corn to feed the cattle—are the major cause of deforestation in the area. The problem is made worse when farmers convert ranches into soy plantations, as they must then clear another area of forest for their cattle to graze.

Combine harvester cuts the soy plant and removes the beans

Conservation

The Amazon rain forest needs protection from the harm caused by human activities. Scientists try and figure out how wildlife survives so that animals can be better cared for. Conservationists work to repair and protect habitats, while lawyers and politicians set rules for people to live in the forest without causing damage to it.

Replanting

When a tall tree falls down in the forest, it leaves a gap that is filled by other plants. Eventually a new tree fills the space in the canopy. Scientists have observed this process and are trying to re-create it. The plants grown in the reforestation nursery above will be used to replenish the Atlantic Forest.

Applying science

The two scientists here—known as ecologists—are looking for plant samples during a research project in the Peruvian Amazon. Their important research shows the damage that is caused when humans alter the natural habitat.

Product bans

These activists are protesting against illegal logging. In 1975, an international ban was introduced on buying and selling endangered species and rain forest products, including hardwood logs from the Amazon rain forest. Sadly, many criminals continue to ignore the ban.

Conservation sites

Many storks and egrets migrate to the Pantanal wetland every year. If this area were drained to make way for fields, these birds would have nowhere to live. The best way to protect animal species is to conserve their habitats. But today, only 2 percent of the Pantanal is protected in reserves.

Wood storks arrive from their wintering grounds

Saving tribes

The traditional cultures of the Amazon region also need to be saved. A fifth of the rain forest belongs to different tribes that have lived in the area for thousands of years. Statistics show that there is less deforestation in tribal areas than in the rest of the rain forest. Still, big portions of tribal land have been taken over illegally by farmers.

Traffic sign

With roads being built through the forest, road signs are a new addition to the Amazon region. This one warns drivers to look out for anteaters that may walk onto the road. Anteaters are slow-moving creatures that may not be able to get out of the way of fast-moving vehicles. This species is endangered, and road signs are one way to help it survive.

Promoting awareness

In 1989, when the problems of deforestation first became known, tribal chiefs from across the rain forest and the rest of North and South America met in Altmira, Brazil, on the banks of the Xingu River. They drew attention to the problems threatening the region. The English musician Sting (far right) also attended the gathering.

Ecotourism

Tourists pay to visit the Amazon rain forest, and the money they pay goes to the local people and toward conservation programs. Turning the rain forest into a world-class tourist attraction is more beneficial than cutting it down to build cities and farms. This region's vacation industry is a prime example of ecotourism, since the hotels and facilities used by the visitors do not create pollution or damage natural habitats.

Handicrafts

Local people in the Amazon region use latex from the trees to make natural rubber, which is used to make souvenir masks, such as the one above. Selling handicrafts to tourists is an important source of income for people who live in remote parts of the region.

Forest resort

Ecotourists stay in comfortable hotels, known as lodges. The buildings are designed to be highly energy-efficient so they do not use a lot of fuel, which has to be brought in by boat. Waste is also kept to a minimum.

Hotel built on stilts in the river

Guided tours

Most visitors to the Amazon rain forest come to see the wildlife. Local guides take tourists on walks through the rain forest or on boat tours. The tourists travel in canoes, not speedboats, since high-speed vessels create waves that would damage the riverbanks. Some guided tours take place at night, when caimans and other nocturnal animals are active.

Bridge made from forest wood and plant fibers

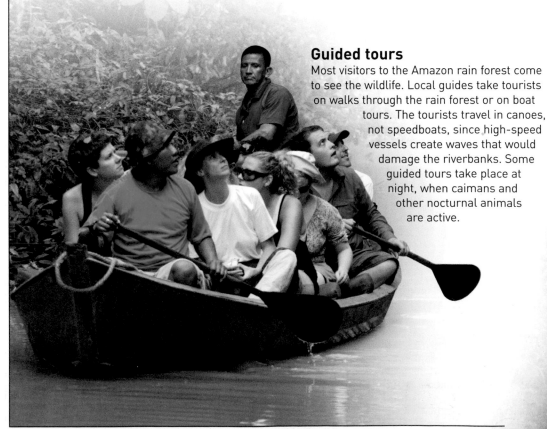

Meeting the locals

Tour groups visit villages, where the residents show off their way of life, such as how they use forest plants to make the things they need. The visits are a chance for Amazonians to make money selling traditional products to visitors.

Straight sticks sharpened into arrows

Saving the animals

Tourists in the Amazon rain forest can help park rangers to care for endangered animals before they are released into the wild. Visitors to Peru are seen here feeding milk to baby manatees. This example of ecotourism helps raise money so that more of the rare manatees can be raised and protected.

Binoculars for viewing wildlife

Walking among the trees

Walkways like this rope walkway, in addition to viewing platforms built in large trees, are the best way to see the rain forest's birds, monkeys, and specialized plants that live high up in the canopy, out of sight from the forest floor.

Farming

Many fruits and nuts eaten the world over come from forest plants. In the Amazon rain forest, local people have been growing their own crops for centuries, using only traditional farming methods. Today, conservation programs are helping them to develop sustainable methods so that they can grow extra crops to sell. Sustainable farms make money for the Amazon communities without causing any damage to the natural habitats.

Açái palm

The açaí palm tree grows naturally in the swampy forests near the Amazon River's mouth. Locals harvest the tree for the soft, edible palm hearts inside its young stems. The berries also taste good, and locals use them to make juices.

Making rubber

Here a farmer is cutting a notch in a rubber tree to release a liquid called latex. This is used to make natural rubber, which is harvested on sustainable farms in the Amazon region. Making things from natural rubber creates much less pollution than artificial rubber—the most common type of rubber, made from petroleum oil.

Agroforestry

The Amazonian farmers above are raking out chiles to dry in the sunshine. These chile peppers come from a rain forest farm in the eastern Brazilian town of Tomé-açu. This farming community was set up by Japanese settlers 90 years ago. When the local pepper crop was killed by pests, the people of Tomé-açu decided to replant the forest trees and grow crops in their shade. This type of farming is called agroforestry.

Bananas

Jungle fruits

Although from southeast Asia, bananas are also grown in South America. The first pineapples came from the forests near the Pantanal wetland. Passion fruit is another Amazon plant, and the region was also home to the first tomatoes, peppers, and chiles.

Pineapple

Passion fruit

Growing coffee

More than 6½ million tons (6 million metric tons) of coffee beans are sold across the world every year, and some of it is grown in the Amazon rain forest. Farmers grow coffee beans on small bushes that are planted among the main forest trees. Rain forest coffee is also good for the environment.

Coffee beans

Coffee plant berries

Five beans grow inside a tough pod

Brazil nuts

Despite the name, these large, tasty nuts are grown all over the Amazon region, not just in Brazil. Wild Brazil nut trees grow along riverbanks. The nuts, which are the trees' seeds, drop to the ground in a round pod. Forest rodents eat some nuts and bury the rest for later. Some of the buried nuts grow into new trees.

Cocoa

Chocolate comes from cocoa beans, which grow wild in the Amazon rain forest. Native American people were using chocolate in food hundreds of years before it became a popular treat around the world. Today, most of the world's cocoa is grown in West Africa, but it can be grown on rain forest farms.

Amazon wonders

The Amazon region is a collection of many wonders. The mountains around the Amazon Basin were home to the most advanced civilizations in the Americas prior to the arrival of the Europeans. There are also incredible natural features down in the vast lowlands, as well as historic cities in which modern life and architecture mix with the wild Amazon rain forest.

Iquitos

This Peruvian city is one of the most remote places on Earth. In the early 1900s, it became a major center in the rubber industry. However, even today, its 420,000 inhabitants cannot leave town by road. They either have to get a boat downriver or catch a plane. The city is 2,235 miles (3,600 km) from the ocean, but the Amazon River is still deep enough here for oceangoing ships to dock in the city's harbor.

Mount Roraima

According to local folklore, Mount Roraima in the Guiana Highlands is the stump of a huge tree that bore all the fruits in the world until it was cut down by a demon. The mountain's rocks are 2 billion years old and were formed when South America was still connected to Africa.

Anavilhanas Archipelago

This is the largest archipelago of river islands in the world. It is a collection of 400 forested islands on the Rio Negro, upstream from the Brazilian city of Manaus.

Tumucumaque National Park

This nature reserve is the world's largest national park; it is bigger than Belgium.

Rio Negro Bridge

Completed in 2010, this 2.2 mile (3.6 km) bridge, located on the Rio Negro, is the first major road bridge on the Amazon River system.

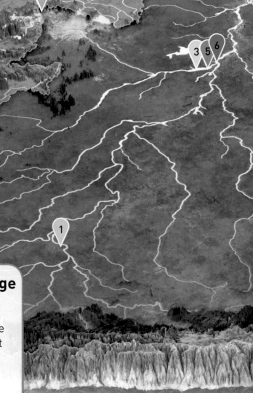

Manaus

The Teatro Amazonas opera house was built in 1884 and is still a famous landmark in the Brazilian city of Manaus. It was paid for with money from the rubber industry, the same industry that made Manaus the largest city in the Amazon Basin. Manaus is located at the meeting point of the Amazon River and the Rio Negro.

Pantanal

The Pantanal is the world's largest wetland. It forms in a hollow basin in the Brazilian Highlands that fills with rainwater flowing down from the surrounding hills. The water never gets more than about 16½ ft (5 m) deep.

Valle de la Luna

Meaning the Valley of the Moon, the Valle de la Luna is a desert region filled with tall rock towers. The towers were created by erosion that washed away the softer clays that once filled the valley. This valley is close to La Paz, the capital city of Bolivia. They are both located on the Altiplano, a high plateau west of the Amazon Basin.

Sacred Valley

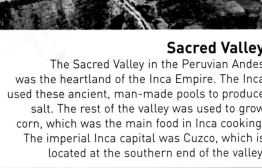

The Sacred Valley in the Peruvian Andes was the heartland of the Inca Empire. The Inca used these ancient, man-made pools to produce salt. The rest of the valley was used to grow corn, which was the main food in Inca cooking. The imperial Inca capital was Cuzco, which is located at the southern end of the valley.

Machu Picchu

The Inca city of Machu Picchu sits high up in the Andes Mountains. It was thought to be a religious center used by the Inca king, but it was abandoned and forgotten after the collapse of the Inca Empire in the 16th century. It lay hidden under jungle until it was rediscovered in 1911.

Amazon facts

The Amazon region is a place of superlatives. It has the world's largest rain forest, its biggest river system, its largest river island, its widest river mouth, and its biggest tributary. Here are many more facts that show what an incredible place this region is and how record-breaking some of its animals are.

Mass of life

Biomass is a measure of how many living things exist in an area. Rain forests have the highest biomass of any land habitat. The biomass in one square mile of the Amazon rain forest is equivalent to the weight of two Nimitz-class aircraft carriers used by the US Navy, each of which weighs nearly 100,000 tons.

Biodiversity

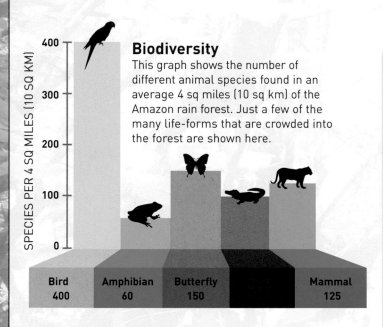

This graph shows the number of different animal species found in an average 4 sq miles (10 sq km) of the Amazon rain forest. Just a few of the many life-forms that are crowded into the forest are shown here.

SPECIES PER 4 SQ MILES (10 SQ KM)

| Bird 400 | Amphibian 60 | Butterfly 150 | | Mammal 125 |

Endangered species

Many Amazonian species are under threat because of damage to their habitat. The international body charged with monitoring endangered species, the International Union for Conservation of Nature (IUCN), has listed 536 animal and 778 plant species as being in danger of extinction in the Amazon region.

Key

Vulnerable
Endangered
Critically endangered

South American manatee

Uakari monkey

Giant anteater

Golden lion tamarin

Pacarana

Giant otter

Rancho Grande harlequin frog

Glaucous macaw

Cherry-throated tanager

LARGEST ANIMALS

The capybara is the largest rodent in the world. This species lives in the rivers and wetlands of the Amazon region. It can grow to more than 3¼ ft (1 m) in length.

Amazonian macaws are the largest types of parrot in the world. Some species can grow to about 3¼ ft (1 m) in length.

At just over 1 in (3 cm) long, the Amazon rain forest's bullet ants are among the largest ants in the world.

The mighty green anaconda hunts in the wetlands and the forest rivers of the Amazon region, using its muscular coils to squeeze prey to death. At about 16½ ft (5 m) long, it may not be the longest snake in the world (some pythons in Asia are longer), but it is certainly the heaviest— a fully grown anaconda can weigh up to 220 lb (100 kg).

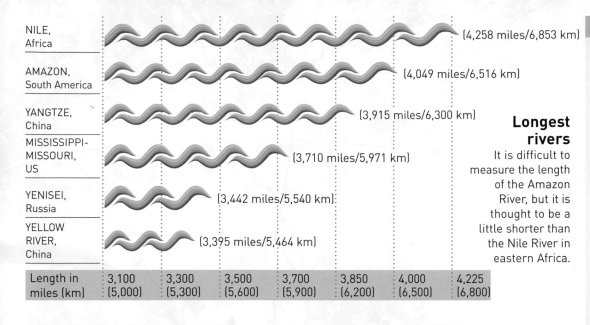

	Length in miles (km)	3,100 (5,000)	3,300 (5,300)	3,500 (5,600)	3,700 (5,900)	3,850 (6,200)	4,000 (6,500)	4,225 (6,800)

NILE, Africa — (4,258 miles/6,853 km)

AMAZON, South America — (4,049 miles/6,516 km)

YANGTZE, China — (3,915 miles/6,300 km)

MISSISSIPPI-MISSOURI, US — (3,710 miles/5,971 km)

YENISEI, Russia — (3,442 miles/5,540 km)

YELLOW RIVER, China — (3,395 miles/5,464 km)

Longest rivers

It is difficult to measure the length of the Amazon River, but it is thought to be a little shorter than the Nile River in eastern Africa.

Amazon milk frog

SMALLEST ANIMALS

At just ½ in (1 cm) long, Izecksohn's toad is the smallest frog in the Amazon rain forest.

The tiny white-bellied woodstar is 3 in (8 cm) long.

RIVER BASIN

Amazon (3.8 million sq miles/ 6.15 million sq km)

Congo (2.4 million sq miles/ 3.82 million sq km)

Mississippi-Missouri (2 million sq miles/ 3.22 million sq km)

Nile (1.7 million sq miles/ 2.8 million sq km)

Ganges (0.7 million sq miles/ 1.07 million sq km)

Largest basin

The Amazon River drains the largest area of any river in the world. The amount of water it collects from its basin is almost twice as much as the Congo River.

1 2 3 4 5 6

Area of drainage basin (million sq km)

Kinkajou

DANGEROUS ANIMALS

The golden poison dart frog of Ecuador is the most toxic vertebrate in the world. Its skin is filled with a powerful poison that protects it from predators. Just touching the frog is enough to make you sick.

The caimans of the Amazon region generally hunt for capybaras and fish, but they have been known to grab people who come too close to the water's edge.

The jaguar has the strongest jaws of any big cat. It can crack skulls and shatter a turtle shell with one bite.

The tropical rattlesnake's venom causes blindness and internal bleeding and makes muscles go limp.

When crowded into a small pool, a school of piranhas can eat a person in minutes.

Amazon by country

The Amazon Basin covers nine separate countries. Most of the rain forest is located in Brazil, and Peru contains the next biggest section. The remaining 20 percent is divided among the seven other countries.

KEY

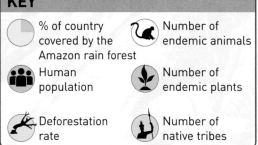

- % of country covered by the Amazon rain forest
- Number of endemic animals
- Human population
- Number of endemic plants
- Deforestation rate
- Number of native tribes

VENEZUELA

The Llanos wetland and Guiana Highlands are located in this country. Venezuela's main forests are around the Orinoco River, which flows into the Caribbean Sea and is connected to the Amazon River near its source in Brazil.

Waterfalls at Jasper Creek

5.56%   313   30 million

8,007   0.6%

26

BRAZIL

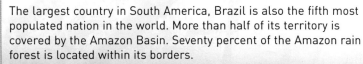

The largest country in South America, Brazil is also the fifth most populated nation in the world. More than half of its territory is covered by the Amazon Basin. Seventy percent of the Amazon rain forest is located within its borders.

Iguazu Falls, on the Iguazu River

ECUADOR

Ecuador gets its name from the Equator, which runs through the middle of the country. The Andes run north to south through the country, dividing the Pacific coastal areas in the west from the Amazon rain forest in the east. The Ecuadorian rain forest is famous for its large areas of flooded forest.

45.7%   383   16 million

4,007   1.9%   27

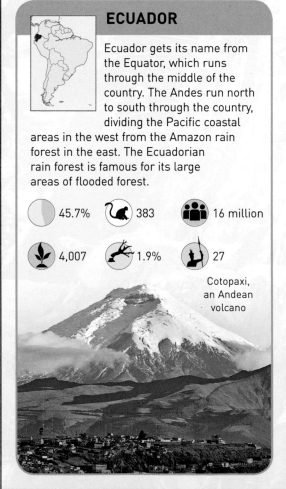

Cotopaxi, an Andean volcano

COLOMBIA

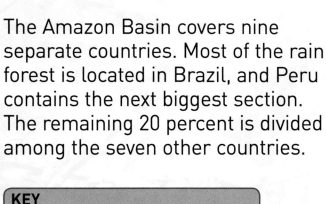

About five percent of the Amazon rain forest is located in the southern part of Colombia. The northern range of the Andes Mountains, which was the site of many important Pre-Columbian cultures, is also found there.

Monserrate Sanctuary in Bogotá, the capital city

42%   604   48 million   15,366

0.16%   87

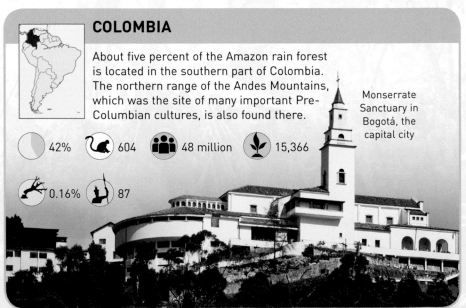

SURINAME

Suriname is almost completely forested, except for its southernmost fringe, which consists of grasslands. This country was once a Dutch colony, the only one in South America.

90.2%   14   540,000   637   0.01%   15

Central Suriname
Nature Reserve

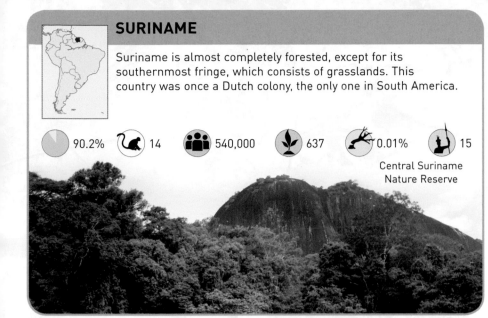

FRENCH GUIANA

French Guiana is an overseas territory of France and its people are French citizens. Much of the forested interior is uninhabited.

94.3%   12   250,000
1,462   0.2%   6

Maroni River

56%   1,051
200 million   16,865
0.4%   240

GUYANA

Once a British colony, Guyana became an independent country in 1966. Much of its land is hilly, and the southern half is covered in rain forest.

70.3%   37   800,000
13   0%   21

Nevado Sajama,
a volcano

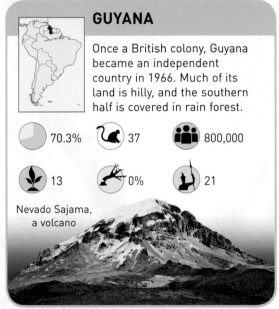

BOLIVIA

Two-thirds of Bolivia lies in the Amazon Basin. Most of this area consists of high mountains, including a high plateau called Altiplano, which is covered in deserts and salt flats.

65%   118   11 million
3,994   4.5%   36

Kanuku Mountains

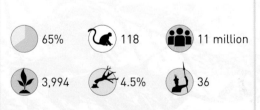

PERU

Peru contains 10 percent of the Amazon rain forest. It is also home to the source of the Amazon River. The eastern half of Peru is covered in lowland rain forest.

60.6%   577   30 million
5,348   0.15%   51

Urubamba Valley

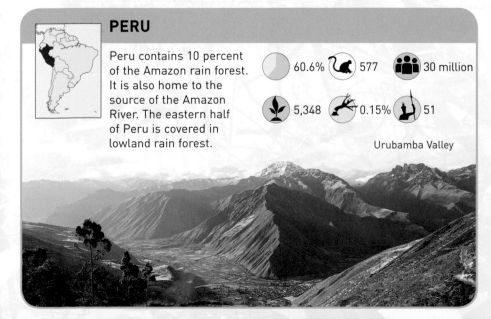

Glossary

Strawberry poison dart frog, an amphibian

AGROFORESTRY
The practice of cultivating agricultural crops among naturally growing trees. Agroforestry helps protect natural habitats.

AMPHIBIAN
A class of vertebrate that generally spends part of its life in water and has to keep its skin moist at all times. Frogs and salamanders are amphibians.

ARID
Describes an area that is dry all the time.

ATLANTIC FOREST
An area of rain forest in Brazil near the coast of the Atlantic Ocean.

BACTERIA
Tiny organisms that are far too small to see without a microscope. Most bacteria live in natural habitats and are harmless.

BASIN
A hollow area of land surrounded by hills or mountains on at least three sides.

BIOMASS
A measure of how much life is contained in an area. Biomass is calculated by adding up the combined weight of all life-forms.

CAATINGA
A type of dry forest found around the edges of the Amazon rain forest. It has sandy soil and is filled with grasses, bushes, and small trees.

CAECILIAN
An unusual amphibian that looks like a snake or worm. While most caecilians live on the forest floor, some swim in water.

CERRADO
An area of mostly shrubs and grasses that grows around the edge of the Amazon rain forest, where the rainfall is not sufficient for a full forest to grow.

CLOUD FOREST
A type of tropical forest that grows on the slopes of mountains. The trees are smaller than those in a lowland jungle, and the area is often covered in fog or mist from low-lying clouds.

DECIDUOUS
Describes a process in which something falls off a living body and then regrows later. It is often used to describe trees that

drop their leaves during harsh seasons. Most deciduous trees shed leaves before winter, but in the tropics they drop leaves in the hottest, driest time of the year.

DEWLAP
A flap of skin that hangs down from the neck or throat.

ENDANGERED
When an animal or other life-form is in danger of becoming extinct.

ENDEMIC
A species that occurs naturally in one place and is found nowhere else on Earth.

EPIPHYTES
Plants that lack roots and grow on the branches and trunks of other, larger plants.

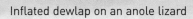

Inflated dewlap on an anole lizard

EVERGREEN
A tree or other plant that is always covered in leaves. New leaves continue to grow even as old leaves fall off.

EXTINCT
When all members of a species have died.

FLOODED FOREST
A forest that is flooded with river water so the tree trunks and roots are submerged in water.

FLOODWATER
Extra water from a river that overflows the riverbanks and covers nearby land.

GEOGRAPHY
A field of science concerned with the study of the lands, features, inhabitants, and phenomena of Earth.

HABITAT
A place where a plant or animal lives. Most species are adapted to live in one type of habitat, such as a rain forest.

HIGHLANDS
An area of hills, mountains, and plateaux. Most highlands are mountains that have been worn down over millions of years.

HUMID
Describes a climate in which the air is full of water vapor.

INDIGENOUS
Originating in, or belonging to, a particular place.

INVERTEBRATE
An animal without a backbone, such as an insect, snail, or worm. Of all the animal species known to science, at least 97 percent are invertebrates.

LIANA FOREST
A forest dominated by lianas—climbing plants that grow out of the ground and snake up around the trunks and branches of trees to reach the sunlight. Lianas use the host tree to support their own weight.

LOGGER
Someone who cuts down trees that are turned into timber products. Some loggers are criminals because they cut down trees that are protected by law.

Liana wrapped around tree trunk

Wandering spider (predator)
eats a beetle (prey)

LOGGING
An industry that provides lumber for construction and paper manufacture. Most of the world's logging is conducted in forests that are grown specially to supply lumber. However, the Amazon rain forest suffers from illegal logging.

LOWLAND
An area of flat land that is not very far above sea level, the point from which the heights of all land forms are measured.

MACHETE
A tool with a thick cutting blade. Machetes help to cut a path through thick jungle.

MARSUPIAL
A type of mammal that carries its young in a pouch on its belly. Most marsupials are from Australia and New Guinea, but a few species also live in the Americas.

NATIVE
Refers to someone or something from the local area. Native Amazonians belong to communities that have lived in the region for perhaps thousands of years.

NOCTURNAL
Active at night.

NUTRIENT
A substance that a living thing needs to survive. Plants absorb nutrients through their roots, while animals get theirs by eating other life-forms. Nutrients include fats and proteins.

PETROLEUM
Also known as rock oil or crude oil. Petroleum is the thick black liquid that is pumped up from underground at oil wells. It is a complex mixture of chemicals that have been created over many millions of years from the remains of living things. Petroleum is then refined to make fuels, chemicals, plastics, and pharmaceuticals.

PLATEAU
A flat area high above sea level.

POLLINATION
The process in which pollen is delivered to a flower by an insect or other animal, or by the wind. Flowers must be pollinated to produce seeds.

POLLUTION
The process by which human activities introduce harmful substances to the natural environment. Chemicals in the air, water, or soil, as well as too much light or noise, are all forms of pollution.

POPULATION
In biology, a group of animals of one species that live in a particular area, such as a forest or even a single tree.

PREDATOR
A hunting animal that catches and kills another animal for food.

PREHENSILE
A body part that can grasp an object, and so functions like a hand or foot.

PREHISTORIC
Referring to the time in a culture's history when no historical events were recorded.

PREY
An animal that is hunted by a predator.

REPTILE
A class of vertebrate that lays its eggs on land and has a body covered in waterproof scales. Reptiles include snakes, lizards, turtles, and crocodiles.

RIVER SYSTEM
A network of rivers that collect water from a particular region.

Napo River, a tributary of the Amazon River

RODENT
A small mammal that has sharp front teeth that are used for gnawing. Rodents include mice, squirrels, and guinea pigs.

SALT FLAT
A region of land that is covered in a crust of salt crystals.

SYMBIOSIS
A partnership between two members of different species. Both partners help each other by providing food or protection.

TIDAL BORE
A tall wave that travels up a river when the tide is very high.

TRIBUTARY
A small river that flows into a larger one.

VENOMOUS
Refers to venom, a poison that is injected by an animal into another one. Also used to describe animals that secrete venom.

VERTEBRATE
An animal that has a backbone.

VOLCANO
A mountain that develops around a crack in our planet's crust. Hot molten rock erupts out of the crack and spreads over the land as lava.

Reventador volcano, Ecuador

Index

Acknowledgments

Dorling Kindersley would like to thank: Ashwin Khurana for text editing; Helen Peters for indexing; Dan Green for proofreading; Simon Mumford for illustrating maps; and Sheryl Sadana for editorial assistance.

The publisher would like to thank the following for their kind permission to reproduce their photographs: (Key: a-above; b-below/bottom; c-center; f-far; l-left; r-right; t-top)

1 Dreamstime.com: Ammit. 2 Alamy Images: Cindy Hopkins (cl). Corbis: DPA / Rolf Wilms (c); Layne Kennedy (b). Dorling Kindersley: The Natural History Museum, London (c). Alamy Images: Amwu (tl). Getty Images: Photodisc / Alex Cao (tc). Thomas Marent: (tc/Fungus beetle). 2-3 Dreamstime.com: Rinus Baak (c). 3 Dreamstime.com: 44kmos (trl); Eric Gevaert (c). 4 Alamy Images: Westend61 GmbH (tl). Corbis: Hugh Sitton (br). Dreamstime.com: Andrea Poole (t); Isselee (tc); Viktarm (cl); Dolphfyn (cr). 5 SuperStock: Iberfoto (b). 6 Corbis: Minden Pictures / Murray Cooper (cl). Dreamstime.com: Antares614 (bc). NASA: GSFC (bl). 9 Alamy Images: Lee Dalton (br). Corbis: Stephanie Maze (br). Photoshot: Imagebroker.net (bl). 10-11 Corbis: Layne Kennedy. 10 Alamy Images: age fotostock / Alvaro Leiva (tl). Dean Jacobs: (tl). 11 Alamy Images: Visual&Written SL (c). Corbis: Reuters / Bruno Domingos (tl). NASA: (tr). 12 Alamy Images: BrazilPhotos.com (cr); Robert Fried (b). Getty Images: Photographer's Choice (t); Photolibrary (cl). 13 Alamy Images: BrazilPhotos.com. Corbis: Minden Pictures / Kevin Schafer. Dreamstime.com: Kschua (b). 14 Alamy Images: Zoonar GmbH (cr). Corbis: Galen Rowell (tr). 15 Alamy Images: David Noton Photography (tr); Martin Harvey (bl). Corbis: Alison Wright (tr). Getty Images: DPA / Rolf Wilms (c); Theo Allofs (tl). 16-17 SuperStock: Minden Pictures (b). 17 Alamy Images: Isselee (br). Corbis: Reuters / PAULO WHITAKER (cra). Glowimages: jspix (cl). 18 Corbis: Minden

Pictures / Mark Moffett (cra). Thomas Marent: (bl). Photoshot: NHPA (tl). 19 Alamy Images: Jacques Jangoux (br). Corbis: Minden Pictures / Mark Moffett (tr). Thomas Marent: (cl). 20 Alamy Images: Westend61 GmbH (tl). Corbis: David Davis (c); Steffen Foerster (bl); Lukas Blazek (bc); Hotshotsworldwide (clb). 20-21 Dreamstime.com: Rinus Baak (c). 21 Alamy Images: Images & Stories (bl); Kuttig - Travel (cr). Chris Jiménez: (tc); Viktarm (cl). Dreamstime.com: 44kmos (br); Hotshotsworldwide (tc). Photoshot: NHPA (tr). 22 Corbis: Arte & Immagini srl (cb); Minden Pictures / Thomas Marent (cla); AsiaPix / Disc Pictures (ca); Minden Pictures / Pete Oxford (cl). 22-23 Dreamstime.com: Eric Gevaert (b). 23 Corbis: Minden Pictures / Murray Cooper (c). Photoshot: Picture Alliance (tc). 24 Alamy Images: Amar and Isabelle Guillen—Guillen Photo LLC (bl); Juniors Bildarchiv GmbH (br). Corbis: Kevin Schafer (cra). FLPA: Photo Researchers (tl). 25 Alamy Images: William Mullins (tc). Corbis: Minden Pictures / Pete Oxford (tl). Dreamstime.com: Andrea Poole (br). 26 Alamy Images: Magica (clb/Euchroma gigantea); The Natural History Museum (clb/Titan Beetle). Corbis: Minden Pictures / Christian Ziegler (tl). Thomas Marent: (clb). 26-27 Getty Images: Piotr Naskrecki (tr). 27 Corbis: Minden Pictures / Piotr Naskrecki (tr). Dorling Kindersley: The Natural History Museum, London (tl). Dreamstime.com: Amwu (br). FLPA: Photo Researchers (tc). Corbis: Minden Pictures / Pete Oxford (tl). Phil Myers, Animal Diversity Web (http://animaldiversity.org): (bl). Science Photo Library: John Devries (br). 30 Photoshot: NHPA (bl). Science Photo Library: Dr Morley Read (br). Jerry Young: (cra). 30-31 Dreamstime.com: Ammit (c). 31 naturepl.com: Nick Garbutt (tl). Rex Features: Gerard Lacz (br). 32 Alamy Images: Nature Picture Library / Pete Oxford (clb). Dreamstime.com: Amwu (br); Dirk Ercken (c, bc). Isselee (b). FLPA: Photo Researchers (tl). Corbis: 123RF.com: Morley Read (br). Dreamstime.com: Isselee (b). 33 Angi Nelson: (t). Dreamstime.com: Isselee (bc,

br); Mgkuijpers (bl). SuperStock: NaturePL (crb). 34 Alamy Images: Joe Blossom (c); Morley Read (tl). Corbis: Minden Pictures / Pete Oxford (tl). Dreamstime.com: Isselee (bl); Mgkuijpers (cl). 35 Getty Images: Edelcio Muscat (b). Igor Siwanowicz (b). 36 Alamy Images: Juniors Bildarchiv GmbH (tl); WaterFrame (b). Pittsburgh Zoo & PPG Aquarium: (b). 37 Alamy Images: Joshua Hee (clb). Getty Images: Alexander Safonov (tr); Photo by K S Kong (c). 38 Alamy Images: Heritage Image Partnership Ltd (tl). Getty Images: National Geographic / Gordon Wiltsie (cra). 38-39 Glowimages: Hermes Images (b). 39 Dreamstime.com: Isselee (crb); Yeolka (tl). Getty Images: AFP / Mauricio Duenas (cra). 40 123RF.com: rook76 (b). With permission from Sociedad Estatal Correos y Telégrafos, S.A. (tl). Alamy Images: Rolf Richardson (br). Antonello Nusca (bra). Science Photo Library: Sheila Terry (clb). 41 Alamy Images: Patrick Pleul / Dpa Picture Alliance Archive (cr). Getty Images: Almir Bindilatti (tl); Photodisc / Alex Cao (tr). naturepl.com: Mark Carwardine (b). 42-43 SuperStock: Iberfoto (b). 42 123RF.com: ammit (br). Artwork © Christine Marsh, www.christinemarsh.com: (bl). 43 Corbis: Alison Wright (br). Getty Images: mlorenzphotography (cra). Mauricio Mercadante https://www.flickr.com/photos/mercadanteweb: (ca). Source: Empresa Brasileira de Correios e Telégrafos: (tr). 44 Ardea: Nick Gordon (br). SuperStock: Jan Sochor / age fotostock (tl). 44-45 © Survival International: (b). Corbis: Ueslei Marcelino / Reuters (tl, cb). naturepl.com: Luiz Claudio Marigo (tr). Photoshot: (br). 46 Alamy Images: peruvianpictures. com (cla); Rolf Richardson (b). Photoshot: NHPA (clb). 46-47 Alamy Images: Paul Harris / John Warburton-Lee Photography (t); Robert Schulten / imageBROKER (b). www.brasil.gov.br: Chico Batata / Agecom—AM (cr). 47 Alamy Images: Paul Harris / John Warburton-Lee Photography (tt); Photo by K S Kong (c). www.brasil.gov.br: Chico Batata / Agecom—AM (cr). 48 Alamy Images: Brasil2 (clb). 48-49 Corbis: Hugh Sitton (b). 49 Alamy Images: Larry Larsen (cf); Carlos Mora (tr). Dreamstime.com: Alex Braga (tl). 50 Alamy Images: Ricardo Beliel / BrazilPhotos (b). Getty Images: Donald Nausbaum (c). NASA: Earth Observatory (tl, cla). 51 Corbis: Reuters (b). 52 Alamy Images: BrazilPhotos. com (c); Nigel Dickinson (tl). 52-53 Science Photo Library: Jacques Jangoux. 53 Alamy Images: Edward Parker (tl); Stock Connection Blue (tr). Dreamstime. com: Jfanchin (cr). Getty Images: AFP / Antonio Scorza

(cl). 54 Corbis: Minden Pictures / Roland Seitre (cr). Dreamstime.com: Musat Christian (tl). 55 Alamy Images: Amazon-Images (r); VWPics / Kelvin Aitken (cl); Westend61 GmbH (b). Getty Images: Danita Delimont (r). 56 Corbis: Reuters / Brazil / Stringer (c). Dreamstime.com: Dolphyn (cla). 56-57 Corbis: Paulo Fridman (b). 57 Getty Images: AFP / Evaristo Sa (tr). Science Photo Library: Alison Wright (tl). 58 Corbis: Reuters / Mariana Bazo (cra). Getty Images: AFP / Xavier Leoty (b); Mint Images / Frans Lanting (c). 59 Alamy Images: Sue Cunningham Photographic (clb). Corbis: Demotix / Ik Aldama (cl); Minden Pictures / Theo Allofs (t); Frans Lanting (br). 60 Alamy Images: Cindy Hopkins (tl); Jan Carroll (br); Paul Springett C (bl). 60-61 Getty Images: Nigel Pavitt (c). 61 Getty Images: National Geographic / Richard Olsenius (t); WIN-Initiative (tr). 62 Corbis: Minden Pictures / Luciano Candisani (b). Photoshot: Nigel Smith (tl). 63 Alamy Images: Ammit (bry); MNS Photo (clb); Fernanda Preto (bc). Dreamstime.com: Goodween123 (cll); Viktarm (bra). Getty Images: Kam & Co. (tr). UniversalImagesGroup (br). 64 123RF.com: Alexandre Braga (bc). Alamy Images: Aaron Chervenak (cl). Dreamstime.com: Anatolii Aleksiaiev (c); Debra Law (tr). Getty Images: Alex Robinson (cl). 64-65 Corbis: Minden Pictures / Kevin Schafer. 65 Dreamstime.com: Brizardh (ca); Gunter Hoffmann (tr). 66 Dreamstime.com: Amaiquez (cra); Pablo Hidalgo (crb). 66-67 Corbis: Minden Pictures / Kevin Schafer. 67 Corbis: Minden Pictures / Mark Moffett (cl). Dreamstime.com: Alslutsky (cra); Feeding White-bellied Woodstar (clb); Mikelane45 (bl); Honourableandbold (cbl); Marek Jelínek (crb); Razvani (br). Thomas Marent: (br/Frog). 68-69 Corbis: Minden Pictures / Kevin Schafer. Dreamstime.com: Attila Jandi (cl). 68 Dreamstime. com: Alexandre Fagundes De Fagundes (br); Natursports (bl). Thomas Marent: (tr). 69 123RF.com: Pawel Opaska (b). Corbis: Remi Benali (tl). Dreamstime.com: Kseniya Ragozina (bl). Getty Images: Ariadne Van Zandbergen (br); Danita Delimont (b). 70 Corbis: Minden Pictures / Kevin Schafer. 70 123RF.com: Dirk Ercken (br). Thomas Marent: (br). 71 Getty Images: (br); ammit (br); Morley Read (br). Dreamstime.com: Kseniya Ragozina (tlr).

All other images © Dorling Kindersley
For further information see: www.dkimages.com

PERENNIALS

COMPLETE GARDENER'S LIBRARY™

Maggie
Oster

PERENNIALS

National Home
Gardening Club
Minneapolis, Minnesota

Perennials

Mike Vail
Vice President, Product & Business Development

Tom Carpenter
Director of Book Development

Dan Kennedy
Book Production Manager

Michele Teigen
Senior Book Development Coordinator

A. Cort Sinnes
Home Gardener's Library Executive Editor

David J. Farr, ImageSmythe
Clarinda Color
Art Direction and Production

Photo Credits

William D. Adams: 119; Jim Block: vi, 23, 33, 38, 39, 40, 50, 54, 67 (2), 69 (2), 70, 72, 74, 75, 77 (2), 78, 81 (2), 82, 83 (2), 85 (2), 88 (3), 90, 91 (2), 92 (2), 93 (3), 97, 99, 101 (3), 102, 106,107, 108, 109, 110 (2), 111 (2), 112, 113 (2), 119 (2), 120, 121, 122, 124 (2), 126, 127, 128, 129 (2), 131, 134 (3), 139, 142 (3), 143, 146, 150, 151 (2), 156 (2), 159, 163, 164,165, 168 (2), 172-3, 173, 174, 175; David Cavagnaro: ii-iii, vi, 4, 7, 20, 66, 68 (2), 69, 70, 71, 72, 74, 75, 76, 78, 79 (3), 80, (2), 81 (3), 82 (2), 83, 84, 85, 87, 88 (3), 89 (2), 90, 92, 94 (2), 95 (2), 96, 97, 98 (2), 99, 100 (2), 101, 102, 104, 106, 108, 111, 112, 114 (2), 115 (2), 116 (3), 117 (3), 118 (3), 120 (4), 121 (2), 122 (2), 123, 124, 125 (2), 128 (2), 129 (2), 130 (2), 132 (2), 135, 136 (2), 137, 138 (3), 139 (2), 140, 141, 142, 143 (2), 145, 146 (2), 148 (2), 150, 152 (2), 153, 154, 155, 157, 158, 159 (2), 160, 162 (2), 163 (2), 164 (4), 165 (2), 166-7, 167, 180; Walter Chandoha: i, v, vii, viii, 5, 6, 9, 12 (2), 13, 14, 17, 23 (2), 24-5, 25, 26 (3), 27 (3), 29, 37, 38, 39, 42, 48 (2), 51, 52, 53, 59, 60, 62, 63 (3), 89, 90, 94, 126 (2), 153, 162, 164, 169, 170 (2), 179; Rosalind Creasy: 99; Thomas E. Eltzroth: 104, 130, 178, 181; Derek Fell: Cover, 16, 18, 19, 41, 43, 44, 50, 55, 56, 58, 60, 61, 70, 73, 78, 102, 108, 122, 134, 139, 143, 144, 156, 159, 160, 162, 179; Marge Garfield: 32, 33, 35, 37, 44; Saxon Holt: v, 6, 21 (2), 28, 46-7, 47, 49, 53, 75, 86; Bill Johnson: 32, 71, 73 (2), 76 (3), 84 (2), 85, 87, 88, 91 (2), 92, 95 (2), 96, 97, 98 (2), 100, 101, 103 (2), 106, 107, 108, 110, 111, 112, 113, 116, 123, 124, 125, 127, 133, 134, (2), 135, 136, 137, 140, 141 (3), 143, 145, 147 (2), 149, 151, 154, 155 (2), 156, 157, 158, (2), 159, 160 (2), 161, 162, 163, 165; Michael Landis: v (2), 2-3, 3, 10-11, 11; Maggie Oster: v, 8, 22, 30, 31, 36 (2), 40, 45, 49, 55, 64-5, 65, 107, 171, 176, 177, 182, 183; Jerry Pavia: 13, 15, 56, 57, 58, 68, 80, 83, 86, 103, 104, 105 (2), 114, 127, 132 (2), 133, (2), 135, 136, 144, 160 (2), 161 (2), 163; Robert Perron: 34; Diane A. Pratt: 180; Stephen R. Swinburne: 106 (3); Mark Turner: 31, 61, 108, 109 (2).

7 8 9 10 11 / 05 04 03 02 01
ISBN 0-914697-89-7

National Home Gardening Club
12301 Whitewater Drive
Minnetonka, Minnesota 55343
www.gardeningclub.com

CONTENTS

PERENNIAL PLEASURE

I can remember it as clearly as if it were yesterday. There was this spectacular flower in our backyard, at just about eye level for a seven-year-old. The top was the purest white, the bottom was a deep purple color, and there was this wonderful fuzzy stuff on the lower petals. Mother called it an iris and said its name was 'Wabash', just like the name of the river in the Indiana state song, "On the Banks of the Wabash," that my father loved to sing.

Certainly, this was not my introduction to flowers, as my parents had gardened since long before I was born. That there were flowers in their lives at that particular moment did speak volumes about the kind of people they were. A year-and-a-half earlier, their lovingly restored, century-old farmhouse had burned to the ground. There was scant insurance or income to rebuild, but somehow they managed, cutting lumber from the farm and doing the building themselves. During that time, my father continued to milk dairy cows, and my mother taught school. Yet, there was also enough time and energy to plant a new flower border. No one will ever accuse my mother of being a spendthrift, so most of the plants were ones moved from around the old house or shared by friends, but for some reason, she splurged that year and ordered a 'Wabash' iris. There were other iris' in the garden, but that was the one that stole my heart.

Perhaps it would make for a better story if I could say that at that specific moment I decided to study horticulture and write books about gardening when I got older. That it was that particular flower or seeing my parents put so much importance on having flowers, even when other matters were so pressing, that immediately and profoundly touched me. The reality is that the process was much more subtle—but no less effective.

My mother's teaching mentor emphasized that children were taught, "Line upon line, precept upon precept." And so it was with me. There were untold numbers of ways that nature and flowers and gardening were a part of my family's everyday life. Sometimes it was being called out to see the first brave crocus in the spring, while at other times it might have been standing together on the front porch to watch a spectacular sunset and make a wish on the evening star,

gathering a bouquet for the dinner table, or appreciating the smells and sounds of the different seasons. No matter what career path I might have chosen, my life would have been inextricably linked with the natural world.

What my parents had learned from their families and friends, and, consequently, passed on to me was a love of the beautiful in nature, especially that of flowers. Without medical research or self-help books, they instinctively knew that when life was difficult and stressful, making time for flowers would raise their spirits. The same is true for any of us today.

But as important as it is to our health and well-being as individuals to have flowers in our lives, the benefits of our

Maggie Oster

flowers and gardens on others can reach greater distances than we might ever imagine. You may never know how you've affected the people who walk by your garden each day. Maybe it will inspire that little child who can look eyeball to petal, or provide happiness for the elderly neighbor who can no longer garden. Or, since one of the overriding characteristics of gardeners is their propensity for sharing, be it divisions, seeds, advice, opinions, information or experiences, you may start a chain reaction with your deeds. The neighbor lady who inspired my mother to grow flowers when she was a little girl never directly knew the child who fell in love with an iris and grew up to write gardening books, but if not for her, you might be reading a very different book. So remember: You sow powerful seeds with your flowers, within your own heart as well as the hearts of others for generations to come.

Maggie Oster

Peonies are among the most popular of all perennials, offering countless forms and colors, splendid fragrance and longevity.

Chapter 1

❦

THE POSSIBILITIES OF PERENNIALS

Perennials, more than any other group of plants, turn a yard into a garden with their diversity of colors, bloom seasons, textures, shapes, sizes and forms. Add a few daylilies around the mailbox or lamp post, a cluster of ornamental grasses at the corner of the house, a ground cover of sweet woodruff under a tree or some rudbeckia among the foundation planting of shrubs, and your yard begins to take on a character of lushness and beauty. Expend a little more effort in creating beds and borders overflowing with the flowers and foliage of perennials, and you'll be on your way to having the kind of garden people fantasize about.

Perennials certainly are nothing if not the stuff of fantasy. For some, it is the nostalgia for a grandmother's garden, overflowing with rainbow-colored iris, sweetly scented peonies and boldly

Perennials bring a yard to life with their many colors, shapes and forms, plus they are adaptable to a wide range of conditions, styles and situations, allowing every garden to be a unique creation.

Whether perennials are short or tall, upright or spreading, with fuzzy, grassy or fleshy leaves, they all have the ability to grow and bloom year after year without replanting.

temperatures, then they send up fresh growth and flowers each spring, repeating the cycle every year. Some perennials, such as peonies and bleeding hearts, often outlive us, while others, like delphiniums, may survive for only a few seasons. Other perennials develop woody stems that lose their leaves but do not die back, while others retain their leaves during winter. To compare perennials with other flowers, annuals complete their life cycle in a single growing season; biennials produce leaves the first year, then bloom, set seed, and die the second year; and bulbs grow and bloom year after year but are classified separately because of their root structure.

Through the centuries, gardeners have been drawn to perennials because of their ability to grow and bloom for years on end, theoretically saving labor, time and money; theoretically, because the tendency for many of us is not to be content with just a few perennials. In fact, the difficult aspect of perennials is not in growing them but in limiting ourselves to a reasonable number. For when the right perennials are chosen for a site, most are remarkably easy to grow, and they often have the good grace to generate new plants for transplanting and sharing.

There are literally tens of thousands of plants from all over the world to choose among for your perennial pleasure. No matter what your given climate, soil, moisture, light conditions or type of design, be it hot and humid, cool and moist, dry soil or wet, acid or alkaline, formal or cottage garden, woodland or meadow landscape, there are perennials that will satisfy. Utilize the chapter on analyzing your garden environment to help you select the plants most suited for your garden. You may want to try a few plants that seem questionable for your conditions, but by choosing the most adapted ones, you will make gardening much easier.

The choices are also many when considering how to use perennials in our gardens. There are any number of

rising spires of delphinium. For others, enticing magazine or book photos or maybe a visit to the gardens of England has beckoned us to perennials like a siren's song. Some people are drawn to perennials because of the many different types of plants available, while others were given transplants by friends explaining how easy they are to grow.

Sometimes, people just tire of planting so many annuals every year. Whatever the reasoning or rationale, perennials have a remarkable ability to fulfill our daydreams.

By definition, perennials are herbaceous, or fleshy, plants that grow, bloom and (usually) die back to the ground in the winter with the roots surviving cold

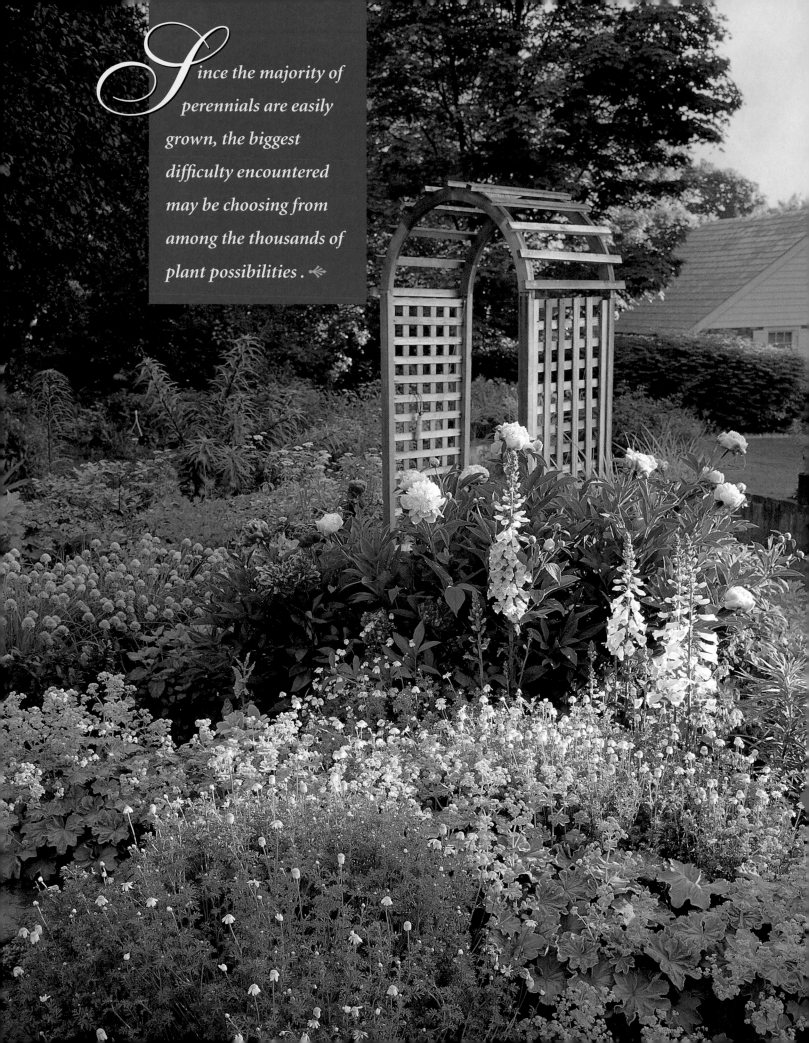

*S*ince the majority of
perennials are easily
grown, the biggest
difficulty encountered
may be choosing from
among the thousands of
plant possibilities . ❦

There is no one right or wrong way to use perennials in the landscape. Some people relish the formality of traditional English-style perennial borders, with their mirror images reflecting each other across the lawn, while others will find this style confining.

When adding perennials to your yard, step back and look at the many places they can be used. Why not start at the beginning, by emphasizing the driveway and mailbox with a colorful planting, such as these long-blooming gaillardia 'Goblin'?

different ways of doing things; the most important person you have to please is yourself. Some people are content to get whatever perennials are available at their local discount department store. Others search out esoteric mail-order nurseries that carry the most obscure plant varieties. One gardener may like beds of flowers while another prefers borders. You may want all one color and straight paths, while your neighbor combines colors with abandon along curving paths. No one method or technique promises either success or failure.

The chapter on the various ways to use perennials, including in borders, beds, foundation and corner plantings as well as groundcovers, along with an assortment of garden themes, is intended to inspire you to look at your

Perennials adapt not only to many different garden styles but also to a wide variety of garden environments, including shade.

erennials offer an amazing diversity of sizes, shapes, textures, colors and forms of both flowers and foliage, affording an unlimited palette. ✦

yard with fresh eyes, opening you to the possibilities of perennials. If you desire artistic success, the chapter on design principles will help you integrate the many elements of perennials into a creative whole.

What may be the most intriguing aspect of perennials is their variety. Some perennials grow only inches tall, while others exceed 8 feet. They may creep, mound, sprawl or reach for the sky. Some have a light airy appearance, with grasslike or feathery leaves, while others present a bold or exotic appearance. You never knew there were so many shades of green, grey, gold and white until you start studying perennial foliage. Not only does flower shape and color run the gamut, but so does the blooming season. By careful selection, you can have flowers in all but the coldest months of the year. With the lists of suggested perennials throughout this book and the detailed descriptions of plants in the plant profile section, you'll have a starting point in choosing the best perennials for different garden sites with a multitude of uses and styles.

Be warned, however, that perennials do require some maintenance. I have heard countless beginning gardeners say that they want to grow perennials because they won't have to do anything. My first reaction is why bother? One of the joys of gardening is the process itself—to get out there in the peace and quiet and putter around. Certainly there are some perennials that you can plant and pretty much forget about, but you should explore the pleasures and rewards when you put some effort into gardening with perennials.

Healthy, flourishing plants, however used in the garden, always bring satisfaction. To achieve that aspect of success, use the best and most efficient ways to care for your perennials. Just as we lead healthier, happier lives when we have a comfortable home, nutritious food, regular medical care and thoughtful attention from family and friends, your plants will respond with enthusiastic growth to well-prepared soil, consistent fertiliza-

Perennials, just as with any living entity, require a certain amount of care and maintenance, but, on the whole, the demands are reasonable and far outweighed by the the beauty and untold amount of pleasure they'll bring to you, your family and friends.

tion and watering, and reasonable care and maintenance.

Among my earliest childhood memories are those of the flowers that my mother, relatives and neighbors grew, shared and enjoyed. Their enthusiasm was contagious, and even many years later, I cannot imagine living anywhere, be it urban or rural, where I would not want to be surrounded by flowers. The

vegetable, herb, fruit and other plants bring their own particular satisfaction, but it is the perennial flowers, with their versatility, adaptability, diversity and sheer beauty that return year after year, some holding a nostalgic place in my heart, others tempting me with their rarity, that keep me looking forward to each new day and new year in the garden.

Chapter 2

THE GARDEN ENVIRONMENT

A well-grown garden has intrinsic beauty, but the first step in attaining that success is not in the work of growing the plants but in selecting those that are most closely adapted to your environment. Considerations include climate, soil, sunlight and the amount of moisture available. Certainly there are ways to modify the soil with amendments; to change the soil moisture with drainage tiles, raised beds or watering systems; to alter the light by trimming, removing or planting trees; or to find a protected microclimate within the yard for less-than-hardy plants. In fact, with only a few minor changes, a wider range of plants than normal can be grown. But to make large-scale, wholesale changes is usually very expensive, and, particularly in the case of irrigation, detrimental to our natural resources. How much more in tune with the natural world to choose wisely at the outset.

The first step in growing beautiful perennial flowers is in selecting ones that are most closely aligned to the climate, soil, sunlight and moisture naturally available in your yard.

survive a minimum winter temperature.

The United States Department of Agriculture has processed data on the lowest temperatures that can be expected each year in the United States and created the USDA Plant Hardiness Zone Map (see page 184). This map includes ten different zones, with each zone representing a difference of 10°F. Almost all plant labels or catalog descriptions carry the hardiness zone for any perennial sold.

What makes gardening complicated and, for many people, an intriguing challenge, are the various other climatic factors that come into play. For example, there are microclimates that exist within these hardiness zones. Those who garden in urban areas often find that they may be an entire zone warmer than the surrounding region. Most likely you'll also find microclimates within your yard, such as a warmer area against a south-facing wall or cooler ones on the north side of the house or at the bottom of a hill.

Then again, even if a plant is considered hardy for an area, other climatic factors can affect its ability to survive winter. In areas with midwinter warm spells, perennials are particularly susceptible to what is known as "heaving," in which the roots are

Be aware of microclimates within your yard. A south-facing stone wall absorbs winter sun, providing warmer winter temperatures at the base, but it's hotter there in the summer.

Fortunately for the generally obsessive gardener, the restrictions put on acquisition are relatively minimal. Perennials epitomize the twentieth-century concept of the global village, with thousands of different plants available from all over the world. Many of these are adaptable to just about any situation. In a backlash to this wealth of flora, some people look to plants native to their area, but even with these, it's smart to consider individual growing requirements. Whether you take the multinational or indigenous approach to plant selection, be sure to allow the time and effort necessary to understand the effects and interactions of climate, soil, moisture and sunlight on plant growth so that you start off with the best plants for your garden.

CLIMATE

When thinking of plants and climate, the first thing that occurs to most people is winter hardiness, or the ability of a plant to

Snow serves as natural protection for roots.

Loosely mulching plants with evergreen branches prevents the plant roots from being heaved out of the ground during alternate freezing and thawing winter temperatures.

literally heaved out of the ground by the soil's alternate freezing and thawing. The remedy for this problem is mulching to keep the soil temperature consistent. Water drainage is another factor that affects hardiness, as many plants will not survive poorly drained soil during the winter. The amount and duration of snow cover during the winter are important, too. Gardeners in areas with a lot of snow are fortunate that snow acts as a natural insulator.

Latitude, elevation and the proximity of a large body of water also have an effect. For example, compare Atlanta, Georgia, to Seattle, Washington. Both of which are classified as Zone 8, but remember that the closer to the equator, the hotter the sun. Large bodies of water tend to cool the surrounding areas in summer and warm them in winter. Often, there is more fog or cloud cover in these areas, too, which also affects plant growth.

Gardeners along a seacoast may have to contend with salt spray and sandy soil, but they have the advantage of temperatures being more moderate in both summer and winter compared to the surrounding region.

An evergreen windbreak protects perennials from damaging winds, plus it provides a dramatic backdrop that accentuates the plants.

Strong prevailing winds are another climatic factor. They affect plant growth by causing the soil to dry out quickly, so plants transpire water faster than the roots can absorb and transport it to the leaves; it also causes tall plants to blow over. For those who live with strong prevailing winds, shorter plants are a better choice, as are those adapted to dry conditions and sometimes even those that are at least a climate zone hardier. A windy site can be remedied by installing a windbreak of trees or shrubs. An open fence will also help, but not a solid one, as it just makes the effect of the wind even greater.

Another climatic factor is the first and last frost dates. Periods of warm weather before the last frost make it difficult to grow perennials that start growth early in the season. Conversely, in the autumn, plants that bloom then may be literally nipped in the bud by early frosts.

Many gardeners in the United States are particularly aware of the effects of summer temperatures and humidity on perennials. Because we tend to look so much to English gardens and gardening books, we are apt to want some of the plants that flourish in English gardens. Unfortunately, many of these simply languish in midwestern and southern heat and humidity. Gardeners, of course, have learned tricks to offset these problems, such as providing light afternoon shade to successfully grow these cool-summer plants, but, even then, they never attain the splendid form they show when grown in their ideal climate.

It is impossible for any gardening book to address all the possible situations and specific adaptability of each plant for each situation. This is where talking with other gardeners in your area, visiting local private and public gardens, and utilizing local experts, such as your local county extension agent, is the best way to learn. The lists in this book will provide a starting point for choosing perennials for your garden. Keep in mind that some plants that will grow in your area may not be included in the lists, just as some plants listed may not grow well in your specific garden.

Among the perennials that withstand the hot days and nights typical of warmer climates are 'Oxbow' sedums, hostas, shasta daisies and gaura.

SOME PERENNIALS FOR WARM CLIMATES

Not only will blistering summer days cause plants to deteriorate and weaken, but so will hot, humid nights. The following plants are ones that, with other growing conditions being correct, should actually flourish in such conditions, even through Zone 9. An even greater variety of perennials with thrive through Zone 8.
(spp. = species in the plural;
cvs. = cultivars)

Acanthus spp.—bear's breeches
Achillea spp. and cvs.—yarrow
Amsonia spp.—blue stars
Aquilegia x *hybrida*—hybrid columbine
Aquilegia longissima—longspur columbine
Armeria plantaginea—plantain thrift
Artemisia absinthium—wormwood
Artemisia ludoviciana cvs.—'Silver King', 'Silver Queen' artemisia
Arum italicum 'Pictum'—variegated Italian arum
Asclepias tuberosa—butterfly weed
Astilbe x *arendsii* cvs.—astilbe
Baptisia spp.—wild indigo
Belamcanda chinensis—blackberry lily
Bletilla striata—bletilla
Boltonia asteroides—boltonia
Ceratostigma spp.—leadwort

Chrysanthemum x *morifolium* (*Dendranthema* x *grandiflorum*)— chrysanthemum
Chrysanthemum x *superbum* (*Leucanthemum* x *superbum*)—Shasta daisy
Chrysogonum virginianum—green-and-gold
Coreopsis spp. and cvs.—coreopsis, tickseed
Crocosmia x *crocosmiiflora*—crocosmia
Cyclamen hederifolium—hardy cyclamen
Dianthus spp. and cvs.—sweet William, pinks
Dicentra spp. and cvs.—bleeding heart
Digitalis purpurea—common foxglove
Eryngium planum—flat sea holly
Euphorbia myrsinites—myrtle euphorbia
Euphorbia wallichii—wallich spurge
Filipendula ulmaria—queen-of-the-meadow
Gaillardia x *grandiflora* cvs.—blanket flower
Gaura lindheimeri—gaura
Gypsophila paniculata—baby's breath
Helianthus angustifolius—swamp sunflower
Heliopsis helianthoides cvs.—sunflower, heliopsis
Helleborus foetidus—bear's foot hellebore
Helleborus orientalis—Lenten rose

By taking into account the climate, soil, rainfall and light in your garden, you can choose plants that are closely adapted to your environment, thereby increasing your chances for success.

Heavy, or dense, shade is the deep, cool shade cast by tall buildings or mature evergreen trees. Very few plants can grow with this type of shade unless there is at least a small amount of reflected light.

Evergreens and mature deciduous trees can create an area of heavy, or dense, shade.

Open, or half, shade gets no direct sun during the brightest daylight hours but lots of reflected or bright light. This includes areas with shade cast by north-facing walls, fences, or low buildings or the area under a fiberglass-roofed patio. Again, most shade-loving plants grow well in this type of shade, and so do some sun-loving plants.

Full, or medium, shade gets no direct sun. It may be on the north side of structures where there are also trees or other structures obscuring the light. It is also the area under large trees that have a dense, wide canopy. Many shade-loving plants can survive here, especially native woodland plants.

A border can be designed for shade-to-sun.

The light under deciduous trees may be full shade in the summer, but in the spring, it will be sunny enough for woodland wildflowers.

Chapter 3

GARDEN STYLES

From the earliest waxen blooms of the Lenten rose battling late-winter winds and snow to the exuberant willfulness of the last asters on a frosty fall morning, the perennial garden offers us the prospect of being surrounded by flowers for many months of the year. The inherent qualities of these flowers are such that even the most casually placed plants bring a charm to the yard. By expending a little effort in considering where and how to place perennials in the landscape, we multiply our pleasures. Whether you have a minuscule urban property or extensive rural acreage, there are rewards in developing planted areas that suit your own particular needs, desires, tastes and lifestyle. Success lies not in rarity or numbers, but in how the plants are used and cared for. It is about passion and vision—and follow-through.

Using perennials in the landscape is somewhat like being handed a giant box of

The glorious beauty of perennial flowers encourages us to use them throughout the yard. In developing areas for planting, think about what garden styles bring you the greatest pleasure.

An informal cottage-style border along the driveway reflects the building design.

Many gardeners find that they like to combine plants in an informal manner but within formally shaped beds. The addition of trees, shrubs, and vines creates a visual whole for the landscape, plus provides visual interest to the garden year-round.

crayons and being told you can't make mistakes—as long as you stay true to yourself. You can create your own lines, and you don't even have to stay inside them. Want a smashing bit of color in a particular corner? Then have it. Since such *carte blanche* can sometimes be a little intimidating, let's consider some ideas to get you started. The first decision in how to use perennials in the landscape is the degree of formality you like to see in a garden. Next, consider the basic ways perennials are used in the landscape: borders, island beds, foundation plantings, corner plantings and ground covers. Then, depending on shade or sun, wet soil or dry, and other factors, you might select plants for certain purposes, such as a shady garden of ferns, a meadow garden of native plants, a garden along a stream or one that attracts butterflies and birds. After you've considered the many different ways that perennials can be used in the landscape, then go to Chapter 4, "Design Considerations," to learn just how to do it.

FORMAL VERSUS INFORMAL

The delineations between the design concepts of formal and informal are essentially a matter of balance, of symmetry versus asymmetry. At their most basic definitions, each side of a formal arrangement matches, or is a mirror image of the other, while an informal arrangement is defined by the two sides being different, but equal in value, or weight.

In translating these design concepts to gardening, formal gardens are generally those based on a central axis with identical plantings on either side. At their most extreme, these are large, elaborate affairs as part of an expansive estate and mansion, such as those built by European and English nobility beginning in the Renaissance. Over time, the concept has been reduced and adapted to more

Whether on an estate or in a back yard, the elements of a classic formal garden are the same: a central axis with identical plantings on each side mirroring one another. Here the beds are edged in lamb's-ears and 'Brilliant' sedum and accented by hollies.

modest plots and dwellings. Among the best examples of small-scale formal gardens are those of Colonial Williamsburg. As exemplified there, formal gardens are composed of beds with clearly delineated geometric shapes, be they rectangular, square, round or pie-shaped, usually outlined by low, clipped hedges and straight paths. Perennial plantings within the beds are also symmetrical, with plants chosen for their ability to stay in place and to maintain a uniform height.

At the opposite extreme is the most informal of gardens, that of the cottage. In its purest form, the true cottage garden is one of necessity, with design elements being of little import. As such it is a higgledy-piggledy mixture of all kinds of plants, including perennials, annuals, herbs, shrubs, trees, roses, vegetables and fruits. A fence, wall or hedge encloses the garden and irregular stepping stones allow passage among the plants. With the introduction of "design" into this garden, it evolves toward more clearly defined beds and borders, often with curving edges and paths, and plants of irregular shapes. In essence, the informal garden draws on

One of the best ways to have a flower border looking good for much of the growing season is to incorporate roses, shrubs, annuals, herbs or other plants with the perennials.

nature. On a large scale, this naturalistic approach to landscape design had its heyday in England with the garden at Stourhead, and in the United States with the gardens of Frederick Law Olmstead. No matter the scale, a well-designed informal garden has an asymmetrical balance at its core.

If straight lines aren't to your liking, try creating borders with softer, flowing edges.

Between the extremes of the formal and informal are infinite combinations. The predominant variation is to have the beds laid out in a formal pattern, but planted in a relaxed, informal way. Both large and small properties can have combinations of the different styles, often with a formal area near the house, while garden areas at the farthest edges of the property are more informally planted.

Perhaps it will be an existing landscape feature, such as a rock wall, that will be a determining factor in what type of planting style you choose.

BASIC THEMES AND VARIATIONS ON THE USES OF PERENNIALS

The most dedicated perennial enthusiast will say that perennials can be used anywhere in the landscape, and there is not even the remotest bit of fibbing in such a declaration. Still, there are certain points where it is most logical to begin. With perennials, these include borders, island beds, foundation plantings, corner plantings and ground cover plantings. With the great wealth of perennials available and wide range of climates and personal preferences, these starting points allow you to develop a somewhat traditional perennial planting, turn problem areas such as boggy soil into an asset or create a garden for a specific purpose, such as attracting butterflies and birds or creating fragrance.

BORDERS

Perennials and flower borders are thought of almost simultaneously by many people. Yet it has really only been in the last hundred years or so that this phenomenon has come about. In reaction to the beds planted with regimented rows of brashly colored flowers so favored by the mid-Victorians, two English gardeners, William Robinson and Gertrude Jekyll, turned the gardening world upside down. They designed long beds at least 9 feet wide, backed by a hedge or brick wall and filled them with masses of subtly colored perennials. Ideally, there were two borders, parallel and separated by a closely-clipped lawn. The tallest plants were placed at the back and the lowest at the front. Colors were soft blues, pinks and white, with only the occasional gold or yellow, all to give the effect of an Impressionist painting. Colors were never to clash, but contrasting forms were put next to each other for interest, and bloom sequence was carefully planned. Significant examples of this type of perennial border still exist in England today, most notably at Wisley, Hampton Court and Great Dixter.

Just as the intervening years have wrought a multitude of changes in society, so too, with the grand perennial border. Such borders require a great deal of space and labor. Most Americans do not have the

Borders derived from the cottage-style of gardening may utilize a wide variety of plants besides perennials, plus have curving edges and meandering paths that beckon one to go exploring. A partially hidden sundial catches the eye in the distance.

advantage of the cool, moist English climate. Still, much has been gleaned from the era of Robinson and Jekyll, with the perennial border of today borrowing from them as well as from the informal cottage garden. The result may best be labeled the mixed border, using as it does a wide range of plants in addition to perennials. These may include both evergreen and deciduous trees and shrubs, roses, bulbs, herbs and annuals. The woody plants provide a year-round framework as well as seasonal color, while the bulbs bring life to the garden in early spring and the annuals give summer-long color.

Certain rules still apply when creating a border, but only insofar as your desired effect. For instance, borders are now thought of in much smaller terms, usually no more than five feet across. A background still shows off the plants, but it now may be a simple fence or an assortment of shrubs planted in a curving line. Shorter, sturdier hybrid varieties are used to minimize the need for staking. The low-in-the-front, medium-in-the-middle and tall-in-the back rule is much more freely interpreted, often with taller plants set more toward the front.

Taking the sequence of bloom into consideration when planning still makes sense, but the use of color is more broadly interpreted. As the section on color in Chapter 4 illustrates, there are many different types of color combinations. The shorter the border, the better to use monochromatic or analagous color schemes. With a longer border, it's possible to use more colors or color schemes, but the effect will be most pleasing if different areas are separated with shrubs or foliage plants.

*U*tilize disparate styles
by combining an
informal border
of perennials and
other flowers with
a formally clipped
boxwood or other low
hedge. ❦

Informal island bed plantings offer the aestheic advantage of their beauty appreciated from all sides, while their free-form shapes fits in with naturalistic landscapes.

FOUNDATION AND ENTRYWAY PLANTINGS

When landscaping a home, the first places most people consider are the foundation of the house, the driveway and the front walk and door. Traditionally, evergreen trees and shrubs form the basis of these plantings that are a first impression of the home and, potentially, the creativity of the owner. They are placed so that they hide the foundation from view, frame the house, outline windows and soften corners. Ideally, the trees and shrubs are not placed in a single row, but arranged in groups of different heights and forms.

But all those evergreens can get a little boring. And so can those rows of petunias put in every year. To shake up this part of the landscape, why not try adding perennials? Use the evergreens as the background for a new perennial border. In the winter, the evergreens provide form and structure to the front of the home, while in the summer, you'll have lots of colorful flowers welcoming people. In addition, a perennial planting will better tie the house to the surrounding landscape and emphasize the trees and shrubs.

Since these flowers are in front, you'll want them to look good for much of summer. That means choosing easily grown perennials with a long blooming season and few pest problems—and providing the best soil preparation, care and maintenance. This is not the site for single specimens or plants that have to be fussed over. You want to make a statement here, so, for the greatest effect, make groupings of perennials, preferably with triangular placement rather than rows. Depending on the space available and your preference, you may want to work up an area three to four feet wide in front of the shrubs. This allows you to have plantings of different heights progressing from back to front.

Don't forget about other areas in front of your home, such as the lamp post, where a large-specimen perennial is effective. Also consider using the space between the walk and the house for a planting of perennials. The strip between the drive and the property boundary is another possible area for perennials.

ISLAND BEDS

The use of beds, open on all sides, is not a new concept in gardening, having been used in ancient times in the courtyard gardens of Persia, then again in the cloistered Medieval gardens and walled Elizabethan *pleasaunce* gardens. Formally arranged beds were the standard in ornate Renaissance gardens, and Victorians took the concept to exaggerated lengths with their stylized plantings of annuals in bedding schemes. Although Gertrude Jekyll is known for her perennial borders, the formally arranged beds she designed at Hestercombe show her willingness and ability to use beds of perennials. For gardens where a formal design is appropriate, beds are certainly still an excellent choice. Using the traditional geometric shapes, these beds are formed into a symmetrical arrangement composing a whole.

A completely different approach to gardening in beds are the island beds promoted by English perennial expert Alan Bloom. These are large and free-form in shape, and fit in with a naturalistic, informal landscape.

No matter their shape or size, the advantages of beds are not only that they can be appreciated from all sides, but also that they can be maintained from any perspective. In addition, light, air and moisture reaches the plants more readily than when they are grown in borders backed by walls, fences or hedges. This means fewer disease problems and less need for staking.

In planting an island bed, the tallest-growing plants are placed near the center, with progressively shorter plants placed outward from the center to the edges. For the most balanced effect, the height of the tallest plants should be half the width of the bed. The overall look will also be more effective if plants of one kind are set out in groups.

No boring planting of yews or junipers at this house. Instead, colorful flowering shrubs like rose-of-Sharon and 'Wonderful' pomegranate are interplanted with long-blooming perennials such as rudbeckia and gloriosa daisies.

LONG-BLOOMING PERENNIALS

The following perennials should bloom at least eight weeks, and even up to 12 weeks, depending mainly on climate and care. Most are summer-blooming, but others will extend the season, either in late spring and early summer or in autumn. This list offers a variety of heights and colors as well as plants for both sun and shade.

Achillea millefolium 'Fire King'
Armeria maritima
Aster x *frikartii* 'Monch'
Aster x *frikartii* 'Wonder of Staffa'
Aster novae-angliae 'September Ruby'
Chrysanthemum rubellum
(*Dendranthema zawadskii*) 'Clara Curtis'
Chrysogonum virginianum 'Mark Viette'
Chrysopsis mariana
Coreopsis grandiflora 'Early Sunrise'
Coreopsis grandiflora 'Sunray'
Coreopsis verticillata 'Moonbeam'
Coreopsis verticillata 'Zagreb'
Corydalis lutea
Dicentra eximia 'Alba'

Dicentra x 'Luxuriant'
Gaillardia x *grandiflora* 'Baby Cole'
Gaura lindheimeri
Geranium sanguineum var. *striatum*
Hemerocallis 'Happy Returns'
Hemerocallis 'Stella de Oro'
Heterotheca villosa 'Golden Sunshine'
Hylotelephium (*Sedum*) x 'Autumn Joy'
Lychnis x *arkwrightii*
Malva alcea 'Fastigiata'
Nepeta x *faassenii* 'Dropmore'
Perovskia atriplicifolia
Phlox paniculata 'Eva Cullum'
Phlox paniculata 'Franz Schubert'
Phlox paniculata 'Sandra'
Platycodon grandiflorus
Rudbeckia nitida 'Autumn Glory'
Rudbeckia nitida 'Goldquelle'
Salvia x *superba* 'East Friesland'
Salvia x *superba* 'Lubeca'
Salvia x *superba* 'May Night'
Scabiosa caucasica 'Butterfly Blue'
Stokesia laevis 'Bluestone'
Verbena bonariensis
Veronica 'Sunny Border Blue'

A stone wall and wrought-iron gate are inviting with plantings of flowers.

Large hostas make a bold corner planting.

GROUNDCOVERS

Plants carpeting the ground are useful, as they prevent the soil washing away, and also bring beauty to the landscape. The most important requirement of a groundcover is that it spreads quickly and efficiently. Plants chosen as groundcovers often have fibrous roots that bind the soil. The second consideration is ease of maintenance. The area to be covered may be large or small, in sun or shade. Groundcover plants may grow close to the ground or with some height. Most often a single type of plant is used as a groundcover in a particular area, but sometimes several can be effectively combined.

The best known and most widely used groundcover for sunny areas is bluegrass. It withstands rugged use, but is, unfortunately, very high maintenance and can be particularly troublesome on slopes or under shrubs. It is also rather boring. For shady conditions, it is superseded by fescue, with the same advantages and disadvantages. Woody evergreen plants, such as creeping junipers or English ivy, are chosen for groundcover use because they are green year-round. For areas where there is little or no foot traffic, certain perennials are the plants of choice because of their various textures, forms and, in many cases, their flowers. Some are for sun, others for various degrees of shade. Using perennial groundcovers not only can make garden chores easier, but also make your garden more interesting.

CORNER PLANTINGS

Corner plantings are not a widespread concept, but quite effective when you want a small, defined space for perennials. Working most effectively on small urban or suburban lots, it involves defining one or more of the outer limits of the property with a short length of fence or hedge. Purchased fencing usually comes in eight-foot lengths, so the basis for a corner planting would be a corner post with lengths of fencing at right angles. Low fencing, such as post-and-rail or picket works best. Of course, the concept can be enlarged, perhaps with an "anchor" plant, such as a spring-blooming or an evergreen tree. Within this triangular area, taller plants are placed near the corner, with progressively shorter plants toward the outside points and across the front.

SOME PERENNIALS AS GROUNDCOVERS

*Ajuga genevensis, A. pyramidalis, A.
   reptans*
Alchemilla mollis
Asarum europaeum, A. hartwegii
*Bergenia cordifolia, B. crassifolia, B.
   stracheyi*
Brunnera macrophylla
Cerastium tomentosum
Ceratostigma plumbaginoides
Chrysogonum virginianum
Convallaria majalis
Corydalis lutea
Dianthus gratianopolitanus 'Bath's Pink'

The corner space between two stairs becomes a focal point near a deck when planted with lilies, clematis, delphiniums and other flowers. Look around your yard for different areas such as this that can provide big rewards with little effort or money.

A steep slope becomes an asset rather than an eyesore or problem area when stone terraces are installed and planted with perennials. The creeping phlox is stunning in the spring with the redbud tree, while other perennials lend interest later in the summer.

Epimedium alpinum, E. grandiflorum, E. pinnatum, E. x rubrum, E. x versicolor, E. x youngianum

Ferns

Festuca cinerea cvs.

Fragaria spp.

Galium odoratum

Geranium x *cantabrigiense* 'Biokovo'

Helleborus argutifolius, H. foetidus, H. niger, H. orientalis

Heuchera americana, H. x brizoides, H. micrantha, H. sanguinea, H. villosa

Hosta spp. and cvs.

Iberis sempervirens

Iris cristata

Lamium maculatum and cvs.

Liriope muscari, L. spicata

Lysimachia nummularia

Miscanthus spp. and cvs.

Myosotis palustris

Ophiopogon japonicus, O. planiscapus 'Nigrescens'

Pennisetum spp. and cvs.

Phlox divaricata

Phlox stolonifera

Among the most versatile of perennials, hostas are among the staples of perennial groundcovers. Hosta foliage may be plain or variegated, in many shades of green.

Polygonum affinis, P. bistorta 'Superba'

Pulmonaria angustifolia, P. longifolia, P. rubra, P. saccharata and cvs.

Sedum acre, S. spurium cvs.

Silphium spp.

Stachys byzantina, S. macrantha

Tiarella cordifolia and cvs.

Waldsteinia fragrarioides

X *Heucherella alba* 'Bridget Bloom', X *H. tiarelloides*

A deciduous woodland area provides an ideal setting for a planting of native spring-blooming perennials, such as these phlox and double trillium. When purchasing native plants, try to make sure that they have been nursery-propagated.

dens, the area of your yard to be used should already show a tendency for such a planting. For example, if an area of the yard has trees, then that would likely be an appropriate spot for a woodland garden. If a stream runs through your property, then planting along it with bog-type plants would be appropriate.

In designing native gardens, it's also logical to take your cues from nature. Study the types of areas you want to emulate. Any translation of a wild garden to a cultivated one should be preceded with a study of the trees, shrubs and flowers that naturally grow together. Observe the type of soil, light and moisture of the area where you will develop your wild garden.

When ready, clear the site, prepare the soil carefully and set the plants out just as you would for any new garden area. Do not dig plants from the wild and be sure purchased plants are nursery propagated. Weeding will also be necessary so that the plants you want to spread can do so. It is a fallacy that a native garden does not require planning or maintenance; a garden is a garden, no matter the style.

SOME PERENNIALS FOR WOODLAND GARDENS

Actaea rubra
Adiantum pedatum
Aquilegia canadensis
Arisaema triphyllum
Asarum canadense
Asplenium platyneuron
Chrysogonum virginianum
Cimicifuga racemosa
Dentaria spp.
Disporum spp.
Dryopteris spp.
Hepatica spp.
Iris cristata
Jeffersonia diphylla
Mertensia virginica
Phlox divaricata, P. pilosa, P. stolonifera
Polemonium reptans
Podophyllum peltatum
Polystichum acrostichoides
Sanguinaria canadensis
Trillium spp.
Uvularia spp.

NATIVE PERENNIAL GARDENS

A native garden is one that contains predominantly native wildflowers in a setting that is as close as possible to the one where they might be found growing in nature.

The three most common native gardens are the spring-blooming deciduous woodland garden, the sunny prairie garden and the bog garden, which may be in sun or shade. When considering any of these gar-

No plant from foreign shores can compete with the stunning appearance, come spring, of the various native woodland phlox.

SOME PERENNIALS FOR PRAIRIE GARDENS

Achillea spp.
Agastache spp.
Amsonia tabernaemontana
Andropogon spp.
Asclepias spp.
Aster spp.
Baptisia spp.
Boltonia asteroides
Coreopsis spp.
Chrysopsis spp.
Echinacea spp.
Eryngium yuccifolium
Eupatorium spp.
Filipendula spp.
Gaillardia spp.
Geranium pratense
Helianthus spp.
Heliopsis spp.
Leucanthemum spp.
Liatris spp.
Miscanthus spp.
Monarda spp.
Oenothera spp.
Panicum spp.
Penstemon spp.
Phlox spp.
Ratibida spp.
Rudbeckia spp.
Solidago spp.
Sorghastrum spp.
Thalictrum spp.
Vernonia spp.

Wide borders of native prairie plants juxtaposed with finely clipped lawn provides an intriguing contrast that is much more interesting than if either were used alone.

SOME PERENNIALS FOR WET SOIL OR STREAMSIDE GARDENS

Acorus spp.
Aruncus spp.
Calamagrostis spp.
Chelone spp.
Filipendula spp.
Helianthus angustifolius
Iris fulva, I. hexagona, I. laevigata, I. pseudacorus, I. versicolor
Ligularia spp.
Lobelia spp.
Meconopsis spp.
Monarda spp.
Osmunda spp.
Ranunculus spp.
Rheum spp.
Rodgersia spp.
Sanguisorba spp.
Silphium spp.
Smilacina spp.
Thelypteris spp.

If you have a stream, pool or any area that is naturally boggy, why not turn the area into a garden by using perennials that thrive and flourish under such conditions?

Foliage takes center stage in this planting of grasses with stachys and santolina.

PERENNIAL GARDENS OF FOLIAGE

The leaves of perennials are usually thought of as an adjunct to the flowers, but in certain situations, focusing on foliage can have a dramatic effect in the garden. A garden where foliage predominates is more likely to produce a feeling of calmness in the viewer. Sometimes it can mean a garden that requires less maintenance. The stars of the perennial garden based on foliage are the hostas, the ferns and the ornamental grasses. Ferns are the only ones that truly do not produce flowers.

Hostas are the premier foliage plant for shaded situations in the landscape. They grow best in a soil that is rich in organic matter, and moist but well-drained. Generally, variegated and golden-leaved varieties tolerate more sun than green- or blue-leaved varieties. The following are some suggested cultivars for various uses in the garden:

Dwarf—eight inches or shorter. They are best suited for rock gardens or containers.
Gold-leaved: 'Little Aurora', 'Blonde Elf'
Green-leaved: 'Baby Bunting', 'Gum Drop'
White-edged: 'Stiletto', 'Verna Lean'
Yellow-centered: 'Just So', 'Kabitan'

Edging—12 inches or shorter.
Green-leaved: 'Snow Flakes', 'Floradora'
White-edged: 'Aristocrat', 'Ginko Craig'
Variegated: 'Emerald Tiara', 'Geisha'

Yellow-edged: 'Scooter', 'Brim Cup'

Groundcover—20 inches or shorter. Vigorous; a good choice for low-maintenance, mass plantings.
Blue-leaved: 'Blue Wedgwood', 'Halcyon'
Gold-leaved: 'Midas Touch', 'Day Break'
Green-leaved: 'Aoki', 'Invincible'
Variegated: 'Bright Lights', 'Janet'
White-edged: 'Francee', 'Fair Maiden'
Yellow-edged: 'Frances Williams', 'Yellow River'

Background—24 inches or more. Use these to fill in at the backs of shade beds and borders.
Blue-leaved: 'Blue Vision', 'Wheaton Blue'
Gold-leaved: 'Gold Regal', 'Sun Power'
Green-leaved: 'Royal Standard', 'Honeybells'

White-edged: 'Antioch', 'Frosted Jade'
Yellow-edged: 'Wide Brim', 'Pizzaz'

Specimen—36 to 48 inches. These are spectacular plants that make a strong focal point in the garden.
Blue-leaved: 'Blue Mammoth', 'Krossa Regal'
Gold-leaved: 'Sum and Substance', 'Golden Medallion'
Green-leaved: 'Edge of Night', 'Green Wedge'
White-edged: 'Regal Splendor', 'Crowned Imperial'
Yellow-edged: 'Sagae', 'Carnival'

Vinca becomes a fine-textured foil to the dramatic clumps of different hosta varieties that invite one to sit upon a bench and enjoy the splendors of the garden.

Dame's rocket not only provides fragrance and excellent cut flowers, it also attracts butterflies, such as this eastern tiger swallowtail, to the garden with its nectar. Remember that butterflies have larvae that eat plants, so grow enough for you and the caterpillars.

Birds and butterflies will make a home in your garden if it provides food, cover, nesting sites and a constant supply of fresh water.

PERENNIAL GARDENS TO ATTRACT BUTTERFLIES AND BIRDS

Any garden is a veritable cosmopolitan ecosystem, complete with a full range of animals, insects and birds as well as assorted microorganisms and other critters large and small. Of these, birds and butterflies are among the most desired, particularly for the bright, flitting colors of both and the songs of the birds.

Some people may contend that the birds will feed on the caterpillars as well as bugs and berries, but unless you're trying to nurture a very rare species of butterfly, a balanced population of each can usually be reached. The one thing that you will have to give up, or at least minimize, in this type of garden is pesticides.

The most important aspect of encouraging birds and butterflies to your garden is providing adequate habitat. Birds need plants that will provide food, cover and nesting sites. Nectar plants for adult butterflies are necessary, along with larval

No bird is more welcome in the garden than the eastern ruby-throated hummingbird, with its glistening feathers and whirring wings. Besides the perennials and other flowers that attract these stunning creatures, you may also want to provide nectar feeders.

food plants for caterpillars. Both birds and butterflies need a constant supply of fresh water.

SOME PERENNIALS THAT ATTRACT HUMMINGBIRDS

Aquilegia
Asclepias
Heuchera
Iris
Lobelia
Monarda
Penstemon
Salvia

SOME PERENNIALS THAT ATTRACT BUTTERFLIES

For nectar:
Achillea
Aster
Centranthus
Coreopsis
Echinacea
Eupatorium
Helianthus
Hemerocallis
Liatris

Lobelia
Monarda
Phlox
Rudbeckia
Salvia
Sedum
Solidago
Verbena

Host Plants for Larvae:
Artemisia
Asclepias
Foeniculum
Viola

SOME PERENNIALS THAT ATTRACT BIRDS WITH THEIR SEEDS

Aster
Boltonia
Chrysanthemum
Coreopsis
Echinacea
Echinops
Gaillardia
Papaver
Penstemon
Rudbeckia

Salvia
Solidago
Spigelia
Vernonia

Rudbeckia and goldenrod are stunning and also produce seeds for birds.

A rock garden in Colorado mimics the surrounding high mountain meadows with its rocks, gravelly soil, windblown tree, evergreens and perennials.

ROCK GARDENS WITH PERENNIALS

People can spend years studying and constructing rock gardens. It requires a keen sense of imagination and practical skill to create an area that takes on the effect of a mountain setting. In planning a rock garden, you should choose a site in full sun with excellent drainage, never too close to trees where roots can take over. It's best to use rocks naturally found in your area so that the artificial outcropping you're going to create looks as appropriate as possible. At least some of these rocks should be of a large size, which means you may need the assistance of a contractor to place them with the bottom three-fourths buried. These rocks should be tilted toward the top of the grade to look natural and to channel water into the soil.

There should be deep pockets of soil between the rocks, with the soil mixture usually composed of one-half part garden loam, one-half part humus, one part half-inch crushed rock and one part coarse sand. Often somewhere in the rock garden is a scree, which is a heap of fine stones representing a rock slide or the tip of a glacial moraine. This should be about 12 inches thick, the bottom three inches composed of two- to three-inch stone, and the rest a mixture of two parts half-inch crushed rock and one part garden loam. Because of the fast drainage, rock gardens must be watered regularly and deeply, but the soil should never be allowed to remain soggy.

The plants most often used in a rock garden are ones that may naturally grow in such a situation. Otherwise, in choosing plants for a rock garden, consider the size of the garden, the size of the plant, how much it spreads, its growing requirements and how it will look in the overall composition.

SOME PERENNIALS FOR ROCK GARDENS

Achillea clavennae, A. tomentosa
Aquilegia
Arabis
Armeria
Artemisia schmidtiana
Aruncus aethusifolius
Asarum
Aster dumosus
Aubrieta
Aurinia
Bellis perennis
Bergenia spp.
Campanula — selected spp.
Cerastium
Coreopsis auriculata 'Nana'
Coreopsis grandiflora 'Goldfink'
Dianthus
Dicentra
Filipendula vulgaris
Gaillardia 'Goblin'
Geum
Helianthemum
Heuchera
Iberis
Linum
Platycodon grandiflorus 'Apoyame'
Santolina
Saponaria
Scabiosa
Sedum — selected spp.
Sempervivum
Teucrium
Veronica — selected spp.

The art in developing a rock garden is in having it look as if the rocks "grew" there naturally. Large boulders should be "planted", with only a quarter of them showing.

The challenge of creating a rock garden seems of little consequence to those who are drawn to its style and character. ❦

Many of grandmother's old-fashioned favorite perennials were chosen for their fragrance, such as these peonies and iris. Not all varieties will have a scent, or a good one, so check out plant descriptions to make sure before you buy.

PERENNIAL GARDENS FOR FRAGRANCE

One of the first things people do when confronted with a flower is smell it to determine if there is fragrance. Creating a perennial garden that focuses on fragrance most often means creating a mixed border or bed that utilizes traditional perennial flowers as well as perennial herbs, old-fashioned and shrub roses, annuals, bulbs, trees and shrubs. Fragrance will come from both flowers and foliage.

SOME PERENNIALS FOR A FRAGRANT GARDEN

Agastache
Artemisia
Centaurea
Centranthus
Cimicifuga
Convallaria
Dianthus
Filipendula
Galium
Hemerocallis (selected cultivars)
Hesperis

Hosta plantaginea
Iris
Lavandula
Monarda
Nepeta
Oenothera
Paeonia
Perovskia
Phlox
Primula
Santolina

SHADE GARDENS

There are many different types of shade and a great variety of shady situations in a landscape. Shade should not be considered a problem in the landscape, but rather a wonderful opportunity for comfortable summer outdoor living surrounded by a wide assortment of beautiful plants. To successfully garden in the shade, it is necessary to analyze your site, matching the plant to the site as much as possible, and, when necessary or possible, adjusting the soil, moisture and degree of shade.

SOME PERENNIALS FOR DRY SOIL AND SHADE

The soil under large trees and shrubs is often especially dry and, because of the competition from roots, low in nutrients. Growing perennials in this situation is difficult, but several plants tolerate this situation. Even so, it's important to incorporate organic matter and fertilizer into the soil before planting and to water regularly.

Alchemilla	*Pulmonaria*
Convallaria	*Stachys*
Epimedium	*Symphytum*
Galium	*Tricyrtis*
Lamium	*Vinca*

SOME PERENNIALS FOR MOIST SOIL AND PARTIAL SHADE

A wide range of perennials will thrive in locations with partial, not deep, shade and moist but well-drained soil.

Acanthus	*Convallaria*
Aconitum	*Corydalis*
Ajuga	*Dicentra*
Alchemilla	*Digitalis*
Aquilegia	*Doronicum*
Artemisia	*Epimedium*
Aruncus	*Filipendula*
Asarum	*Galium*
Astilbe	*Gaura*
Bergenia	*Geranium*
Brunnera	*Hakonechloa*
Campanula	*Helleborus*
Carex	*Heuchera*
Chelone	*Heucherella*
Cimicifuga	*Hosta*

Lamium	*Oenothera*	*Sanguinaria*	*Vinca*
Ligularia	*Phlox (some)*	*Symphytum*	*Viola*
Liriope	*Polemonium*	*Thalictrum*	*Waldsteinia*
Lobelia	*Polygonatum*	*Tiarella*	
Monarda	*Pulmonaria*	*Tricyrtis*	
Nepeta	*Ranunculus*		

On a stifling hot summer's day, the cooling breezes in a shady area of the yard seems the best place in the world. Don't neglect these areas when deciding where to have perennials.

DROUGHT-TOLERANT PERENNIAL GARDENS

If you live in an area with little rainfall, have a garden with fast-draining soil or have other conditions that make the soil particularly dry, don't give up on creating a garden, or think that a massive amount of watering is the only solution. Consider creating a dry landscape, or xeriscape, composed of plants that are adapted to dry growing conditions. By utilizing plans from various arid regions of the world, you can have a garden that is beautiful and makes thoughtful use of limited natural resources.

SOME DROUGHT-TOLERANT PERENNIALS FOR SUN

Achillea	Gaillardia
Andropogon	Gaura
Anthemis	Kniphofia
Artemisia	Liatris
Asclepias	Miscanthus
Baptisia	Rudbeckia
Belamcanda	Salvia
Coreopsis	Solidago
Cortaderia	Stachys
Disporum	Thermopsis
Echinops	
Elymus	
Euphorbia	

Low rainfall or sandy soil needn't be a deterrent to gardening. By carefully choosing the plants, this entrance garden is lush and welcoming without irrigation.

With less natural rainfall, gardeners often set plants farther apart from each other so that the roots of each have a wide area from which they can draw nutrients and water.

No matter your climate or means, a garden should be your own unique expression, a place that is your joy and passion, a testament to your spirit and beliefs.

Chapter 4

❧

DESIGN CONSIDERATIONS

Great garden designers are generally born not made, but even the artistically challenged can learn to utilize the design principles of applied art to significant effect.

What the use of repetition, balance, sequence, contrast and rhythm in conjunction with the elements of form, texture and color bring to any design, be it fabric, a centerpiece, a room or a garden, is a visually satisfying appeal.

This isn't to say that designing a garden isn't a challenge. Because of the dynamic nature of plants combined with the complicating factors of climate, soil, moisture, light and different bloom seasons, it takes careful planning to create a breathtaking picture-book garden. This is why it's so important to first take the time to evaluate your garden environment, then decide how you want your garden to look before you ever being creating a garden plan. Making lists of

Even those who don't consider themselves artistic can create a stunning garden if they take the time to consider the various principles of applied art when developing a garden plan.

By planting clumps of the white foxglove throughout the garden, the gardener has utilized the design principle of repetition, which gives a feeling of movement in the garden.

DESIGN PRINCIPLES

Repetition is the reappearance of the same plant, form, texture or color throughout an area. Whether naturalistic or stylized, this creation of a pattern provides visual pleasure plus a feeling of security and simplicity with its rhythm and movement. Think of it as the catchy chorus to a song. Repetition is used both within a single area and throughout the entire landscape.

Contrast accentuates the differences rather than the similarities. The juxtaposition of different sizes, textures, forms and colors of perennials creates interest in a garden. Or, to use the cliché, variety is the spice of life. Just remember that with too much spice you get heartburn. The use of a focal point in your garden is a prime example of good use of contrast. First your eyes are drawn to a particular plant or garden ornament, then gradually you examine adjacent elements.

Tall spiky irises provide visual contrast with the rounded dianthus.

plants is also helpful, including lists of the best plants for your site and those you like, as well as lists of plants representing each of the elements of size, form, texture, color and bloom season. This way when you're looking for a bold-textured perennial with yellow autumn flowers for that moist, shady site, you'll see that *Kirengeshoma* is just the plant to use.

The planning stage can be some of the most fun of gardening, because that's when we all have the perfect garden. So get lots of notepads, graph paper and tracing paper ready, with sharp pencils and those all-important erasers, get out the sketches and measurements of the areas you want to work on, surround yourself with plant catalogs and books and settle down for some serious doodling.

Make your goal a final plan drawn to scale on graph paper. Designing to scale helps you get a sense of space and proportion as well as the number of plants needed. First, determine the dimensions of the site and outline the shape of the bed or border on the graph paper. Next, lay a sheet of tracing paper over the graph paper. Using your plant lists, begin drawing in the clumps of plants on tracing paper.

As you design, it helps to include plant characteristics, such as height, form, color and bloom season. To save space, develop your own code for each of these. Using colored pencils or markers is a good way to indicate colors. Overlaying layers of tracing paper helps in experimenting with different combinations or seeing how the garden might look at different seasons. In spacing plants on the plan, consider that placing at least three of the same plants together gives the greatest impact.

As you go about this planning and design process, remember that no matter how good the plan, it is not foolproof. Acknowledging that fact in the beginning can make the whole process seem much less intimidating. Some plants will grow differently than you expected, or a color combination that seemed like such a good idea in your mind in January doesn't quite work in the light of June. A good spading fork can rectify any number of design errors.

Balance may be symmetrical or asymmetrical, real or perceived, but there is always a sense of stability. To achieve balance, the size, form, texture and color must all be taken into consideration. With symmetrical balance, one side of a design will be a mirror image of the opposite side. In an asymmetrical arrangement, the two halves are different, but are of equal visual weight.

Straight lines, geometrical shapes and mirror images are the components of this symmetrically balanced garden designed by Gertrude Jekyll in England.

An asymmetrically designed garden has two halves that are very different, but the effect is still one of balance, or equal weight.

By repeating the use of yellow flowers in this garden, a rhythm is created that moves the eyes around this garden from the iris in the front, to the right, then to the back.

Sequence, or scale and proportion, is the orderly relationship of sizes of plants and landscape materials to each other and to the landscape as a whole. In other words, a tall plant isn't used directly next to a short plant; rather a tall and a medium or a medium and a short are placed together. Or, for another example, a tiny planting area looks lost in a large yard. The ratio of size from one plant or planting to the next should be ½ to ⅓.

Rhythm is another method for moving the eyes around the garden, be it in a straight, circular or meandering line, or by a curve into a straight line (known as arc and tangent). It is achieved by the use of repetition of patterns punctuated by contrasts, causing the eye to hesitate, then be drawn onward. Such repetitions and contrasts should not be exact, or the effect will be as monotonous as a metronome. Think of how your favorite drummer might "play" a garden.

DESIGN ELEMENTS

Size is both the mature height and width of the plant. In considering the width of perennials, keep in mind how quickly the plant spreads, or multiplies. Some perennials spread rapidly from the cen-

ter of the plant, while others remain relatively compact. The ultimate height of a plant will affect where in a garden the plant is placed, with taller plants usually going to the back of a border or the center of an island bed. The width has more effect on the spacing of the plants. A newly—and correctly—planted area can look sparse, so the temptation is to plant too closely. In what seems like no time at all, the plants are competing for light, water and nutrients, and you're out there digging up half the garden. Even in a perennial garden, where we're used to seeing plants close together, there should be a feeling that each plant has its own distinct space.

Just as in those group photos from class trips, perennial borders are usually planned with the tall plants in the back, medium-sized ones in the middle and the short ones in the front. Some plants confound the issue by being ground-hugging except when in flower. In this case, plants are most often placed according to their foliage height. As described in the design principle of contrast, just to shake things up a little and make them interesting, taller plants are sometimes jutted out further toward

the front of a border. The following lists are meant as a general guideline; sometimes there are taller or shorter cultivars of certain plants available that push them into another category, and, some genera have plants of all sizes.

SOME PERENNIALS BY SIZE

Short—up to 18 inches tall

Alchemilla	*Hosta*
Arabis	*Iberis*
Armeria	*Iris*
Asarum	*Linum*
Aubrieta	*Mertensia*
Aurinia	*Nepeta*
Bergenia	*Oenothera*
Campanula	Ornamental
Cerastium	grasses
Chrysogonum	*Phlox*
Dianthus	*Primula*
Dicentra	*Pulmonaria*
Euphorbia	*Scabiosa*
Ferns	*Sedum*
Galium	*Stachys*
Gypsophila	*Veronica*
Heuchera	*Viola*
Heucherella	

Utilize plants of different sizes.

Utilizing the principles of scale and proportion between the plants, landscape and building have allowed this bold garden to delight the eye.

Try incorporating the design elements of size, form, texture and color into your garden plan. ❦

Plant form, or the three-dimensional shape of the plant, is one of the design elements to consider when developing a garden plan. These mums are an example of rounded form.

Medium—18 to 36 inches tall

Achillea	Helleborus
Adenophora	Hemerocallis
Amsonia	Hesperis
Anaphalis	Hosta
Anthemis	Iris
Aquilegia	Lavandula
Artemisia	Liatris
Asclepias	Lupinus
Astilbe	Lychnis
Belamcanda	Lysimachia
Brunnera	Ornamental
Campanula	grasses
Chrysanthemum	Paeonia
Coreopsis	Papaver
Dicentra	Phlox
Dictamnus	Platycodon
Doronicum	Salvia
Erigeron	Sedum
Eupatorium	Solidago
Euphorbia	Stokesia
Ferns	Tradescantia
Filipendula	Veronica
Gypsophila	

Tall—36 inches and above

Aconitum	Filipendula
Anchusa	Helenium
Anemone	Heliopsis
Aruncus	Hemerocallis
Aster	Iris
Baptisia	Kniphofia
Campanula	Liatris
Centranthus	Lobelia
Cimicifuga	Macleaya
Clematis	Monarda
Delphinium	Ornamental
Digitalis	grasses
Echinacea	Phlox
Echinops	Physostegia
Eryngium	Polygonatum
Eupatorium	Rudbeckia
Ferns	Thalictrum
Filipendula	Thermopsis

Form is the three-dimensional shape of a plant. These shapes can be broken down into any number of categories, but most perennial forms fall into five types: ❶ spiky, or vertical; ❷ mounding, or rounded; ❸ upright and spreading; ❹ low and creeping, or prostrate and ❺ open, or filler. Keep in mind that plants may take on a different form when they're in bloom. Perennial gardens usually have a mix of these forms, but, once in awhile, it's interesting to use only one form. Since the majority of plants are upright and spreading, that is probably the shape that will predominate in your garden, with the other shapes providing contrast. Most important to remember is that as living, growing entities, plants do not always fit rigid categorization, but the element of form is one that, with practice, can be used to make a garden more striking.

Most plants are spreading or creeping.

The foliage of irises provides a strongly spiky and vertical effect in the garden, while forget-me-nots have an open, or filling, effect.

Some upright and spreading perennials

Achillea	Ligularia
Amsonia	Mertensia
Anemone	Monarda
Aquilegia	Oenothera
Arisaema	Paeonia
Artemisia	Papaver
Aster	Phlox
Baptisia	Physostegia
Boltonia	Platycodon
Campanula	Polemonium
Centaurea	Rodgersia
Chelone	Rudbeckia
Chrysanthemum	Salvia
Dicentra	Sanguisorba
Doronicum	Scabiosa
Echinacea	Sedum
Echinops	Solidago
Erigeron	Stokesia
Eryngium	Thalictrum
Eupatorium	Tradescantia
Gaillardia	Tricyrtis
Helenium	Uvularia
Helianthus	Veronica
Heliopsis	

Some low and creeping, or prostrate, perennials

Ajuga	Euphorbia
Arabis	Iberis
Asarum	Phlox
Aubrieta	Pulmonaria
Aurinia	Saponaria
Bergenia	Stachys
Cerastium	Tiarella
Ceratostigma	Viola
Epimedium	

SOME PERENNIALS BY FORM

Some spiky, or vertical, perennials

Acanthus	Digitalis
Aconitum	Erianthus
Anchusa	Gaura
Aruncus	Hemerocallis
Astilbe	Iris
Belamcanda	Kniphofia
Campanula	Liatris
Centranthus	Lobelia
Cimicifuga	Lupinus
Crocosmia	Macleaya
Delphinium	Penstemon
Dictamnus	Polygonatum
Smilacina	Verbascum
Thermopsis	Yucca

Some mounding, or rounded, perennials

Alchemilla	Festuca
Armeria	Geranium
Artemisia	Helleborus
Brunnera	Hosta
Coreopsis	Lavandula
Dianthus	Nepeta
Euphorbia	Santolina

Some open, or filler, perennials

Alchemilla	Lychnis
Astrantia	Ornamental
Gypsophila	grasses
Heuchera	Perovskia
Heucherella	Patrinia
Limonium	Verbena

Texture relates to how the plant looks in terms of fine, medium or coarse, not to how it actually feels to the touch. What determines texture is the size and density of the foliage and flowers. One of the complications is that the foliage may have one texture, while the plant in bloom has another. The element of texture has the ability to create spatial illusions in the garden. For instance, coarse-textured plants appear closer, while fine-textured ones seem farther away. Using coarse-textured plants at the back of a garden will make it seem smaller. Placing fine-textured plants in a narrow border gives it the illusion of appearing wider than it actually is.

SOME PERENNIALS BY TEXTURE

Some fine-textured perennials

Achillea	Gypsophila
Aquilegia	Hemerocallis
Armeria	Lavandula
Artemisia	Liatris
Astilbe	Nepeta
Coreopsis	Perovskia
Dianthus	Polemonium
Dicentra	Santolina
Foeniculum	Thalictrum

Some bold-textured perennials

Acanthus	Ligularia
Bergenia	Macleaya
Cynara	Mertensia
Digitalis	Polygonatum
Echinops	Rodgersia
Helleborus	Sedum
Hosta	Verbascum

Fine-textured plants provide the illusion of space in the garden. They will appear farther away than coarse-textured ones, plus give the appearance that an area is wider.

Bold-textured plants appear closer than they actually are, plus they will make an area seem smaller than it really is.

warm or cool, based on the feelings they impart. Warm colors, including red, yellow and orange are the colors of passion. In the garden, they tend to stand out, seeming to advance toward the viewer. They make for dramatic displays, but also make an area appear smaller than it is. Cool colors, including green, blue and violet, are those of tranquility. They recede from the eye, making an area appear larger; they are best when viewed close up, and will make a hot location seem cooler.

If you're wondering where red-violet and yellow-green fit in, they have both warm and cool properties. Their effect in the garden depends on the other colors used with them.

Warm colors, including reds, yellows and oranges, stand out in the garden and make a passionate statement.

Color is what the garden is all about, for it's the flowers, in their rainbow of colors, that continually inspires us. The best way to begin thinking about color in the garden is to first of all be aware of your favorite colors and what colors in the garden please you most. Remember, too, that what catalog and book writers describe as red or pink, you may call magenta, and what goes for blue in the plant world is usually purple everywhere else.

In planning a garden, it's helpful to understand some of the basic principles of color, with a standard color wheel providing assistance. The color wheel is based on the three primary colors of yellow, red and blue. All other colors are derived from these three colors. For instance, green is made from blue and yellow, purple from red and blue and orange from yellow and red. A pure color is called a hue. When white is added, the color becomes lighter, or a tint. With the addition of black, the color becomes darker, or a shade.

When considering colors for your garden, the first aspect to consider is their effect. Colors are considered either

Blues and violets are the cool colors that are relaxing and give a feeling of tranquility. Used in the garden, they will make an area appear larger, but they are best viewed close up.

A garden of golden yellow flowers imparts a sense of laughter and happiness as it reflects the sunshine and joyful days spent outdoors.

A garden with a monochromatic color scheme focuses on using flowers or foliage that is all of one color, such as this white garden of stachys, foxglove, Shasta daisy and pansies.

In creating a garden, there are four basic ways to use color. These include monochromatic, analogous, complementary and polychromatic color schemes. Because there are so many perennials, with innumerable shades and tints, these four basic schemes multiply exponentially.

Monochromatic color schemes in the garden utilize flowers in various tints and shades of one color. Of course, no garden is truly monochromatic because there is always the green foliage. A monochromatic garden gives a feeling of harmony; it is relatively easy to carry out, perhaps with a color that complements the color of the house. The predominance of pink flowers in the plant world makes this a good choice, but the "white garden" at Vita Sackville-West's Sissinghurst Castle in England is the most famous monochromatic garden.

Analogous color schemes are meant to utilize the tints and shades of three adjoining colors on the color wheel, such as blue, blue-violet and violet. The reality in the garden is that the rule book doesn't always work. Taking those three colors as an example, what most often happens is that pink flowers are also included, and are actually what makes the combination come alive. Since pink is essentially a tint between red and red-violet, you're actually using four analogous colors. Call on your common sense.

Complementary color schemes combine colors that are opposite on the color wheel, such as yellow-orange and blue-violet. They are stunning and dramatic, with a definite vitality. Mismanage them, and the effect quickly becomes a nightmare. Again, don't be afraid to bend the rules a bit. In this case, the dogma is to stick to pure hues and use gray foliage or white flowers for softening. Maybe an artist would know a pure hue, but most of us just sort of scratch our heads. And flowers don't always bloom in the exact color we want. As an example, take a look at the color wheel, and think about analogous and complementary simultaneously. For instance, consider orange, yellow-orange and yellow opposite violet, blue-violet and blue. Now those are colors that can be thought of in terms of plants. The most important thing to keep in mind with an example like this is to plant the analogous colors in groups. Interplant all six colors randomly, and it won't be a pretty sight.

A color combination composed of colors opposite on the color wheel is a complementary color scheme. Here golden achilleas are combined with blue-violet delphinium.

The analogous golds and oranges of lilies, rudbeckias and achilleas provide a dynamic effect when combined in the garden. ❦

A well-planned polychromatic garden softly blends the entire gamut of color.

Finally, the color scheme for the rest of us: the polychromatic garden. In other words, any and every color. So who needs a book to tell you this? With either great skill or pure dumb luck, such combinations can give a rich and lively effect. A variation on this theme is when a garden progresses from one color scheme to another. Usually this is best attempted when both skill and a large property are present.

SOME PERENNIALS BY COLOR

Some perennials with yellow flowers

Achillea	Heliopsis
Alchemilla	Hemerocallis
Adonis	Iris
Anthemis	Ligularia
Aquilegia	Lysimachia
Aurinia	Oenothera
Baptisia	Primula
Centaurea	Rudbeckia
Chrysanthemum	Santolina
Chrysogonum	Sedum
Chrysopsis	Solidago
Coreopsis	Thalictrum
Corydalis	Thermopsis
Doronicum	Trollius
Epimedium	Uvularia
Helenium	Verbascum
Helianthus	

Some perennials with orange flowers

Aquilegia	Hemerocallis
Asclepias	Kniphofia
Belamcanda	Ligularia
Crocosmia	Lychnis
Gaillardia	Papaver
Geum	Primula
Helenium	Trollius

Some perennials with red flowers

Achillea	Helleborus
Aquilegia	Hemerocallis
Aster	Heuchera
Astilbe	Lobelia
Bergenia	Monarda
Chrysanthemum	Paeonia
Dianthus	Papaver
Dicentra	Penstemon
Epimedium	Primula
Gaillardia	

Daylilies, lychnis and roses offer an assortment of orange, pink and red flowers.

White forms of flowers are especially striking when viewed in moonlight.

Some perennials with blue, lavender or purple flowers

Aconitum	Iris
Adenophora	Lavandula
Ajuga	Limonium
Amsonia	Lupinus
Anchusa	Mertensia
Aquilegia	Perovskia
Aster	Phlox
Baptisia	Platycodon
Brunnera	Polemonium
Campanula	Primula
Centaurea	Pulmonaria
Ceratostigma	Salvia
Corydalis	Scabiosa
Delphinium	Stokesia
Echinops	Thalictrum
Erigeron	Tradescantia
Eryngium	Veronica
Geranium	Viola
Hosta	

Some perennials with white flowers

Acanthus	Erigeron
Achillea	Galium
Anemone	Gaura
Aquilegia	Geranium
Arabis	Gypsophila
Aruncus	Hosta
Aster	Iberis
Astilbe	Iris
Baptisia	Monarda
Boltonia	Phlox
Campanula	Platycodon
Centranthus	Polemonium
Cerastium	Primula
Chelone	Scabiosa
Chrysanthemum	Verbascum
Cimicifuga	Veronica
Dianthus	Yucca
Dicentra	
Dictamnus	
Echinacea	

Some perennials with pink or magenta flowers

Achillea	Heuchera
Ajuga	Iris
Anemone	Liatris
Aquilegia	Lychnis
Armeria	Monarda
Aster	Oenothera
Astilbe	Paeonia
Astrantia	Papaver
Aubrieta	Penstemon
Bergenia	Phlox
Campanula	Platycodon
Centaurea	Primula
Centranthus	Pulmonaria
Chelone	Rodgersia
Chrysanthemum	Saponaria
Delphinium	Scabiosa
Dianthus	Sedum
Dicentra	Stachys
Dictamnus	Stokesia
Digitalis	Thalictrum
Echinacea	Tricyrtis
Erigeron	Verbascum
Filipendula	Verbena
Geranium	Veronica
Gypsophila	Viola
Helleborus	

Delphinium and veronica are among the perennials grown for their blue flowers. Both of these perennials also have varieties in shades of purple, pink, rose and white.

BLOOM SEASON

Now, for the real test. Can you coordinate all the other factors in this chapter with when the plants come into bloom? And for the length of time that they are in bloom? If you think about this for too long, you're apt to take up another pastime. For those taking this chapter to heart, you may want to start with a perennial border that focuses the bloom time on just one of the three seasons of spring, summer or fall. Another way to alleviate the problems is to include annuals for their long bloom period, as well as some shrub roses. Another way is to use perennials with a longer blooming period than the average of two to four weeks. As you gain experience and confidence, the three- or even four-season perennial planting can be planned and, ultimately, enjoyed.

Some perennials flowering in spring

Alchemilla	Galium
Amsonia	Geranium
Anchusa	Helleborus
Anemone	Hesperis
Arisaema	Iberis
Aquilegia	Iris
Arabis	Mertensia
Armeria	Paeonia
Aubrieta	Phlox
Aurinia	Primula
Bergenia	Pulmonaria
Brunnera	Sanguisorba
Chrysogonum	Smilacina
Euphorbia	Trillium
Dicentra	Trollius
Dianthus	Viola
Filipendula	

Spring and early summer is the easiest time of the year to have a garden filled with glorious flowers. Many people plan parties around the height of the bloom in their gardens.

Some perennials flowering in summer

Achillea	Helenium
Adenophora	Heliopsis
Anaphalis	Hemerocallis
Anthemis	Heuchera
Aruncus	Hosta
Asclepias	Iris
Astilbe	Kniphofia
Baptisia	Lavandula
Belamcanda	Liatris
Campanula	Linum
Centaurea	Lobelia
Chrysanthemum	Lychnis
Cimicifuga	Lysimachia
Clematis	Macleaya
Coreopsis	Monarda
Delphinium	Nepeta
Dictamnus	Oenothera
Digitalis	Papaver
Echinacea	Phlox
Echinops	Physostegia
Erigeron	Platycodon
Eryngium	Rudbeckia
Filipendula	Salvia
Gaillardia	Scabiosa
Gaura	Stokesia
Geranium	Thalictrum
Geum	Thermopsis
Gypsophila	Veronica

Some perennials flowering in autumn

Aconitum	Perovskia
Anemone	Rudbeckia
Aster	Scabiosa
Boltonia	Sedum
Chrysanthemum	Solidago
Coreopsis	Stokesia
Gaillardia	Tricyrtis
Helenium	Vernonia
Heliopsis	Viola
Ornamental grasses	

This gardener let bulbs take center stage in a mixed border.

Later in the summer, perennials and summer-blooming bulbs are the focus.

In the fall, ornamental grasses, kale and mums bring the season to a close.

Chapter 5

❦

PERENNIALS

$\mathcal{T}$he goal in choosing the perennials profiled in this book was to offer a wide range of plant types. Some have been grown by gardeners for centuries, while others have become favored only recently. One criterion was that a perennial plant should make an aesthetic contribution to the garden for as much of the growing season as possible, either from a long or repeat blooming period or with foliage that remains attractive. In cases where this criteron is not met but the plant is still included, the rationale was the popularity of the plant or that it has the good grace to disappear, allowing other plants to fill in.

Maintenance was another important criterion. Life is complicated enough, and, however much relaxation and pleasure gardening gives us, there is a point of diminishing returns. Again, we grow certain plants in spite of their fussiness. Overall, flower gardening pleasure is best enhanced with perennials that are seldom bothered by pests, sturdy enough to stand on their own without staking and adaptable to a wide range of soils, moisture conditions, heat and humidity.

Among the great quantity of perennials best suited for specialty situations such as rock gardens native woodland gardens or bog gardens, only a small number were included. Most of the perennials profiled have a wide adaptability and availability. As we become more sensitive to the environmental impact of gardening, the use of native plants naturally adapted to our locales has increased in importance, and hence many native plants are included here. With ten different climate zones in the United States, climatic criteria was another factor in selection. With most gardeners in Zones 4 through 8, the vast majority of profiled perennials fall into this range. Sometimes, though, others were included because of their importance to the garden.

BOTANIZING

The plant descriptions include both the botanical name, or Latin binomial, as well as the most widely used of the common names. While common names vary among locales, the Latin names are the same throughout the world. To ease the pain of learning these, a pronunciation guide is included with each one.

Scientists have devised a system of classifying all creatures, both plant and animal, into a hierarchical system. The system of botanical names is based on varying degrees of taxonomic differences—and similarities—between plants, mainly focused on flower structure. Plants with certain characteristics in common are grouped into a genus. This generic name is the first word in a Latin binomial. To differentiate between the members of a genus, a species name is given as the second part of the binomial. Sometimes this is broken down further, either into a subspecies (spp.) or variety (var.) name. The major frustration with this system occurs when, with research, taxonomists regroup or

rename plants. To help alleviate the resulting confusion, both old and new names are included in the descriptions. Finally, either in nature or with the help of plant breeders amateur or professional, further differences are created among plants. A garden form, sport, clone or result of a hybrid cross is called a cultivar, with the cultivar name enclosed in single quotation marks.

a

Acanthus
(ah-*kan*-thus)
Bear's breeches
Acanthaceae—acanthus family

The large mounds of stiffly arching leaves give the various species of acanthus an architectural quality, fitting as the leaves inspired the decoration on Corinthian columns. Evergreen and invasive in milder climates, acanthus make a striking statement in the garden. The spikes of hooded, mauve flowers can be used fresh or dried.

GROWING GUIDE Full sun to partial shade, especially in hot, humid climates. Fertile, humus-rich, moist but well-drained soil. Winter mulching is necessary to prevent cold damage until plants become well established. Cut off flower stems when finished blooming.

PROPAGATION Division, root cuttings or fresh seed.

USES As an accent or focal point, singly or *en masse*. Give plenty of space.

SPECIES, VARIETIES, CULTIVARS AND HYBRIDS

A. mollis (*mol*-lis). Bear's breeches. Mediterranean. Grows 4 feet tall and 3 feet wide. Long, deeply cut leaves with spikes of white and mauve flowers in summer. The variety most often seen is 'Latifolius.' Can become invasive. Although it can tolerate

Acanthus mollis.

colder temperatures, it grows best in those areas of Zones 8 and 9 that are not hot and humid.

A. spinosus (spin-oh-sus). Spiny bear's breeches. Southeastern Europe. Grows 4 feet tall and 3 feet wide. Dark green, glossy, deeply divided leaves to 3 feet long and 1 foot wide. Abundantly produced spikes of spiny white and mauve flowers in summer. More tolerant of both heat and cold and more free-flowering than *A. mollis*. The variety *spinosissimus* has leaves more deeply divided with silvery points, making it more beautiful but decidedly more vicious. Zones 6 to 10.

Achillea
(ah-*kil*-lee-ah or ah-kil-*lee*-ah)
Yarrow
Compositae—daisy family

A staple of perennial gardens for their beauty, ease of growth and long life, achilleas are prized for their feathery foliage and long-blooming, flat-topped flower clusters of white, yellows, pastels or reds. Cut when the pollen is visible, the flowers are excellent for arrangements. For dried use, pick them just as they become fully open.

GROWING GUIDE Full sun. Well-drained average to poor soil. Deadhead for repeat bloom.

PROPAGATION Division, stem cuttings.

USES Beds, borders, foundation, corner and meadow plantings. Use dwarf species and cultivars at the front of the border or in rock gardens. Fresh or dried flower.

SPECIES, VARIETIES, CULTIVARS AND HYBRIDS

Pale Achillea x 'millefolium'.

A. x 'Coronation Gold'. Grows 2 to 3 feet tall and wide. Well branched, aromatic, gray-green leaves and golden flower heads 3 to 4 inches across. Does not need staking. Will bloom for eight to 12 weeks. Zones 3 to 9.

A. x 'Moonshine'. Grows 2 feet tall and 18 inches wide. Gray-green leaves and pale yellow flower head to 3 inches across. Susceptible to leaf diseases in hot, humid climates. Will bloom for 8 to 12 weeks. Zones 3 to 8.

A. grandifolia (grand-i-*foh*-lee-uh). White yarrow. Southeast Europe. Grows 2 to 3 feet tall and wide. Gray-green foliage and white flowers on strong stems 3 to 4 feet tall. Seldom available but a much better white-flowered form than *A. millefolium.*

Achillea rilipendulina.

A. millefolium (mil-luh-*foh*-lee-um). Common yarrow. Europe. Grows 2 to 3 feet tall and wide. A spreading plant with white or pink flowers and aromatic, dark green foliage, it has a long-standing medicinal herb tradition. A number of cultivars and hybrids are available, including 'Cerise Queen', intense pink-red; 'Fire King', red fading to pink; 'Red Beauty', dark red; 'White Beauty', white; 'Summer Pastels'; and the 'Galaxy' hybrids, including 'Appleblossom', medium pink; 'The Beacon', crimson; 'Great Expectations', amber; 'Paprika', red with a white eye; 'Salmon Beauty', salmon pink.

In summer heat, many of these grow thin, flowers fade and plants need staking. Zones 3 to 8.

For the rock garden, consider *A. chrysocoma, A. clavennae* and *A. tomentosa.*

Aconitum

(ak-oh-*nye*-tum)
Monkshood, wolfsbane
Ranunculaceae—buttercup family

Lovely, underused plants, aconitums have delphinium-like leaves and spires of hooded, one-inch flowers, mainly in shades of purple or blue, which contrast particularly well with yellow-flowered perennials. A few species have yellow or rose-colored flowers. Depending on the species, bloom may be in summer or early fall. Roots, leaves and stems are poisonous, and, as one common name attests, this quality has caused it to be used as a poison for wolves. The heart sedative aconite is derived from one species.

GROWING GUIDE Full sun to light afternoon shade in hotter climates. Humus-rich, moist but well-drained soil. Mulching and regular fertilization are especially beneficial.

Leave in place as they do not transplant well. Staking may be required.

PROPAGATION Division; seed, if sown as soon as ripe, but it is slow to germinate and will not flower for two to three years.

USES Middle or back of beds or borders; bog edges; wild gardens; planted in masses. Cut flowers.

SPECIES, VARIETIES, CULTIVARS AND HYBRIDS

A. x bicolor (bye-kul-or) (*A.* x *cammarum*). Bicolor monkshood. Grows 3 to 4 feet tall and 18 to 24 inches wide. Hybrids of *A. napellus* and *A. variegatum.* Dark green, glossy, deeply cut leaves and branching stems. Blooms in summer. Varieties include 'Bicolor', white with blue edges; 'Bressingham Spire', violet-blue; 'Ivorine', ivory-white; 'Newry Blue', navy blue; 'Spark's Variety', dark blue and 'Night Sky', deep-violet. Zones 3 to 7.

A. carmichaelii (kar-mye-*keel*-ee-eye). Azure monkshood. Eastern Asia. Grows 4 feet tall and 18 inches wide. Thick, leathery, dark green leaves. Blooms in early fall with short spikes of flowers in various shades of blue. *A. c. wilsonii* grows to 6 feet tall with violet-blue flowers. 'Kelmscott' has lavender-blue flowers. 'Barker's' has deep blue flowers and comes true from

Aconitum napellus.

seed. The best variety is 'Arendsii', with intense amethyst-blue flowers. Zones 3 to 7.

　　A. napellus (nap-*pell*-us). Common monkshood. Europe. Grows 4 feet tall and 12 inches wide. Glossy, dark green leaves and branched spikes of indigo-blue flowers in mid- to late summer. There are cultivars with white or flesh-pink flowers. Zones 3 to 8.

Acorus
(ah-*koh*-rus)
Sweet flag
Araceae—arum family

With semievergreen, grasslike leaves, this is a popular plant for boggy areas, especially in its variegated form. Because the leaves emit a spicy odor when crushed, they were used in earlier times for strewing on the floors of castles and manor homes.

GROWING GUIDE Full sun to partial shade. Constantly moist to wet soil.

PROPAGATION Division.

USES As specimen plants or mass plantings in bog and water gardens.

Acorus calamus variagatus.

SPECIES, VARIETIES, CULTIVARS AND HYBRIDS

　　A. calamus (*kah*-lah-mus). Sweet flag. Asia, North America. Grows 3 feet tall and 12 inches wide. Aromatic, sword-shaped leaves. Insignificant flowers. The form 'Variegatus' has green and white striped leaves, sometimes flushed pale pink in spring. Grows in up to 10 inches of water. Zones 4 to 9.

　　A. gramineus (grah-*min*-ee-us). Japanese sweet flag. Asia. Grows 12 inches tall and five inches wide. Dark green, grasslike leaves. 'Pusillus' grows to 10 inches tall; 'Variegatus' has leaves striped with white. Zones 6 to 9.

Adenophora
(ad-e-*noff*-o-ruh)
Ladybells
Campanulaceae—bellflower family

Perennials with an old-fashioned charm, ladybells are appreciated for their spikes of nodding, light blue flowers, which give them an appearance similar to campanulas.

GROWING GUIDE Full sun to partial shade. Fertile, well-drained soil.

PROPAGATION Seed; stem cuttings. Avoid division as the deeply growing, fleshy roots are easily damaged.

USES Front or middle of borders. Use *A. tashiroi* in rock gardens or as an edging, as it grows 4 to 12 inches tall. Cut flowers. Fragrant.

Adenophora liliifolia.

SPECIES, VARIETIES, CULTIVARS AND HYBRIDS

　　A. liliifolia (lil-ee-eye-*fol*-lee-uh). Lilyleaf ladybells. Europe. Grows 2 feet tall and spreads to 12 inches. Stout spikes of nodding, pale blue, bell-shaped flowers bloom in mid- to late summer above egg-shaped foliage. Spreads rapidly in proper conditions. White-flowered form available. *A. confusa* has deeper blue flowers, but it is less heat tolerant. Zones 3 to 8.

Agastache
(ah-*gah*-sta-kee)
Giant hyssop
Labiatae—mint family

Agastache 'Licorice Blue'.

A genus of about 30 species, all native to North America and Mexico except for one from Japan, agastache is appreciated by herb gardeners for its aromatic foliage and spikes of small, edible flowers. Recommending it for the perennial garden is its ease of growth, adaptability and mid- to late summer flowers. The name comes from the Greek *aga*, "very much," and *stachys*, "spikes," referring to the many flower spikes.

GROWING GUIDE Full sun to light shade. Just about any soil with good drainage. Plants do not live long, but readily reseed, which can be good or bad.

PROPAGATION Seed, stem cuttings.

USES Bed and borders, cottage, meadow or native plant gardens.

SPECIES, VARIETIES, CULTIVARS AND HYBRIDS

A. foeniculum (fee-*nik*-yew-lum). Giant blue hyssop. Eastern North America. Grows to 3 feet tall and 18 inches wide. Coarse, triangular leaves are toothed. Many cylindrical 4-inch spikes of small, dusky indigo-violet flowers are produced in summer. There is a white form, as well as hybrids in pastels. Zones 4 to 9.

Ajuga
(ah-*joo*-guh)
Bugleweed
Labiatae—mint family

The common bugleweed (*A. reptans*) is a widely adaptable, vigorous perennial groundcover grown mainly for its foliage, with a number of highly colorful cultivars available. The slightly taller-growing species are less vigorous, which can be considered an advantage in this case, with somewhat more prominent flowers. In the right place, the ajugas are wonderful plants.

GROWING GUIDE Partial to half shade. Just about any moist but well-drained soil.

PROPAGATION Division is easy at any time during the growing season.

USES Groundcover, but not where it will overtake a lawn or less robust plants.

SPECIES, VARIETIES, CULTIVARS AND HYBRIDS

A. genevensis (gen-e-*ven*-sis). Geneva bugleweed. Europe. Grows to 12 inches tall and at least as wide. Rounded, toothed leaves to 4 inches long and 2 inches wide with whorled spikes of blue, pink or white flowers in summer. Although robust, it is not invasive. With constant soil moisture, it will tolerate more shade than other ajuga. 'Brockbankii' is a hybrid with bright blue flowers. Zones 4 to 9.

A. pyramidalis (peer-ruh-mid-*ah*-lis). Upright bugleweed. Europe. Grows to 9 inches tall and as wide. A handsome plant with dark semievergreen leaves and blue flowers. The cultivar 'Crispa', sometimes listed as 'Metallica Crispa', has deep blue flowers and red-brown, crinkled leaves with a metallic sheen; it is outstanding. Zones 3 to 9.

A. reptans (*rep*-tanz). Common bugleweed. Europe. Grows to 8 inches tall and spreads as far as it wants to go. Plant where its invasive qualities will

Ajuga reptans.

not be a problem, such as under trees or on banks. Used as an edging, it can potentially take over a lawn. There are a number of cultivars selected for unusual foliage, which can revert to plain green; remove these to maintain the unique coloring. Selections, all with blue to violet flowers, include 'Atropurpurea', dark bronze-purple leaves with best color in full sun; 'Bronze Beauty', dark bronze-purple leaves with metallic sheen; 'Burgundy Glow', 'Multicolor' and 'Rainbow' are

Ajuga reptans 'Burgundy Glow'.

all similar, with white, pink, rose and green variegation on leaves; 'Gaiety', bronze-purple leaves; 'Silver Beauty' and 'Variegata', leaves variegated silver and green, with best coloring in shade. Zones 3 to 9.

Alchemilla
(al-kuh-*mill*-uh)
Lady's mantle
Rosaceae—rose family

Mounds of velvety, pale green, scalloped leaves make alchemilla endearing, especially to those of us who work to grow it in hot, humid climates. With cooler summers and more abundant growth, it may be taken for granted. The froth of yellow-green flowers rising in an airy cloud above the leaves in summer is like icing on the cake; these are also very good for bouquets. The genus name is derived from the use of the plant by alchemists, while the common name is a Latinized version of an Arabic name.

GROWING GUIDE Full sun in cooler climates to partial shade in hotter ones. Humus-rich, moist but well-drained soil. In hot climates, cut back in midsummer to stimulate fresh growth as days begin to cool.

PROPAGATION Division. Readily grows from fresh seeds. Deadhead unless you want it to self-sow.

USES Informal edging plant or ground-cover. Looks particularly good as a foil for other flowers. Cut flowers.

SPECIES, VARIETIES, CULTIVARS AND HYBRIDS

Alchemilla mollis.

A. mollis (*mol*-lis). Lady's mantle. Asia Minor. Grows 12 to 18 inches tall and 24 inches wide. Sprays of tiny, chartreuse-colored flowers are held six inches or more above the rounded, 4-inch-wide leaves during summer. Plants sold as *A. vulgaris* are usually *A. mollis*. There are more than 200 other species, the smaller ones being useful for the rock garden. Zones 4 to 7.

Amsonia
(am-*sohn*-ee-uh)
Blue stars
Apocynaceae—dogbane family

Although they'll never be traffic stoppers, amsonias are easily grown North American natives that deserve greater use in perennial gardens. They emerge early in the spring with fine-textured, dark green leaves and are unusual in that they have significant fall color, in this case a bright gold. Loose, rounded clusters of star-shaped, pale blue flowers cover the upright clumps for about a month in spring and early summer. The genus is named after Charles Amson, an 18th-century physician.

GROWING GUIDE Full sun if soil is constantly moist, or partial to light shade. Widely adaptable but does best in deep, humus-rich moist soils that are mulched.

PROPAGATION Division, seed or stem cuttings.

USES Beds and borders, along the edges of woodlands or streams, native plant gardens.

SPECIES, VARIETIES, CULTIVARS AND HYBRIDS

Amsonia tabernaemontana.

A. tabernaemontana (ta-bur-nee-mon-*tay*-nuh). Willow blue star. North America. Grows to 3 feet tall and 2 feet wide. Thin, willow-like leaves to 6 inches long on upright stems. Open clusters of numerous, star-shaped, pale

blue flowers to 1 inch across in early summer followed by soft, hairy seed pods. Golden fall color. Zones 3 to 9.

Gardeners in the South should also consider downy amsonia, *A. angustifolia* (*A. ciliata*). Zones 7 to 10.

Anaphalis
(ah-*nah*-fa-lis)
Pearly everlasting
Compositae—daisy family

A tough plant long prized for its woolly, silvery-gray foliage and large heads of small white flowers that are easily dried, anaphalis is particularly suited to gardens with moist soil where other gray-leaved plants might perish. To dry the flowers, cut when the blooms just begin to show their centers; put in a vase of water for several hours, then hang upside down in a dark, dry place.

GROWING GUIDE Full sun to partial shade in moist but well-drained soil. Can benefit from midsummer pruning if growth becomes leggy. May host fungal diseases in hot, humid summers or suffer caterpillar damage in early summer.

PROPAGATION Division, seed or stem cuttings.

USES Near the front of beds or borders; naturalized areas. Use in white gardens or to tone down warm colors.

SPECIES, VARIETIES, CULTIVARS AND HYBRIDS

Anaphalis triplinervis.

A. triplinervis (tri-plee-*ner*-vis). Himalayan pearly everlasting. Himalayas. Grows to 18 inches tall and 12 inches wide. Growing in a zigzag, the stems form bushy, compact plants with woolly leaves and tight masses of small, creamy white, yellow-centered flowers from mid- to late summer. 'Summer Snow' is shorter-growing and flowers are a brighter white. Zones 3 to 8.

Also consider Indian pearly everlasting, *A. cinnamomea* (*A. yedoensis*), a taller-growing plant that takes several years to become established, and American pearly everlasting (*A. margaritacea*), growing to 4 feet tall and more tolerant of drought.

Anchusa officianalis.

Anchusa
(an-*kew*-suh)
Italian bugloss
Boraginaceae—borage family

Its life in the garden may be short, but anyone who has been smitten by the intense blue flowers of anchusa doesn't mind; better a brief, stunning affair than a long, boring one. The airy clusters of flowers, resembling forget-me-nots, bloom in early summer. The genus name is from a Greek word meaning "to paint," a reference to the use of the root as a dye. The common name is also from a Greek word, this one translating as "ox tongue," referring to the shape and roughness of the leaves.

GROWING GUIDE Full sun to very light shade. Deep, humus-rich, moist but well-drained soil. Cut back and fertilize after flowering to encourage a second blooming. May need staking.

PROPAGATION Division, seed or root cuttings.

USES At the back of beds or borders.

SPECIES, VARIETIES, CULTIVARS AND HYBRIDS
A. azurea (a-*zoo*-ree-uh). Italian bugloss, Italian alkanet. Caucasus. Grows to 5 feet tall and 2 feet wide. Coarsely textured, the oblong leaves grow to 8 inches long. The bristly stems bear spiralling clusters of ½-inch, deep blue flowers in early summer for about 4 weeks. A number of selections have been developed, including 'Dropmore', to 4 feet tall with deep blue flowers; 'Little John', to 18 inches tall with dark blue flowers; 'Loddon Royalist', to 3 feet tall with azure blue flowers; and 'Royal Blue', to 3 feet tall with dark blue flowers. Zones 3 to 8.

Anemone
(ah-*nem*-oh-nee)
Windflower
Ranunculaceae—buttercup family

The many and varied anemones found around the world provide us with flowers from early spring through autumn on plants of different shapes and sizes. While the early blooming ones are charmers (and highlighted as a group later), it is the fall-blooming anemones that are the stars of this clan, with their tall, elegant foliage and a profusion of pastel flowers at a time of year when we cherish every single blossom.

GROWING GUIDE Full sun to partial shade. Fertile, moist but well-drained soil. Requires several seasons to get established enough to bloom their best.

PROPAGATION Division.

USES Specimens, mass plantings or back of beds and borders.

SPECIES, VARIETIES, CULTIVARS AND HYBRIDS
A. x *hybrida* (*hib*-ri-duh). Japanese anemone. May also be listed as *A. japonica*. Grows to 4 feet tall and 2 feet wide. Each leaf composed of 3 leaflets. Open, branching clusters of single or double flowers to 3 inches across in white or shades of pink to rose. There are a number of excellent named hybrids from which to choose. Zones 4 to 8.

Anemone tomentosa.

A. tomentosa (toe-ment-*toe*-suh). Grape-leaved anemone. May also be listed as *A. vitifolia*. Asia. Grows to 3 feet tall and 18 inches wide. Very similar to *A.* x *hybrida* but with lobed leaves, more rapid spreading, and bloom beginning earlier. White flowers. 'Robustissima' grows to 4 feet with pale pink flowers. Zones 5 to 8.

There are a number of low-growing, spring-blooming perennial species particularly suited either for planting in masses, especially with spring bulbs, or for naturalized plantings. All have white flowers; they include *A. canadensis* (Zones 3 to 7), *A. magellanica* (Zones 2 to 7), *A. nemerosa* (Zones 4 to 8) and *A. sylvestris* (Zones 4 to 8). For the front of the border, *A.* x *lesseri* (Zones 5 to 8) blooms in early summer with white, yellow, rose or red flowers.

Anthemis
(*an*-them-is)
Chamomile
Compositae—daisy family

The anthemis of choice for the perennial garden has sunshine yellow daisy-like flowers along with fine-textured foliage and an ability to thrive in dry soil.

Anthemis tinctoria 'Golden Marguerite'.

GROWING GUIDE Full sun. Well-drained, average to poor soil. May need staking.

PROPAGATION Division, stem cuttings.

USES Middle to back of beds and borders.

SPECIES, VARIETIES, CULTIVARS AND HYBRIDS
   A. tinctoria (tink-*toe*-ree-uh). Golden marguerite. Europe. Grows 2 to 3 feet tall and 2 feet wide. Leaves resemble parsley. Abundant yellow flowers to 1½ inches across. Does best in areas with cool summers. A number of hybrids between this species and *A. sancti-johannis* are available, with plants ranging in height from one to three feet and flowers in shades varying from cream through yellows to golds and oranges. Zones 3 to 7.

Other species to consider include *A. cupaniana*, dwarf chamomile, forming dense, gray-green mats with white flowers (Zones 5 to 8) and *A. marschalliana* (*A. bierbersteinii*), with fernlike, silvery foliage and golden flowers (Zones 5 to 7).

Aquilegia.

Aquilegia
(a-kwil-*lee*-gee-uh)
Columbine
Ranunculaceae—buttercup family

Their springtime bloom period and life span may be short but the gaily colored, unusually shaped flowers of easily-grown columbine have endeared it to generations of gardeners. Besides the many hybrids, there are a number of species that make excellent garden plants. The resemblance of the flowers to birds is illustrated in the names: *columba* for dove and *aquila* for eagle.

GROWING GUIDE Partial to half shade in most climates, but can tolerate full sun in cooler ones. Humus-rich, moist but well-drained soil. Destroy foliage riddled by leaf miner insects.

PROPAGATION Seed as soon as ripe or in spring. Division in spring of young plants only. Plants readily hybridize among themselves and self-sow, with the resulting colors a surprise.

USES Massed in shaded wild gardens. Beds and borders. Use shorter types in rock gardens.

SPECIES, VARIETIES, CULTIVARS AND HYBRIDS
   A. x *hybrida* (*hib*-ri-duh). Hybrid columbine. Grows 1½ to 3 feet tall and 1 foot wide. Gray-green, finely divided leaves and spurred flowers in shades of white, yellow, pink, purple, red and orange. Many excellent named hybrids are available. Zones 3 to 9.
   Among the species, consider *A. alpina*, to 3 feet with blue or white flowers (Zones 3 to 8); *A. caerulea*, to 2 feet with blue and white flowers; *A. canadensis*, to 2 feet with red and yellow flowers (Zones 3 to 8); *A. chrysantha*, to 3 feet with yellow flowers (Zones 3 to 9); *A. flabellata*, to 18 inches with light blue flowers (Zones 3 to 9); and *A. longissima*, to 3 feet with yellow flowers and very long spurs (Zones 4 to 9).

Arabis
(*air*-uh-bis)
Rock cress
Cruciferae—mustard family

A large genus with many plants for the rock garden collector, one species is more widely adapted for garden use. It celebrates spring with a cascade of tiny, fragrant white flowers. The name is derived from Arabia, referring to its preference for dry soils.

GROWING GUIDE Full sun. Average to poor, neutral to alkaline soil. Cut back the flowers after blooming.

PROPAGATION Division, stem cuttings.

USES Edging or accent along walls, banks or the front of beds and borders.

Arabis causasia.

SPECIES, VARIETIES, CULTIVARS AND HYBRIDS

A. caucasica (kaw-*kas*-ee-kuh). Rock cress. Mediterranean. Also known as *A. albida*. Grows 10 inches tall and 18 inches wide. Small, oval, toothed, gray-green leaves form a loose mat that is particularly effective climbing over rocks or cascading down walls. Fragrant white flowers are held above the leaves in loose sprays. There are variegated and pink-flowered varieties as well as one with double flowers that is especially long blooming. Zones 4 to 7.

Arisaema
(air-ris-*ee*-muh)
Jack-in-the-pulpit
Aracae—arum family

Jack expounding from his sylvan pulpit is one of the treasures of the woodlands of eastern North America, but the perennial cogniscenti are all aflap over the Asian varieties with their striking forms and colorations.

GROWING GUIDE Partial to half shade. Humus-rich, moist but well-drained soil.

PROPAGATION Division; fresh seed in fall.

USES Woodland shade gardens. Mass plantings are most effective.

SPECIES, VARIETIES, CULTIVARS AND HYBRIDS

A. candidissimum (kan-duh-*dees*-

Arisaema sikokianum.

si-mum). China. Grows 12 inches tall and 18 inches wide. The white-striped, pink-hooded spathe appears in early summer, followed by broad, lobed leaves. Zones 7 to 9.

A. sikokianum (sik-koke-ee-*ah*-num). Japan. Grows 18 inches tall and as wide. Silvery-green leaves and a dark-purple hooded spathe striped white. Zones 5 to 9.

Besides the beloved Jack (*A. triphyllum*), another North American native is *A. dracontium*, dragonroot, with a rather bizarre form. There are about 75 Asian species, more of which are being offered by specialty mail-order nurseries.

Armeria
(ar-*mee*-ree-uh)
Thrift
Plumbaginaceae—plumbago family

Would thrift be such a widely seen plant if it was not so easy for garden centers to propagate the plants? Probably not. Still, ready availability should not preclude it from the garden. Though diminutive, thrift

is a sturdy, neat plant that does its job well.

GROWING GUIDE Full sun to partial shade in hotter climates. Sandy to average, well-drained soil. Deadhead regularly.

PROPAGATION Division, seed.

USES Rock gardens, between flagstones, along walls or at the front of beds and borders.

Armeria maritima 'Splendens'.

SPECIES, VARIETIES, CULTIVARS AND HYBRIDS

A. maritima (mah-*ri*-tah-mah). Common thrift, sea pink. Europe. Grows 6 to 12 inches tall and 12 inches wide. Dense tufts of grasslike, evergreen leaves. Rounded, 1-inch clusters of tiny flowers on leafless stems. Depending on selections, flowers may be pink, lilac, red or white. Found growing naturally along coastlines. Zones 4 to 8.

Other species to consider include *A. juniperifolia* (*A. caespitosa*), Pyrenees thrift, 6 inches tall with lilac flowers (Zones 4 to 8); and *A. plantaginea*, 18 inches tall with wider leaves, pink flowers, and the cultivar 'Bee's Ruby' usually chosen (Zones 4 to 9).

Artemisia
(ar-tem-*meez*-ee-uh)
Wormwood
Compositae—daisy family

Artemisia schmidtiana.

With a cast of hundreds, the artemisias run the gamut from sagebrush to tarragon, with aromatic foliage a common thread in their use for thousands of years. For the ornamental garden, the focus is placed on those with fine-textured foliage that mainly runs to silver. An added bonus is that many of these are staples for making dried arrangements and crafts. The genus name is from the goddess Artemis, while the common name of wormwood refers to early herbalists' use of the plant to kill parasitic worms.

GROWING GUIDE Full sun. Dry, well-drained soils. Cut back in midsummer to get fresh growth, particularly in hot, humid climates where rot can occur.

PROPAGATION Division, stem cuttings.

USES One of the best foliage plants for sunny beds and borders, providing a foil to flowering plants with its texture and color. Fresh and dried arrangements.

SPECIES, VARIETIES, CULTIVARS AND HYBRIDS

A. abrotanum (ab-*roh*-tan-um). Southernwood. Southern Europe. Grows 3 feet tall and 18 inches wide. A woody plant with threadlike leaves having a fruity scent. Insignificant yellow flowers. Zones 5 to 8.

A. absinthium (ab-*sin*-thee-um). Wormwood. Europe. Grows 3 feet tall and 2 feet wide. Woody plant with finely divided, silvery-gray leaves to 5 inches long. Insignificant, tiny gray flowers. Was used in the French liqueur absinthe, which turned out to have deleterious effects beyond the alcohol, as evidenced by Degas. Selections to be sought out include, 'Lambrook Silver' and 'Huntington Gardens', plus *A.* x 'Powis Castle'. Zones 3 to 9 for species, variably less for cultivars.

A. lactiflora (lak-ti-*flor*-uh). White mugwort. Asia. Grows to 6 feet tall and 4 feet wide. This is the oddball ornamental artemisia, what with dark green leaves and spectacular sprays of creamy flowers in late summer and fall. Good for background plantings and fresh-cut flowers. Needs moist soil. Zones 5 to 8.

A. ludoviciana var. **albula** (lew-doe-vik-ee-*ah*-nah *al*-buh-luh). White sagebrush. Western North America. Grows 3 feet tall and 2 feet wide, but watch out; it can spread fast and far. Both stems and leaves are silvery white. Long and pointed, the jagged-edged leaves are up to 4 inches long. Insignificant gray flowers in late summer. Prime candidate for summer

Aruncus didicus.

pruning to freshen growth. Selections include 'Silver Frost', 'Silver King', 'Silver Queen', and var. *latiloba*.

A. schmidtiana (shmit-ee-*ah*-nah). Silvermound artemisia. Japan. The form almost universally offered is 'Nana', or 'Silver Mound'. Grows 12 inches tall and 18 inches wide. Forms a silken mound of finely cut silver foliage. Tiny yellow flowers in summer. Superb in cool-summer climates, less so with heat and humidity. Zones 3 to 7.

Aruncus
(ah-*run*-kus)
Goatsbeard
Rosaceae—rose family

Large and stately, the North American goatsbeard is a long-lived, must-have plant for shaded areas. Magnificent clusters of creamy-white flowers in early summer create a striking effect.

GROWING GUIDE Partial shade. Tolerant of a wide range of soils, but best with humus-rich, moist but well-drained soil.

PROPAGATION Division, seed.

USES Back of the shade border, among shrubs, woodland wildflower garden, near a stream or pool.

SPECIES, VARIETIES, CULTIVARS AND HYBRIDS

A. dioicus (dee-oh-*ee*-kus). Goatsbeard. Eastern North America. Also listed as *A. sylvester*. Grows 5 feet

Asarum europaeum.

tall and and as wide. Compound, serrated leaves resemble those of astilbe. Plume-like clusters of tiny ivory flowers in early summer. The variety *astilbioides* grows to 2 feet, 'Kneiffii' grows to 3 feet with finely divided foliage and 'Child of Two Worlds' has dropping flower clusters. Zones 3 to 8.

Another aruncus to search out is *A. aethusifolius* from Korea. It is a diminutive plant growing to 12 inches tall.

Asarum
(ah-*sah*-rum)
Wild ginger
Aristolochiacae—wild ginger family

These are not the culinary gingers, which are *Zingiber*, but the leaves and roots do emit a similar fragrance. The value of the asarums lies in their low-growing, heart-shaped leaves; they make a good groundcover for moist, shady conditions. Taxonomists have now classified the evergreen types as *Hexastylis*, so you may find plants under that listing.

GROWING GUIDE Partial to full shade. Humus-rich, moist but well-drained soil.

PROPAGATION Division.

USES Edgings, front of shade borders, groundcover.

SPECIES, VARIETIES, CULTIVARS AND HYBRIDS
A. europaeum (oy-roh-*pye*-um). European wild ginger. Europe. Grows 8

inches tall and as wide. Glossy, dark green, evergreen leaves to 3 inches across. Purple-brown, urn-shaped flowers at ground level under foliage in early spring. Zones 4 to 7.

A. shuttleworthii, native to the Southeastern United States, is more tolerant of heat; it has lovely silvery-white markings on the evergreen leaves (Zones 6 to 8). *A. caudatum* (Zones 4 to 8) and *A. hartwegii* (Zones 6 to 8), both evergreen species, are native to western North America. More hardy (Zones 3 to 8) is the deciduous native wild ginger, *A. canadense.* There are also species native to Asia just coming into commerce.

Asclepias
(uh-*sklay*-pee-us)
Milkweed, silkweed, butterfly weed
Asclepiadaceae—milkweed family

Long-lived and easy to grow, butterfly weed is true to the name, attracting scores of butterflies to the clusters of waxy orange, yellow or scarlet flowers in summer. All plants of the milkweed family have a sticky white sap, hence the name. The canoe-shaped seed pods are distinctive, too, with the silken threads attached to the seed giving the group another common name. The flowers can be used for cutting if the cut end is seared in a flame to seal off sap flow.

Asclepias tuberosa.

GROWING GUIDE Full sun. Sandy to average well-drained soil. Plants are slow to emerge in the spring, so mark their site well. Deadhead to extend the bloom season beyond 6 weeks.

PROPAGATION Division, but with caution as the fleshy roots go deep. Fresh seed in fall. Root cuttings.

USES Sunny borders, meadows.

SPECIES, VARIETIES, CULTIVARS AND HYBRIDS
A. tuberosa (tew-bah-*roh*-suh). Butterfly weed. Eastern North America. Grows 3 feet tall and 2 feet wide. Stocky stems with narrow, pointed, bristly leaves to 4 inches long. Somewhat flat, tightly packed clusters of waxy flowers, mainly orange but with yellows and reds sometimes occurring. Zones 4 to 9.

Asphodeline
(as-fod-eh-*lee*-nee)
Jacob's rod
Liliaceae—lily family

Asphodeline lutea.

The grassy leaves of asphodeline provide fine texture to the garden, while the spikes of yellow flowers in early summer offer vertical form. They are sturdy and easy to grow in warmer climates.

GROWING GUIDE Full sun to partial shade in average to humus-rich, well-drained soil.

PROPAGATION Division, seed.

USES Groups in middle to back of beds and borders. Mass plantings. Cut flowers. Fragrant.

SPECIES, VARIETIES, CULTIVARS AND HYBRIDS

A. lutea (*lew*-tee-uh). Jacob's rod. Mediterranean. To 3 feet tall in bloom and 1 foot wide. Gray-green, grassy leaves to 10 inches long. Slim stalks of star-shaped, fragrant yellow flowers in early to midsummer. 'Flore Pleno' has double flowers. Zones 6 to 8.

Aster amellus.

Aster
(*ass*-ter)
Aster, michaelmas daisy
Compositae—daisy family

Asters are indispensable in the sunny landscape in the summer and fall. With over 600 species and thousands of selections, choosing is a process of elimination by intimidation. Ranging in size from 6 inches to 8 feet tall, all have small, daisylike flowers, usually with yellow centers, in shades of blue, lavender, purple, pink, red or white. Foliage is relatively small, oval, pointed with smooth or jagged edges. The name is from the Latin for "star."

GROWING GUIDE Full sun to light shade. Humus-rich, well-drained soil. They grow best in cool-summer climates and need a winter mulch. Stake taller varieties. Pinch back in early summer to encourage branching, shorter growth and more flowers. Choose disease-resistant varieties.

PROPAGATION Division in spring, at least every 2 years, to keep plants vigorous. Terminal stem cuttings in spring or early summer.

USES Short ones near the front or middle of beds and borders; taller ones to the back. Meadow gardens. Cut flowers.

SPECIES, VARIETIES, CULTIVARS AND HYBRIDS

A. alpinus (ahl-*pine*-us). Alpine aster. Europe, Asia. Grows 10 inches tall and 18 inches wide. Tufts of gray-green, spoon-shaped leaves. Blue to purple, to 1-inch flowers in early summer. Best for cool-summer climates.

A. amellus (ah-*mel*-us). Italian aster. Southern Europe. Grows 2 feet tall and as wide. Rough-textured stems and leaves. A number of selections available in various colors, with 2-inch flowers in fall. Drought tolerant. Does best in Zones 5 to 6, but hardy in Zones 4 to 8. *A. x alpellus* is a cross between *A. alpinus* and *A. amellus*; it grows 15 inches tall and as wide. Sometimes listed as 'Triumph'. Blue flowers with orange centers.

A. divaricatus (duh-var-ah-*cah*-tus). White wood aster. North

Aster x frikartii 'Monch'.

America. Grows to 3 feet tall and as wide. Great quantities of 1-inch white flowers from summer through fall. Good for dry soil and light shade. Zones 4 to 8.

A. x frikartii (fri-*kart*-ee-eye). Grows 3 feet tall and as wide. One of the best asters for the garden. Long-blooming, with 2- to 3-inch lavender-blue flowers. Selections include 'Monch' and 'Wonder of Staffa'. Zones 5 to 8.

Aster novae-angliae.

A. novae-angliae (*noh*-vee-*ang*-lee-ee). New England aster. North America. Grows to 6 feet tall and 4 feet wide. Many selections available, but especially look for 'Alma Potschke' and 'Harrington's Pink', both shorter cultivars with pink flowers. May need staking. Do not overfertilize. Zones 4 to 8.

Aster novi-belgi 'Professor Kippenburg'.

A. novi-belgi (*noh*-vee-*bell*-gee-ee). New York aster. Eastern North America. Size varies greatly, depending on the selection, of which there are many. Full aster color range, with some beginning to bloom in summer, but most with late-summer and autumn flowers. Zones 4 to 8.

A. tartaricus (tar-*tar*-eh-cus). Tartarian daisy. Asia. Grows 6 feet tall and 3 feet wide. Blue to purple flowers are particularly late blooming. Stout stems seldom need staking. Zones 4 to 8.

Astilbe
(ah-*stil*-bee)
Astilbe
Saxifragaceae—saxifrage family

Among the best plants for shaded areas, astilbes are long-lived and easily grown. Although each individual flower is tiny, the overall effect is of a fluffy plume in shades of pink, red or white. The foliage composed of divided leaves may be deep green to bronze. The name comes from the Greek *a*, without, and *stilbe*, brightness, referring to the dull color of the leaves of some species.

GROWING GUIDE Can be grown in all but the deepest shade. Needs a humus-rich, moist soil. Boggy soils can be tolerated, but dry soils cannot.

PROPAGATION Division.

Astilbe x *arendsii* (red).

USES Shade beds and borders, along streams and pools. At their best planted in masses. Cut flowers.

Astilbe x *arendsii* (pink).

SPECIES, VARIETIES, CULTIVARS AND HYBRIDS

A. x arendsii (ah-*rendz*-ee-eye). Astilbe. Hybrid origin. Hybrids under this classification were originally developed by German plantsman Georg Arends (1862–1952), with others following. Selections range in height from 2 to 4 feet tall and to 2 feet wide, with various colors and bloom times from early to late summer. Zones 4 to 9.

Although the vast majority of astilbes sold each year come under *A.* x *arendsii*, there are others with merit. These include *A. simplicifolia*, growing to 18 inches tall with starry, white flowers (Zones 4 to 8), and two that are more tolerant of dry soil: the creeping *A. chinensis* 'Pumila', growing to 18 inches tall with magenta-pink flowers (Zones 3 to 8), and the late-blooming *A. taquetii* 'Superba', growing to 4 feet with magenta-pink flowers (Zones 4 to 8).

Astrantia
(ah-*stran*-tee-uh)
Masterwort
Umbelliferae—carrot family

Much-touted perennials by aficionados, masterworts are not showy plants and can be a bit difficult to grow. Their charm lies in their subtleties, including airy branches of small but unusual flowers over a long period in summer and the long life of these flowers when cut. With a domed center surrounded by pointed bracts, the whitish, pink or red flowers are the source of the name, an allusion to their star shape.

GROWING GUIDE Does best in partial to light shade but tolerates full sun in cooler climates. Must have humus-rich, moist but well-drained soil. Grows best with cool night temperatures, partial shade and consistently moist soil.

PROPAGATION Division. Self-sows.

USES Toward the front of beds and borders so the flowers can be seen closely. Near streams and pools. Massed under open trees.

SPECIES, VARIETIES, CULTIVARS AND HYBRIDS

A. major (*may*-jor). Great masterwort. Europe. Grows to 3 feet tall and 18 inches wide. Deeply lobed and toothed leaves. Wiry stems topped by open clusters of flowers. Starts blooming in early summer, stops during heat, then resumes in the fall. 'Involucrata' has a particularly large "ruff." Other selections differ mainly in the color of the flowers. Zones 5 to 7.

Aurinia
(aw-*rin*-ee-uh)
Basket-of-gold
Cruciferae—mustard family

Formerly classified as an *Alyssum*, the form remains the same—mounds of

Aurinia saxatalis.

creeping or cascading plants are covered with bright yellow flowers in early spring.

GROWING GUIDE Full sun. Average to poor, well-drained soil. Cut back after flowering. Does best in cool-summer climates.

PROPAGATION Division, seed, stem cuttings.

USES Edging for paths, steps, or front of beds and borders. Rock gardens. Cascading over stone walls.

SPECIES, VARIETIES, CULTIVARS AND HYBRIDS

A. saxatilis (saks-ah-*til*-us). Basket of gold. Europe. Grows 12 inches tall and 18 inches wide. Mounds of fine-textured, gray-green leaves. Tiny, four-petaled flowers of bright golden or lemon yellow in early spring, depending on the cultivar. Zones 3 to 7.

b

Baptisia
(bap-*tis*-ee-uh)
False indigo
Leguminosae—pea family

North American natives, the baptisias hold their own in perennial plantings. Long-lived and easy to grow, they are shrubby plants with leaves divided into pointed, oval segments. The pea-like flowers are blue, yellow or white, depending on the species. The flowers were used at one time as a dye, substituting for true indigo. Baptisias are attractive even after flowering, as they develop black seed pods that last through fall.

GROWING GUIDE Full sun to partial shade. Humus-rich, moist but well-drained soil. Because of the deep taproot, they are somewhat tolerant of dry soil.

Baptisia australis.

PROPAGATION Seed, sown outdoors as soon as ripe. Division is possible, but difficult because of the taproot.

USES Back of beds or borders. Cut flowers; seed pods for dried arrangements.

SPECIES, VARIETIES, CULTIVARS AND HYBRIDS

D. australis (ah-*strah*-lis). False indigo. Eastern United States. Grows to 4 feet tall and as wide. Branching, upright stems with bright blue-green leaves. Blooms for a month in early spring with spikes of indigo-blue, 1-inch flowers, followed by the black seed pods. Zones 3 to 9.

White-flowered species for the garden include *B. alba*, from the southeastern United States (Zones 5 to 8), and *B. leucantha*, from the Midwestern prairies (Zones 4 to 8).

The most widely grown yellow-flowered form is *B. tinctoria*, from the Southeast (Zones 5 to 9).

Begonia
(buh-*gon*-ee-uh)
Hardy begonia
Begoniaceae—begonia family

Among the thousand-plus species of begonias, only one has any significant hardiness. To make it feel at home, grow in shade among ferns, hostas, and Japanese anemones.

GROWING GUIDE Partial to light shade. Humus-rich, moist but well drained soil. Needs a protective winter mulch in Zone 6.

PROPAGATION Small bulbs form in the leaf axils. These can be allowed to "self sow," or can be gathered and stored over winter in dry peat moss, potted up the following spring, then transplanted several months later. Stem cuttings.

USES Front to middle of shade borders, woodland gardens.

Begonia grandis.

SPECIES, VARIETIES, CULTIVARS AND HYBRIDS

B. grandis (*gran*-dis). Hardy begonia. Asia. May also be listed as *B. evansiana* or *B. discolor*. Grows to 2 feet tall and 1 foot wide. Waxen, glistening heart-shaped leaves are red-tinted beneath. Succulent, angular stems. Sprays of drooping red buds open to 1-inch pink flowers from late summer into fall. There is a also a variety with white flowers. Zones 6 to 9.

Belamcanda chinensis.

Belamcanda
(bell-am-*kan*-duh)
Blackberry lily
Iridaceae—iris family

Not a flashy plant, but delightful for small charms. Leaves resemble those of iris, and, in midsummer, thin stalks bear sprays of 2-inch yellow-orange flowers marked with red-purple dots. As the flowers fade, the seed pods ripen to reveal clusters of shiny black seeds that look like blackberries.

Flower stems may be cut for fresh use, while the seed pods can be used in dried arrangements. Easy to grow, with no appreciable pests. Why not try it?

GROWING GUIDE Full sun to partial shade. Average to humus-rich, well-drained soil.

Belamcanda chinensis seeds.

PROPAGATION Division, seed. Self-sows, but is not invasive.

USES Middle of beds and borders. Meadow and dappled woodland gardens. Cut flowers.

SPECIES, VARIETIES, CULTIVARS AND HYBRIDS

B. chinensis (chin-*nen*-sis). Blackberry lily. East Asia. Grows to 3 feet tall and 1 foot wide. Sword-shaped leaves and yellow-orange, six-petaled flowers on zigzagged stems in summer, followed by seeds resembling blackberries. Yellow-flowered forms are available. Zones 5 to 10.

Bergenia.

Bergenia
(ber-*jen*-ee-uh)
Bergenia
Saxifragaceae—saxifrage family

Bergenias are noted for the bold-textured effect of their foliage, variously described as cabbage-like, leathery, waxy or thick, with leaves growing up to 10 inches long. Although the leaves are evergreen,

sometimes changing to burgundy in the winter, they can become tattered-looking during the colder months. Even so, the foliage is attractive for many months of the year. The leaves are also prized for use in flower arrangements. As another bonus, thick stems rise up in the spring, topped by clusters of bell- or cup-shaped pink, red or white flowers.

GROWING GUIDE Full sun in cooler climates to partial shade in hotter ones. A wide range of soils are tolerated, except in hot climates, where the soil must be moist but well drained. Remove faded flowers.

PROPAGATION Division, with each start having at least a 4-inch piece of rhizome. Seed.

USES Front of beds and borders, massed along paths, groundcover under shrubs and trees.

SPECIES, VARIETIES, CULTIVARS AND HYBRIDS The best selections for the garden are the hybrids between species. The differences between the various ones are the flower color and winter or summer coloration of the leaves. Most grow 12 to 18 inches tall and as wide. Some to look for include 'Bressingham White', 'Evening Glow', 'Morning Red', 'Red Bloom', 'Silver Light' and 'Sunningdale'. Zones 4 to 8.

Boltonia
(bol-*ton*-ee-uh)
Boltonia, false starwort
Compositae—daisy family

Rather like an aster on steroids, boltonias produce profuse quantities of small, starry flowers in late summer and fall. The most widely available species is a North American native, usually seen with white flowers, but lilac also occurs. Although its 7-foot height is a bit intimidating, to say nothing of floppy, a selection called 'Snowbank', at 4 feet, adds lightness and grace to the fall garden. It is an especially good choice for hot climates, where other fall-blooming plants may not fare so well.

GROWING GUIDE Full sun. Adapts to a wide range of soils that are well-drained.

PROPAGATION Division.

USES Backs of bed and borders.

Boltonia asteroides 'Snowbank'.

SPECIES, VARIETIES, CULTIVARS AND HYBRIDS

B. asteroides (as-ter-*roy*-deez). White boltonia. Eastern North America. Grows to 7 feet tall and 4 feet wide. Willow-like, blue-green leaves to 5 inches long. Airy, open sprays of white or lilac, daisy-like, 1-inch flowers. Selections include 'Snowbank', 4 feet tall with white flowers; 'Pink Beauty', 4 feet tall with pink flowers; and one most often listed as *B. a. latisquama* var. *nana*, 3 feet tall with larger, purple flowers. Lower stems may become bare, so place boltonias behind other plants. Zones 4 to 9.

Brunnera
(*brun*-ah-rah)
Siberian bugloss
Boraginaceae—borage family

The common name may be a bit off-putting, but the effect of Siberian bugloss, particularly when planted in

Brunnera macrophylla.

masses beside a pool or along a stream, is one of pure romance. When the conditions are right, brunnera are long-lived and easy to grow.

GROWING GUIDE Partial to half shade. Humus-rich, moist but well-drained soil. Remove faded flowers unless self-sowing is desired.

PROPAGATION Seldom necessary, but possible by division, seed or, preferably, root cuttings.

USES Any moist, shady area, but especially around water features in the garden; groundcover.

SPECIES, VARIETIES, CULTIVARS AND HYBRIDS

B. macrophylla (mak-ro-*fill*-uh). Siberian bugloss. Caucasus. Grows 12 to 18 inches tall and as wide. Mounding, with light green, roughly textured, heart-shaped leaves. Sprays of blue flowers resembling forget-me-nots in spring. Selections are offered with different types of leaf variegation; these must be propagated by division, and reversions to plain green leaves must be weeded out. Zones 3 to 7.

Campanula
(kam-*pan*-yew-luh)
Bellflower
Campanulaceae—bellflower family

Campanulas are among the most beloved of perennials, partly because there are so many species and selections, but also because campanulas are strikingly beautiful. Liberty Hyde Bailey has written, "They are for those who love to grow plants for the joy of growing them." Most often thought of for their blue, bell-shaped flowers, colors are also available in lavenders and purples, pinks and whites. This is not an easy group to typify, since the ones for the garden range from tiny species for the rock garden to behemoths over 5 feet tall. The showiest campanula, Canterbury bells (*C. medium*), is a biennial.

GROWING GUIDE Full sun, with partial shade preferred in hotter climates. Humus-rich, moist but well-drained soil. Deadhead regularly for recurrent bloom. Apply protective winter mulch.

PROPAGATION Division, seed, stem cuttings, root cuttings.

USES Because of the many sizes and forms of campanulas available, they can fit in just about anywhere in the garden except deep shade. Plant in clumps of at least three. Taller forms are good cut flowers.

Campanula carpatica.

SPECIES, VARIETIES, CULTIVARS AND HYBRIDS

C. carpatica (kar-*pa*-ti-kuh). Carpathian harebell. Eastern Europe. Grows 8 to 12 inches tall and 12 inches wide, forming trailing clumps of small heart-shaped leaves. The 1- to 2-inch violet-blue or white cup-shaped flowers bloom throughout the summer on wiry stems. Use in the rock garden or the front of the border. Zones 3 to 8.

Campanula latiflora.

C. latifolia (lah-tee-*fo*-lee-uh). Great bellflower. Europe. Grows 3 to 5 feet tall and 3 feet wide. Rapidly spreading clumps with large leaves at the base of plants. Blooms in summer with 2-inch purple-blue or white flowers. Readily self-sows. May need staking. Zones 3 to 7.

Campanual persicifolia.

bellflower. Southern Europe. Grows to 6 inches tall and 18 inches wide. Smooth, kidney-shaped leaves on mat-forming plants. Funnel-shaped, lilac-blue or white, 1-inch flowers cover the plants in late spring and early summer. Self-sows. Zones 4 to 8.

Campanula glomerata.

C. glomerata (glom-er-*rah*-tuh). Clustered bellflower. Eurasia. Grows 12 to 18 inches tall and 12 inches wide. Leaves are dark green and coarsely textured. Tightly packed clusters of 1-inch purple or white flowers at the ends of erect stems bloom from early to midsummer. Zones 3 to 8.

C. lactiflora (lak-ti-*floh*-ruh). Milky bellflower. Caucasus. Grows 3 to 5 feet tall and 3 feet wide. Small leaves on bushy plants. Pale blue, violet-blue, pink or white 1-inch, bell-shaped flowers borne on long stiff spikes in summer. Readily self-sows. Especially easy to grow, but may need staking. Zones 5 to 7.

Campanula latifolia.

C. persicifolia (per-si-ki-*foh*-lee-uh). Peach-leaf bellflower. Europe, Asia, North Africa. Grows 2 to 3 feet tall and 2 feet wide. Clump-forming plants with narrow, leathery leaves that are evergreen in mild-winter regions. Borne on spikes, the open, upward-facing, 1- to 2-inch flowers are available in shades of blue or white, as singles or doubles. Zones 3 to 8, with best growth in Zones 3 to 6.

C. portenschlagiana (por-ten-shlag-ee-*ah*-nuh). Dalmatian

Campanula portenschlagiana.

C. rotundifolia (roh-tun-di-*foh*-lee-uh). Harebell. Europe. North America. Grows to 12 inches tall and as wide. Famous as the "bluebells of Scotland." Rounded, 1-inch leaves on dainty, tufted plants. Slender flower stems bear lavender-blue or white, 1-inch, nodding, bell-shaped flowers in summer. Zones 2 to 7.

Centaurea
(sen-*taw*-ree-uh)
Knapweed
Compositae—daisy family

Of the over 500 species of centaurea in the wild, only about a dozen are useful garden plants. These include such familiar annuals as cornflower, or bachelor's buttons. Among the perennial garden plants, they distinguish themselves with a tolerance of neglect and freely produced, thistle-like flowers that tend to strong colors and an excellence for cutting. The genus was named after the centaur Chiron, who is said to have been healed by the plant and went on to heal others.

GROWING GUIDE Full sun. Almost any well-drained soil. Deadhead for repeat flowering and to prevent self-sowing. Staking may be necessary.

PROPAGATION Division; seed, particularly when fresh; root cuttings.

USES Middle of beds and borders. Cut flowers.

Centaurea Montana.

SPECIES, VARIETIES, CULTIVARS AND HYBRIDS

C. dealbata (dee-al-*bah*-tuh). Persian cornflower. Asia Minor. Grows 2 feet tall and as wide. Small, coarsely cut leaves, dark green above and downy white beneath. For about 4 weeks in summer, stiff stems bear pinkish-purple to deep-rose flowers 2 to 3 inches across. May need staking. Zones 5 to 7.

C. hypoleuca (hye-po-*loo*-kuh). Knapweed. Asia Minor. Grows 2 feet tall and 18 inches wide. Very similar in appearance to *C. dealbata*, except that growth is more compact, foliage more gray-green and flowers are centered with white. Rarely needs staking, but spreads rapidly. The variety 'John Coutts' may be listed under either *C. dealbata* or *C. hypoleuca*, but wherever, it is an excellent, long-blooming plant with deep-rose flowers. Zones 4 to 7.

C. macrocephala (mak-roh-*sef*-ah-luh). Globe knapweed. Caucasus. Grows 4 feet tall and 2 feet wide. Bold plants with large, hairy leaves with wavy edges. Bright yellow flowers 3- to 4-inches across attract butterflies.

Centaurea macrocephala.

Bloom period is shorter in areas with hot, humid summers. Use the flowers both fresh or dried.

C. montana (mon-*tah*-nuh). Mountain bluets, Montana cornflowers, mountain knapweed. Europe. Grows 18 inches tall and as wide. Downy, silver-gray leaves. Deep violet-blue, dark pink or white flowers in late spring and early summer. Spreads very rapidly by underground stems and self-sowing. Excellent for meadow gardens. Zones 3 to 8.

Centaurea montana.

Centranthus
(sen-*tran*-thus)
Valerian
Valerianaceae—valerian family

Best for areas with cool summers, centranthus is adaptable enough to make it worth the effort in hotter climates. The lure is the large, showy spires of small, fragrant red, pink or white flowers. These are excellent for cutting and attract butterflies as well. The bushy plants of blue- or gray-green leaves have their own appeal.

GROWING GUIDE Full sun. Poor to average, well-drained soil that is neutral to alkaline. Deadhead to encourage repeat blooming.

PROPAGATION Division, seed, stem cuttings.

USES Sunny borders or rock walls. Cut flowers. Butterfly gardens.

SPECIES, VARIETIES, CULTIVARS AND HYBRIDS

Centaurea ruber.

C. ruber (*rue*-ber). Red valerian, Jupiter's beard, keys of heaven. Europe. Grows 2 to 3 feet tall and 18 inches wide. Branching, woody-stemmed plants with pointed, oval leaves. Branching, pointed clusters of ½-inch flowers in shades of pink, red or white. Zones 5 to 8.

Cerastium
(ser-*ras*-tee-rum)
Snow-in-summer
Caryophyllaceae—pink family

"One person's weed is another's treasured plant" certainly applies to cerastium. It is also one of those plants that grows rapaciously in England, but that struggles with heat and humidity. But even a small mound of "snow" can bring pleasure, so where summers are not too stressing, the creeping cerastium should be included.

GROWING GUIDE Full sun. Poor to average, well-drained soil. Shear plants after flowering to prevent self-sowing.

PROPAGATION Division, seed, stem cuttings.

USES Groundcover, cascading over stone walls, edging.

SPECIES, VARIETIES, CULTIVARS AND HYBRIDS

Cerastium tomentosum.

C. tomentosum (toe-men-toe-sum). Snow-in-summer. Italy. Grows 6 inches tall and spreads to 24 inches. Forms dense mats of downy, silvery gray, fine-textured foliage. Masses of ¾-inch, white, star-shaped flowers in early summer. Zones 2 to 7.

Ceratostigma
(ser-at-oh-*stig*-muh)
Leadwort, plumbago
Plumbaginaceae—plumbago family

Ceratostigma plumbaginoides.

Where hardy, leadwort is an easily grown, widely adaptable ground cover. As an added bonus, there are deep blue flowers from late summer into fall and glorious bronze-red foliage color, as well. Just be patient for it to leaf out in the spring.

GROWING GUIDE Full sun to light shade. Average, well-drained soil.

PROPAGATION Division, stem cuttings.

USES Front of the border, groundcover, especially good interplanted with small spring bulbs.

SPECIES, VARIETIES, CULTIVARS AND HYBRIDS

C. plumbaginoides (plum-bah-ji-noi-deez). Leadwort, plumbago. China. Grows 12 inches tall and 18 inches wide. Small, pointed, oval, dark green leaves on woody stems; leaves turn bronze-red in fall. Small clusters of gentian-blue flowers in late summer and fall. Zones 5 to 9.

Chelone
(kee-*loh*-nay)
Turtlehead
Scrophulariaceae—figwort family

Chelone.

Maybe you have to use a lot of imagination to see the turtle's head, but, even so, these are attractive perennials that adapt to both sun and some shade. Native to moist woodlands and prairies of the North America, chelones bring color to the garden in summer and fall.

GROWING GUIDE Full sun to light shade. Humus-rich, moist but well-drained soil. Full sun tolerated if soil is constantly moist. Tolerant of acid soil. Pinch the growing tips in the spring for best growth and flowering.

PROPAGATION Division, seed, stem cuttings.

USES Shaded beds and borders, native areas, near pools and streams.

SPECIES, VARIETIES, CULTIVARS AND HYBRIDS

C. glabra (*glay*-bruh). White turtlehead. North America. Grows 3 feet tall and 2 feet wide. Clumps of sturdy stems with narrow, lance-shaped leaves to 6 inches long. Spikes of 1-inch, white or rose-tinted flowers for 3 to 4 weeks in late summer. Zones 3 to 8.

Chelone lyonii.

C. lyonii (lye-*oh*-nee-eye). Pink turtlehead. Higher elevations of the southeastern United States. Grows 3 feet tall and 18 inches wide. Dark green, broadly lance-shaped, serrated leaves to 6 inches long. Tight clusters of 1-inch pink flowers produced for about 4 weeks in late summer to early fall. Zones 4 to 8.

C. obliqua (oh-*blee*-kwuh). Rose turtlehead. Wetlands of eastern North America. Grows 3 feet tall and 2 feet wide. Very similar in appearance to *C. lyonii*, but the flowers are a deeper rose color. The flowers and handsome appearance make it a good companion to other fall-blooming plants. Zones 6 to 9.

Chrysanthemum
(kris-*anth*-ah-mum)
Compositae—daisy family

Among the oldest of cultivated plants, chrysanthemums are usually thought of in terms of those plants that fill the garden with fall blooms as well as the florist's flowers and plants. Hundreds of different forms have been developed, but there are dozens of other species and selections for the garden. With their daisy-like flowers, albeit in many forms and all colors but blue, and ease of growth, the entire clan constitutes an important addition to the sunny garden. In recent years, taxonomists have scattered this group to the winds; their new names are given below.

GROWING GUIDE Full sun. Humus-rich, moist but well-drained soil, with a few exceptions as noted below. The ubiquitous garden chrysanthemum transplants easily, even when in full bloom. Plants set out in the spring or grown from year to year in the garden should have the growing tips of the stems pinched out several times until mid-July. The types referred to as cushions don't need this pinching. Taller or weaker-stemmed types must be staked. Deadhead regularly. A summer mulch is beneficial to keep the soil moist, and a winter mulch is needed for protection.

PROPAGATION Division, stem cuttings. Painted and Shasta daisies and feverfew from seed.

USES Depending on the form and size, chrysanthemums can be used singly, in groups, massed in beds and borders or used as an edging. Cut flowers.

SPECIES, VARIETIES, CULTIVARS AND HYBRIDS

Dendranthema grandiflora (den-*dran*-thuh-muh gran-*duh*-flor-uh). Chrysanthemum. China, Japan. Thousands of selections developed over the centuries, ranging in size from 1 to 4 feet tall and up to 3 feet wide. Shape varies from short, fat mounds to tall and thin. The 1- to 6-inch flowers may be single or double, with special shapes like button, spoon, quill or spider. Special care includes extra feeding, pinching back the growing tips and staking the taller varieties. Hardiness varies greatly among selections, but the overall range is Zones 5 to 9.

Chrysanthemum (Dendranthema) zawadski 'Clara Curtis' (x *rubella*).

Dendranthema rubella (rue-*bell*-uh). Red chrysanthemum. Probably a hybrid of Asian origins. Grows 2 to 3 feet tall and as wide. Compact, branching, free-flowering plant with 2- to 3-inch, muted red or deep-pink, single, fragrant flowers held singly or in small clusters. Flowering starts in late summer. Most commonly found in the

Chrysanthemum (Leucanthemum).

pink-flowered form 'Clara Curtis'. Zones 5 to 9.

Leucanthemum pacificum (lew-kan-thuh-mum pah-*sif*-uh-cum). Grows 2 feet tall and 18 inches wide. Grown mainly for its unusual foliage, which is small and rounded with silvery edges. Clusters of tiny, yellow, button-like flowers in mid- to late fall. Zones 6 to 9.

Chrysanthemum x *superbum* 'Shasta Snow'.

Leucanthemum x superbum (sue-*pur*-bum). Shasta daisy. Of hybrid origin, originally produced by Luther Burbank. Grows 18 to 30 inches tall and as wide. Produces a great quantity of stems with white, 2- to 3-inch daisies throughout summer. Is not long lived. Zones 5 to 8.

Tanacetum coccineum (tan-ah-*see*-tum cok-*sin*-ee-um). May also be listed as *Pyrethrum roseum*. Pyrethrum, painted daisy. Western Asia. Grows 1 to 3 feet tall and 1 to 2 feet wide. Ferny, dark green leaves. Single or double, 3-inch, daisy-like pink, red or white flowers with yellow centers on tall,

Chrysanthemum (Tanacetum) coccineum.

single stems from early to midsummer. Best planted in groups of three. Most suited for areas with cooler summers, but with light shade, can do well in hotter areas. Use dwarf cultivars to eliminate the need for staking. This plant is the source for the insecticide pyrethrum. Zones 3 to 7.

Tanacetum parthenium (par-*thin*-ee-um). May also be listed as *Matricaria parthenium*. Feverfew. Europe. Grows to 2 to 3 feet tall and 1 to 3 feet

Tanacetum parthenium.

wide. Strongly aromatic, deeply divided leaves. Masses of long-blooming, 1-inch, daisy-like flowers are white or yellow, single or double, and superb for cutting. Cut plants back by half when 12 inches tall to lessen sprawling. Single-flowered forms readily self-sow. A number of selections are available. Zones 5 to 8.

Chrysogonum
(kris-*sog*-oh-num)
Goldenstar, green-gold
Compositae—daisy family

A local plant makes good, at least in the eastern United States, where this yellow-flowered edging plant or ground-cover sells out quickly for use in shaded gardens and woodland plantings.

GROWING GUIDE Partial to full shade. Humus-rich, moist but well-drained soil.

PROPAGATION Division, seed.

USES Edging or groundcover for shady beds and borders, woodland gardens, near pools or streams. Does not become invasive. A winter mulch is necessary in Zone 5.

Chrysogonum virginianum.

SPECIES, VARIETIES, CULTIVARS AND HYBRIDS

C. virginianum (vir-jin-ee-*ay*-num). Goldenstar, green-gold. Eastern United States. Grows to 8 inches tall and 12 inches wide. Dark green, rounded triangular, 1- to 2-inch long leaves with serrated edges. Bright yellow, 1-inch flowers mainly in the spring, but some flowering off and on all season. A number of selections have been made, with somewhat indistinguishable differences. Zones 5 to 9.

Chrysopsis
(kris-*op*-sis)
Golden aster, goldaster
Compositae—daisy family

For those in hot climates looking for an adaptable, easily grown, late-blooming plant, the golden aster fills the bill to a "T". The only problem is in following the name trail left by taxonomists; if chrysopsis doesn't turn up anything, try *Heterotheca*.

GROWING GUIDE Full sun. Any well-drained soil. When the first frost blackens plants, immediately cut back almost to the ground.

Chrysopsis villosa.

PROPAGATION Division, seed.

USES Back of beds or borders, meadow gardens.

SPECIES, VARIETIES, CULTIVARS AND HYBRIDS

C. villosa (vil-*loh*-suh). Hairy golden aster. North America. Grows 3 to 6 feet tall and 2 to 4 feet wide. A coarse plant with woody, branched stems and lance-shaped leaves. Multi-branched clusters of 1-inch, yellow, daisy-like flowers from late summer until frost. The cultivar 'Golden Sunshine' grows 3 to 4 feet tall, with 2-inch flowers. Zones 4 to 9.

Other species to consider include *C. mariana*, growing 1 to 3 feet tall and *C. bakeri*, growing 12 inches tall.

Cimicifuga
(sim-*mi*-suh-*few*-guh)
Bugbane
Ranunculaceae—buttercup family

Graceful and dramatic, bugbanes offer low-maintenance for a wide range of garden sites. Although the long-lived plants are large, the foliage is fine-textured. White flowers resembling bottle brushes top the plants in summer and autumn. These may be used as fresh or dried flowers, and the seed spikes are good for dried arrangements. Both the genus and common names refer to the scented leaves of some species, said to repel insects.

GROWING GUIDE Best in light shade, although more or less light is tolerated. Deep, humus-rich, moist but well-drained soil. May need staking when in bloom. Plants take several years to become established.

PROPAGATION Division.

USES Beds and borders or woodland gardens. Effective combined with blue-leaved hostas and rodgersias and other bold-textured plants or when planted in masses.

Cimicifuga racemosa.

SPECIES, VARIETIES, CULTIVARS AND HYBRIDS

C. racemosa (ray-sem-*oh*-suh). Black cohosh. North America. Grows 6 feet tall and 3 feet wide. Clump-forming plant with dark green, deeply cut leaves. Thin spikes of tiny ivory-white flowers may reach 2 feet in length. Depending on the climate, flowering may start in mid- to late summer, lasting 4 weeks. Must have even, constant moisture. Zones 3 to 8.

C. simplex (*sim*-plex). Kamchatka bugbane. Siberia, Japan. Grows 3 to 4 feet tall and 2 to 3 feet wide. Clump-forming plant with dark green, deeply cut leaves and purplish stems. Thin, arching spires of tiny, slightly fragrant white flowers in late summer and fall. The cultivars 'White Pearl' and 'Elstead Variety' are definite improvements over the species. Zones 3 to 8.

Clematis
(*klem*-ah-tis)
Clematis
Ranunculaceae—buttercup family

The vining clematis may be more familiar, but there are also short, bushy varieties that fit right in among the perennials. Easy to grow and long-lived, most types also have plumed seeds that are showy, prolonging the garden display. Both the flowers and seed heads may be used in arrangements.

GROWING GUIDE Full sun to partial shade. Humus-rich, moist but well-drained soil. Additional lime may be necessary. Cool soil is a must, so mulch in summer. Roots are easily damaged, so cultivate around them carefully. Place them next to tall plants that can provide some support or surround by twigs. Trim perennial clematis back to 6 inches in late fall or early spring.

PROPAGATION Division, terminal stem cuttings.

USES The slightly sprawling nature of

Clematis heracleifola var. *davidiana*.

perennial clematis makes them useful as a textural contrast in beds and borders.

SPECIES, VARIETIES, CULTIVARS AND HYBRIDS

C. heracleifolia (he-ra-klee-i-*foh*-lee-uh). Tube clematis. China. Grows 2 to 3 feet tall and as wide. Dark green, three-parted, slightly hairy leaves. Clusters of 6 to 12, tubular, blue, 1-inch flowers in late summer and fall are followed by fluffy seedheads. Several selections are available. Zones 3 to 8.

C. integrifolia (in-teg-ri-*foh*-lee-uh). Solitary clematis. Southern Europe. Grows 2 to 4 feet tall and as wide. Prominently veined, pointed leaves to 4 inches long.

Flowers bloom in late summer, with each borne singly at the end of a stem, hence the common name. They are 1- to 2-inch, nodding, bell-shaped blooms of lavender to violet-blue. Plumy seed heads follow. The most popular cultivar is 'Hendersonii', with larger, dark blue flowers; its proper name is *C.* x *eriostemon.* Zones 3 to 8.

C. recta (*rek*-tuh). Ground clematis. Southern Europe. Grows 3 to 4 feet tall

and as wide. Slender, twining stems with finely divided leaves. Clouds of 1-inch, fragrant, star-shaped white flowers cover the plants in summer, followed by silken fruits. 'Flore-pleno' is a double-flowered variety, and 'Purpurea' has purple foliage. Zones 3 to 8.

Convallaria
(kon-val-*lah*-ree-uh)
Lily-of-the-valley
Liliaceae—lily family

Convallaria majalis.

What would spring be without the heavenly scent or a simple bouquet of the small, perfectly formed white bells of lily-of-the-valley? This is one of the easiest plants to grow, providing a quickly spreading groundcover in shade. The name comes from the Latin *convallis*, for valley.

GROWING GUIDE Any type of shade. Humus-rich, moist but well-drained soil. Growth is considered rampant only by those with no taste or character.

PROPAGATION Division.

USES Groundcover. Cut flowers. Fragrant garden.

SPECIES, VARIETIES, CULTIVARS AND HYBRIDS

C. majalis (ma-*jah*-lis). Lily-of-the-valley. Europe, Asia, North America. Grows 12 inches tall and as wide. Single, dark green, broad, pointed leaves arise from creeping rhizomes. Arching flower stems carry drooping white bells along one side. Intensely fragrant. Among the selections are those that are slightly taller, double- or pink flowered or with palely striped leaves. Zones 2 to 7.

Coreopsis
(koh-ree-*op*-sis)
Coreopsis, tickseed
Compositae—daisy family

The ease of growth and production of sunshine-yellow, daisy-like flowers for much of the summer has endeared the perennial coreopsis to gardeners. The name is from the Greek *koris*, for bug and *opsis*, in that the seeds somewhat resemble a bug or tick. The flowers are longlasting when cut.

GROWING GUIDE Full sun. Average to humus-rich soil that must be well-drained. Deadhead or cut plants back by one-third after the first flush of bloom.

PROPAGATION Division, seed.

USES Beds and borders, either as specimens or massed. Cut flowers.

SPECIES, VARIETIES, CULTIVARS AND HYBRIDS

C. verticillata (ver-ti-sil-*lah*-tuh). Threadleaf coreopsis. North America. Grows 1 to 3 feet tall and as wide. Very finely divided, almost threadlike, 2- to 3-inch leaves on clump-forming, spreading plants. In various shades of yellow, 2-inch flowers are produced in

Coreopsis verticillata 'Moonbeam'.

Coreopsis verticillata.

masses for a long time during the summer. If the plants are deadheaded or sheared back, a second flush of bloom occurs in the fall. The best selections include 'Golden Showers', growing 18 to 24 inches tall with bright yellow flowers; 'Moonbeam', growing 18 to 24 inches tall with yellow flowers in a soft, muted shade (it even does well in the South); and 'Zagreb', growing 12 to 18 inches tall with deep yellow flowers. Zones 3 to 9.

Coreopsis verticillata 'Zagreb'.

Coreopsis lanceolata.

Coreopsis lanceolata.

Other coreopsis to consider include *C. auriculata*, mouse-eared coreopsis (Zones 4 to 9); *C. grandiflora*, tickseed, (Zones 5 to 9); *C. lanceolata*, lance-leaved coreopsis (Zones 3 to 8); and *R. rosea*, pink tickseed (Zones 4 to 9).

Corydalis
(kor-*ri*-dah-lis)
Fumaria
Fumariaceae—fumitory family

Low-growing plants with finely divided leaves, fumarias add a graceful note to lightly shaded areas of the garden. The flowers resemble those of the smaller forms of bleeding heart, but are in shades of yellow, white or blue. It is the blue form that has particularly caught the attention of gardeners, especially since the availability of 'Blue Panda'. The generic name is derived from the Greek word meaning lark, in reference to the spurs on both the flowers and European larks.

GROWING GUIDE Partial to light shade. Humus-rich, moist but well-drained soil with a neutral to alkaline pH.

PROPAGATION Division, seed. Readily self-sows; old seed is difficult to germinate.

USES Shaded beds and borders, as groundcovers under shrubs or trees, in rock walls, among stepping stones. Cut flowers.

SPECIES, VARIETIES, CULTIVARS AND HYBRIDS
  C. flexuosa (flex-*yew*-oh-suh). Blue

Corydalis flexuosa 'Blue Panda'.

corydalis. China. Grows 15 inches tall and as wide. Forms clumps with finely divided leaves. Electric-blue, ¾-inch flowers produced off and on throughout the growing season. Several named varieties, with different shades of blue flowers as well as one with purple blotches on the leaves. Zones 5 to 7.

Coydalis lutea.

  C. lutea (*lew*-tee-uh). Yellow corydalis. Europe, Britain. Grows 1 foot tall and as wide. Clumps of lacy, cool-green leaves. Bright yellow, ¾-inch flowers produced throughout the growing season. *Ochroleuca* is similar but with white flowers. Zones 5 to 7.

Crambe
(*kram*-bee)
Colewort
Cruciferae—mustard family

As might be suspected from a plant related to cabbage, the leaves of crambe are bold. What may be

Crambe cordifolia.

unexpected are the enormous clouds of fragrant, starry white flowers in early summer. Some find the fragrance sweet, while others call it malodorous. One member, *C. maritima*, or sea kale, is edible and, what a surprise, does well in seaside locations.

GROWING GUIDE Full sun. Poor to average, very well-drained soil. Deadhead. Susceptible to the same pests as any cabbage-family member, especially caterpillars, so treatment with Bt may be necessary.

PROPAGATION Seed, root cuttings. Self-sows.

USES Back of beds or borders, meadow gardens.

SPECIES, VARIETIES, CULTIVARS AND HYBRIDS

  C. cordifolia (kor-di-*foh*-lee-uh). Colewort. Caucasus. Grows to 6 feet tall and 4 feet wide. Forms mounds of hairy, crinkled, coarsely toothed, dark green leaves growing up to 2 feet across. Airy, open branched stalks of ¼-inch white flowers in early summer, giving an appearance like a behemoth baby's breath. Zones 6 to 8.

Crocosmia
(krow-*kos*-mee-uh)
Crocosmia, montbretia
Liliaceae—lily family

Except in warm and damp climates where croscosmia literally grows like a weed, it is little known. Yet it has proven to be a widely adapted plant and not invasive in colder areas. The benefits are vertical iris-like foliage and many arching stems of bright, funnel-shaped, scarlet, orange or yellow flowers for a long period in late summer and fall. These are excellent as cut flowers.

Crocosmia 'Lucifer'.

GROWING GUIDE Full sun to partial shade. Moist but well-drained soil.

PROPAGATION Division, necessary every 2 or 3 years or plants may become overcrowded and stop producing flowers.

USES As a vertical element in beds and borders. Where the color can be worked in, the form offers a pleasing diversion to all the daisy-like flowers of late summer and autumn. Combines well with yellow-flowering plants.

SPECIES, VARIETIES, CULTIVARS AND HYBRIDS

  C. x *crocosmiiflora* (krow-kos-mee-eh-*floh*-ruh). Montbretia. Hybrid origin. Original crosses made by Lemoine in France in the 1880s. Grows 2 to 3 feet tall and to 12 inches wide. Bright green, grassy leaves and arching, branching stems of funnel-shaped flowers in shades of red, orange, orange-red, apricot and yellow in late summer and early fall. Zones 6 to 9.

  C. x *curtonus* (kur-*tone*-us). Crocosmia. Hybrid origin. From crosses made of the two genera by Alan Bloom. Grows 2 to 3 feet tall and 1 foot wide. Bright green, grassy leaves and arching, branching stems of funnel-shaped flowers in shades of scarlet, orange-red and yellow. The most widely available one is 'Lucifer', with scarlet-red flowers. Zones 6 to 9.

Cynara
(suh-nar-uh)
Cardoon
Compositae—daisy family

For those who want to have their perennials and eat them, too, cardoon is the plant of choice. This is a "statement" plant, with a decided boldness and elegance with its large mounds of long, gray-green, thistle-like leaves.

GROWING GUIDE Full sun. Well-drained soil a must. Benefits from winter protection.

PROPAGATION Division, seed, root cuttings.

USES As an architectural focal point in beds or borders.

Cynara cardunculus.

SPECIES, VARIETIES, CULTIVARS AND HYBRIDS

  C. cardunculus (kar-dun-kew-lus). Cardoon. Europe. Grows to

Cynara cardunculus.

6 feet tall and 3 feet wide. Mounds of foliage are created from the arching, 3- to 4-foot long, silvery-grey, pointed and divided leaves. In late summer, stout grey stems bear large purple flowers resembling thistles. Zones 6 to 8.

---

d

Delphinium
(del-*fin*-ee-um)
Delphinium, larkspur
Ranunculaceae—buttercup family

Delphinium.

Delphiniums are reminiscent of the rhyme about the little girl who "when she was good, she was very, very good, but when she was bad, she was horrid." So it is with these breathtaking flowers when they are in the right climate and grown with the best care. But, otherwise, why bother? Well, because of the striking spires of blossoms in shades from sky-blue to lavenders, purples, pinks and white. Okay, so where's the compromise for those of us who don't live in England, the Pacific Northwest, or the Maine coast? Basically, either treat them as annuals or grow the ones that give you the best bet for at least a modicum of success.

GROWING GUIDE Full sun to partial shade in the hottest climates. Humus-rich, moist but well-drained, slightly alkaline soil. Mulching in the summer and fertilizing in early spring and again in early summer is almost compulsory, as is staking and protection from the wind. Remove faded flowers to encourage reblooming. Cut all stems back to the ground in the fall. Susceptible to slugs and an assortment of fungal diseases. Even in the best of situations, they are usually replaced every 2 to 3 years.

PROPAGATION
D. x belladonna—division, seed;
D. elatum—seed, stem cuttings.

USES Middle to back of beds and borders. Cut flowers.

SPECIES, VARIETIES, CULTIVARS AND HYBRIDS
   D. x belladonna (bell-uh-*don*-uh). Belladonna delphinium. Hybrid origin, first introduced in 1900. Grows 3 to 4 feet tall and 2 feet wide. Large, many-branched plants that are relatively heat tolerant and that produce blooms for much of the summer in various shades of blue or white. Zones 3 to 7.
   D. elatum (ee-*lay*-tum) **hybrids**. Hybrid delphinium. Western Europe to East Asia. This is the most frequent parent of the plethora of hybrid delphiniums available, including 'Pacific Hybrids', 'Mid-Century Hybrids', 'Giant Imperial Series',

Delphinium elatum.

'Connecticut Yankee Series' and others. Height ranges from 30 inches to 6 feet and to 3 feet wide. The full range of flower colors and forms, including singles, doubles and those with "bees." Zones 3 to 7.

Dianthus
(dye-*an*-thus)
Pinks
Caryophyllaceae—pink family

Beloved through the centuries for their delicious, spicy fragrance, long life as cut flowers and easy cultivation, dianthus remain integral to gardens today. From the 300 or so species, hundreds more selections have been hybridized, with much confusion over proper classification, but the essence of the best ones for the garden remains the same. Most of them form mounds or mats of grassy, gray-green to dark green leaves. Flowers may vary from only a half-inch to 2 inches across, be single, semi-double or double, with fringed or toothed petals either in a solid color or marked with a contrasting color, and in shades of pink, red or white. Although dianthus may be short-lived, propagation is easy, adaptability is wide and growth rapid but not rapacious. From the Greek words *dios*, divine, and *anthos*, flower, the name says it all.

GROWING GUIDE Full sun to partial shade. Best growth is in a humus-rich, sandy, slightly alkaline soil, but they do admirably well in any well-drained soil. The important aspect to avoid is poor drainage in winter. Winter protection may be necessary in colder regions. Deadhead regularly to prolong blooming or prevent self-sowing. Slugs, aphids, spider mites and fungal diseases may occasionally be a problem.

Dianthus x allwoodi 'Clove Pink'.

PROPAGATION Readily from division, but also stem cuttings and seed.

USES Front of beds and borders, edging, cascading over walls. Cut flowers.

SPECIES, VARIETIES, CULTIVARS AND HYBRIDS

D. x *allwoodii* (all-*wood*-ee-eye). Allwood pinks. Hybrid origin. Original crosses made by Montague Allwood in the 1920s. Size is highly variable, depending on the selection, with a range of 6 to 18 inches tall and up to 18 inches wide. Compact mats of gray-green, grassy leaves. Usually 2 flowers per stem, mostly doubles, and fragrant, for up to 8 weeks. Many selections. Zones 4 to 8.

D. barbatus (bar-*bah*-tus). Sweet William. Europe, Asia. Grows to 18 inches tall and 1 foot wide. Dark green leaves and leafy stems bearing tight

Dianthus barbatus.

3-inch clusters of ½-inch flowers with no scent. Officially a biennial, but it readily self-sows, keeping it coming back year after year; in warmer climates, it acts as a true perennial if faded flowers are removed. Many selections, with 'Newport Pink' among the favorites. Zones 3 to 9.

D. deltoides (del-*toy*-deez). Maiden pinks. Europe, temperate Asia. Grows 6

Dianthus deltoides.

to 12 inches tall. Forms spreading mats of grassy, bright, semi-evergreen leaves. Most selections have fragrant, single flowers of white or red, usually 2 to a stalk. Plants bloom for many weeks in early summer, with some repeat bloom if faded flowers are removed. Many selections, with 'Zing Rose' most widely available. Zones 3 to 9.

Dianthus gratianopolitanus 'Bath's Pink'.

D. gratianopolitanus (grah-tee-ah-na-pah-leh-*tah*-nus). Cheddar pinks. West and Central Europe. Grows to 12 inches tall and as wide. Gray-green, grassy leaves form compact mounds. The fragrant, 1-inch flowers are borne singly or 2 to a stem, mainly in shades of pink, rose and red. Can bloom from spring to late summer if faded flowers are removed. Many selections, with 'Bath's Pink' one of the oldest and best. Zones 3 to 9.

D. plumarius (plew-*mah*-ree-us). Cottage pinks, grass pinks. Eastern Central Europe. Grows 18 inches tall and 12 inches wide. The parent of many of today's hybrids. Grassy, gray-green leaves forming mounds. Selections have fragrant flowers up to 1½-inches wide with just about

Dianthus plumarius.

every flower form and color possible with the genus. Deadhead to prolong bloom. Many selections. Zones 3 to 9.

Dicentra
(dye-*sen*-truh)
Bleeding heart
Fumariaceae—fumitory family

How bereft shaded gardens would be without both the large and small bleeding hearts, with their unique flowers and fine-textured, blue-green foliage. These popular, easy-to-grow plants deserve all the credit they receive. For those who want to create a native woodland garden, be sure to include the related squirrel corn (*D. canadensis*), Dutchman's breeches (*D. cucullaria*) and golden eardrops (*D. chrysantha*), hardy in Zones 4 to 8.

GROWING GUIDE Partial to full shade. Humus-rich, moist but well-drained soil. Provide a summer mulch to keep the soil cool and moist. Deadhead regularly to prolong blooming of *D. exima* and *D. formosa* and their cultivars.

PROPAGATION Divison, seed. Some self-sowing but not invasive.

USES Shaded beds and borders; cottage, rock and wildflower gardens.

Dicentra eximia 'Luxuiant'.

SPECIES, VARIETIES, CULTIVARS AND HYBRIDS

D. eximia (ex-*im*-ee-uh). Fringed bleeding heart. Eastern United States. Grows to 18 inches tall and as wide. Forms neat mounds of gray-green, feathery foliage. Sprays of 1-inch, rose-pink, heart-shaped flowers borne on slender, branched stalks. Most of the blooming is in late spring and early summer, but there is some all summer long. *D. formosa*, native to the Pacific Northwest, is very similar. Cultivars and hybrids of these two species have created several improved selections. These include 'Adrian Bloom', 'Bountiful', 'Luxuriant and 'Zestful', all with flowers in various shades of red or pink. There are also white-flowering forms. Zones 3 to 9.

Dicentra spectabilis 'Alba' *and Dicentra spectabilis (pink).*

D. spectabilis (spek-*tab*-i-lis). Common bleeding heart. Siberia, Japan. Grows 2 feet tall and 18 inches wide. Forms irregular mounds of divided leaves. Bears branching arches of pink, heart-shaped, 1½-inch flowers in late spring. A white-flowered form is available. Plants go dormant by midsummer, so they must be surrounded by other plants. Zones 2 to 9.

Dictamnus
(dik-*tam*-nus)
Gas plant
Rutaceae—rue family

Long-lived and low-maintenance, gas plant has a shrubby form with glossy, dark green leaves that are attractive all summer. The highlight of the early summer is the numerous spikes of 1- to 2-inch white flowers. The star-shaped seed pods are useful in dried arrangements. Both flowers and foliage produce a volatile oil with the scent of lemons. On a hot summer night, a lighted match at the base of the flower spike will send a flame shooting up, gratefully without harming the flowers. Some people have an allergic reaction to this oil.

GROWING GUIDE Full sun or partial shade. Humus-rich, moist but well-drained soil. Will tolerate some drought once well established. Plants are slow to sprout in the spring, so mark the site.

PROPAGATION Seed, root cuttings. Deep roots make it difficult to divide.

USES Sunny beds and borders.

SPECIES, VARIETIES, CULTIVARS AND HYBRIDS

D. albus (*al*-bus). Gas plant. Europe, Asia. Grows 3 feet tall and 2 feet wide. Glossy, dark green, aromatic

Dictamnus albus.

leaves divided into leaflets up to 3 inches long. Spikes of fragrant, white flowers in early summer, each having 5 petals and 10 showy stamens.

'Purpureus' and 'Rubra' have mauve-purple flowers with darker veins. Zones 3 to 8.

Digitalis
(dij-i-*tah*-lis)
Foxglove
Scrophulariaceae—figwort family

Digitalis.

With tall spires of velvety, dotted bells rising from low clumps of large, rough, oval leaves, foxgloves provide drama to the early summer garden. A necessity for cottage gardens, they are equally lovely in formal beds and borders. Although most are either biennials or short-lived perennials, they can be easily started from seed, allowed to self-sow or divide. They are also long-lasting as cut flowers. Various tales go with the common name, but each flower resembles a glove finger and "fox" probably started out as "folks," or the fairies. The drug digitalis is obtained from one species.

Digitalis.

GROWING GUIDE Partial to light shade. Humus-rich, moist but well-drained soil. Remove the central flower spike when faded to encourage side shoots to grow and bloom.

PROPAGATION Division, seed.

USES Shady beds and borders, open woodlands, cottage gardens. Cut flowers.

SPECIES, VARIETIES, CULTIVARS AND HYBRIDS

D. ferruginea (feh-roo-*jin*-ee-ah). Rusty foxglove. Europe, Asia. Grows 5 feet tall and 2 feet wide. Two-foot spikes of rusty-red and white flowers in midsummer. Zones 4 to 8.

D. grandiflora (gran-duh-*flor*-ah). Also listed as *D. ambigua*. Yellow foxglove. Europe. Grows 3 feet tall and 18 inches wide. From late spring to early summer, produces yellow flowers with brown-speckled throats. Other yellow foxgloves include *D. lanata*, growing 2 feet tall with creamy yellow flowers in mid- to late summer, and *D. lutea*, growing 3 feet tall with pale yellow flowers in early summer. Zones 3 to 8.

D. x mertonensis (mer-toe-*nen*-sis).

Strawberry foxglove. Hybrid origin. Original hybrid raised in Merton, England, in 1925. Grows 4 feet tall and 2 feet wide. Foliage remains particularly fresh. Large, bright pink flowers in early summer. Divide every year or two to maintain vigor. Zones 5 to 8.

Digitalis grandiflora.

D. purpurea (pur-pur-*ee*-ah). Common foxglove. Europe. Grows 3 to 5 feet tall and 2 to 3 feet wide. A true biennial; leave flower stalks on long enough to produce seed for a new crop, then pull out the original plant. Many selections available, with 'Foxy' growing only 30 inches tall and producing many blooming side shoots in the first year from seed. Zones 4 to 9.

Doronicum
(doh-*ron*-i-kum)
Leopard's bane
Compositae—daisy family

Of the 35 or so species, only one is widely used in gardens. It is prized for the early spring, yellow, daisy-like flowers that are good for cutting, even though they close up at night. Plants go dormant during the summer, but return with the cooler days of autumn. The common name is said to come from the use of the juice of a particular species on the tips of arrows when hunting leopards. Perhaps that explains the paucity of leopard in the garden.

GROWING GUIDE Full sun in cooler climates to partial shade in hotter ones. Humus-rich, moist but well-drained soil. Deadhead faded flower to prolong blooming. Remove faded leaves when plants go dormant in the summer.

PROPAGATION Division, seed.

Doronicum orientale.

USES Spring border, rock garden, cut flowers. Interplant with spring bulbs.

SPECIES, VARIETIES, CULTIVARS AND HYBRIDS

D. orientale (oh-ree-en-*tay*-lee) May also be listed as *D. columnae, D. cordatum* or *D. caucasicum*. Leopard's bane. Europe. Asia. Grows 18 inches tall and 2 feet wide. Forms neat mounds with heart-shaped, deeply toothed leaves. Single or double daisy-like, 2- to 4-inch yellow flowers in early spring. Several selections available. Zones 4 to 8.

e

Echinacea
(ek-eh-nay-see-uh)
Purple coneflower
Compositae—daisy family

Purple coneflower is another case of local plant makes good. A wildflower of the central United States, it is one of the finest plants for sunny gardens. Tough, long-lived plants with a wide range of adaptability, they produce pink, daisy-like flowers for a long period during summer. The name is derived from the Greek word *echinos*, or hedgehog, because the base of the plant is rather prickly. Extracts from the thick, black roots are used for their efficacious properties, while the flowers are excellent for cutting and attracting butterflies.

GROWING GUIDE Does best in full sun but tolerates partial shade. Any humus-rich, well-drained soil. Staking is sometimes needed with the taller-growing forms when grown in very rich soil. Deadhead regularly to prolong blooming.

PROPAGATION Division, seed.

USES Middle to back of beds and borders. As specimens or massed. Butterfly gardens. Cut and dried flowers.

Echinacea purpurea.

Echinacea purpurea 'White Swan'.

E. purpurea (pur-pur-ree-uh). Purple coneflower. Central United States. Grows 2 to 4 feet tall and 2 feet wide. Coarse, hairy stems and leaves. Tall, leafless stalks bear 4- to 6-inch flowers in summer. A number of selections are available, mainly differing either in size of plant or flower, with colors ranging from light to dark pink or white. There are also several other similar species native to other parts of the United States. Zone 3 to 8.

Echinops
(*ek*-eh-nops)
Globe thistle
Compositae—daisy family

Globe thistles are easily grown, eye-catching plants, both for their gray-green, spiny-looking foliage and the globes of tiny lavender to blue flowers produced for a long period during the summer. Bees buzz around them during the day, while moths visit at night and flower arrangers prize them anytime, either fresh or dried. Because of their bristly appearance, the generic name is derived from the Greek word *echinos*, for hedgehog. There is much confusion not only as to the correct naming, but also in that two plants with the same name can appear very different. The search for a good one is worth it.

GROWING GUIDE Full sun. Almost any well-drained soil. Because of their deep root, heat and drought are tolerated once the plant is established. Staking may be required if the soil is rich.

PROPAGATION Division, root cuttings, seed.

USES Middle to back of beds and borders. Specimen among shrubs. Meadow gardens. Cut or dried flowers.

SPECIES, VARIETIES, CULTIVARS AND HYBRIDS

Echinops ritro.

E. ritro (*rit*-roh). Also listed as *E. bannatus.* Globe thistle. Europe, Western Asia. Grows to 4 feet tall and 3 feet wide. The deeply serrated gray-green leaves grow to 8 inches long and are downy-gray on the underside. The 1- to 2-inch diameter globes of tiny blue flowers form on branching stems during summer. The most popular cultivars are 'Taplow Blue' and 'Veitch's Blue'. Zones 3 to 8.

Epimedium
(ep-eh-*mee*-dee-um)
Barrenwort
Berberidaceae—barberry family

When only a few of these plants are grown, barrenworts can be easily overlooked. Plant them in masses as a groundcover and they come into their own. Delicate-looking yet sturdy, the low-growing, deciduous or evergreen, heart-shaped leaves provide a foil for the small but unusually shaped, columbine-like flowers borne in spring. Depending on the species and cultivar, these can range from white or

cream to yellow, pink, red or violet. Leaves often have a pinkish cast in the spring, and may turn yellow, red or bronze in the fall. The common name is from the early herbal use as a contraceptive.

GROWING GUIDE Partial to full shade. Can be grown in full sun in cooler climates with plenty of moisture. Humus-rich, moist but well-drained soil. Slow to establish and spread. To better appreciate the flowers, some gardeners clip the leaves low to the ground very early in spring.

PROPAGATION Division.

USES Groundcover.

SPECIES, VARIETIES, CULTIVARS AND HYBRIDS

E. alpinum 'Rubrum' (al-*pine*-um *rue*-brum). Alpine barrenwort. Europe. Grows to 9 inches tall and 12 inches wide. Loose clusters of 12 to 20 flowers of red and yellow. Vigorous and spreads rapidly. Zones 3 to 8.

E. grandiflorum (gran-di-*flor*-rum). Longspur barrenwort, Bishop's hat. Japan. Grows to 15 inches tall and as wide. Among the largest of the species, with leaves to 3 inches long. Long-spurred flowers are cream and reddish-purple, with about a dozen 1-inch flowers in a cluster. Cultivars include 'Rose Queen', 'White Queen' and 'Violaceum'. Zones 5 to 8.

E. pinnatum (pin-*nay*-tum). Persian epimedium. Caucasus. Grows to 12 inches tall and as wide. Foliage is red-bronze in spring and fall. Bright

Epimedium x *versicolor* 'sulphereum'.

yellow flowers in loose clusters of 12 to 30 blooms. *E. p.* var. *colchicum* has larger yellow flowers. Crosses between it and *E. grandiflorum* produce *E.* x *versicolor*, with either solid yellow flowers or flowers of both rose and yellow. It is one of the toughest epimediums. Zones 5 to 8.

Epimedium rubrum.

E. x **rubrum** (*rue*-brum). Red barrenwort. Hybrid origin. Grows to 12 inches tall and as wide. Vigorous offspring of *E. alpinum* and *E. grandiflorum.* Produces clusters of 15 to 20 1-inch, bicolored flowers of red and yellow. Leaves are tinged with red in spring and fall. Zones 4 to 8.

Epimedium x *youngianum* 'Niveum'.

E. x **youngianum** (yung-ee-*ah*-num). Young's barrenwort. Hybrid origin. The result of a series of crosses. Grows 8 inches tall and as wide. Compact plants with reddish leaves in spring, turning to green in summer. Clusters of 3 to 8¾-inch, pink or white flowers on each stem. Zones 5 to 8.

Erigeron
(ee-*rij*-er-on)
Fleabane
Compositae—daisy family

Resembling small-growing asters with their 2-inch daisy-like, yellow-centered flowers of blue, pink or white, fleabanes are easily grown and bloom well even in hotter climates. They are a source of cut flowers for many weeks in summer. Perhaps because most of the species are roadside natives in North America, they are not readily appreciated, but the many cultivars offer choice, low-maintenance plants. The early British herbalist Culpepper wrote that the name fleabane refers to the appearance of the seeds.

GROWING GUIDE Full sun in cooler climates to partial shade in hotter ones. Almost any well-drained soil, preferably enriched with humus.

PROPAGATION Division.

Erigeron 'Azure Fairy'.

USES Front to middle of beds and borders. Lower-growing types as edging. Cut flowers.

SPECIES, VARIETIES, CULTIVARS AND HYBRIDS

E. speciosus (spee-see-*oh*-sus). Fleabane, Oregon fleabane. Western United States. Grows 2 feet tall and as wide. Well-branched, upright, clump-forming plants. Spoon-shaped, 3- to 6-inch leaves with hairy edges. Numerous clusters of 1- to 2-inch flowers. A number of cultivars are available, varying in size from 12 to 30 inches tall and flowers ranging from shades of pink to lavenders, violets or white. Among these, 'Darkest of All' grows 2 feet tall with deep violet-blue flowers; 'Dimity'

grows 12 inches tall with light pink flowers; and 'Foerster's Leibling' grows 18 inches tall with double pink flowers. Zones 4 to 8.

Eryngium
(er-*rin*-jee-um)
Sea holly
Umbelliferae—carrot family

Eryngium yuccifolium.

For a genus with over 220 members distributed widely around the world, including a number of highly distinctive, attractive perennial members that are undemanding and heat-loving, sea hollies don't make enough garden appearances. Go search them out, for their silvery-blue flowers surrounded by a spiny ruff are highly prized for their appearance in the garden and their use for both fresh and dried arrangements. The long-lived, thistle-like, gray-green foliage and flowers contrast well with fine-textured plants, especially ornamental grasses.

GROWING GUIDE Full sun. Adaptable to a wide range of well-drained soils. Deadhead to prevent self-sowing, unless desired.

PROPAGATION Because of the deep taproot, plants do not divide easily. If absolutely necessary, take root cuttings in spring. Seed sown outdoors as soon as ripe will germinate the following spring.

USES Use as an accent in bed or borders.

SPECIES, VARIETIES, CULTIVARS AND HYBRIDS

There are a great many species and cultivars with garden value. Most are relatively similar in appearance, with a few noted exceptions. There is much disagreement about proper naming by the taxonomists, a problem that is compounded by the discrepancies in which plants are actually being sold. Most grow about 2 to 3 feet tall and 2 feet wide. Among those worth searching out are *E. alpinum* and its cultivars 'Amethyst', 'Opal' and 'Superbum'; *E. x zabelii, E. bourgatti* and cultivars of *E. planum*. All of these are hardy in Zones 5 to 8. For colder areas, *E. amethystinum* is hardy in Zones 2 to 8. For those who like the truly unusual, there is the gray-white biennial *E. giganteum*; growing to 6 feet tall in Zones 4 to 8, it is commonly called 'Miss Wilmott's Ghost' in Britain, where the Victorian gardener, Ellen Wilmott, supposedly scattered seeds in gardens she visited. For a North American native, there is *E. yuccifolium*, or rattlesnake master, that, surprise, looks like a yucca; Zones 3 to 8.

Eupatorium
(yew-pah-*toe*-ree-um)
Boneset, mist flower, Joe Pye weed
Compositae—daisy family

Of the 600 or so species of eupatorium, many of which are native to North America, only a handful are valued as ornamentals. Even among these, they are more prized by the English than in their own country. Although they vary widely in size, all are noted for the billowy clusters of tiny flowers in shades of blue or pink during late summer and fall. The name commemorates Mithridates Eupator, physician and king of Pontus, acknowledging the medicinal qualities of certain members of the genus.

GROWING GUIDE Full sun to partial shade in a wide range of average to moist soils, preferably well-drained. Pinch or cut back *E. coelestinum* several times during to the summer to encourage branching.

PROPAGATION Division.

USES Beds and borders, meadow gardens, butterfly gardens. Cut flowers.

SPECIES, VARIETIES, CULTIVARS AND HYBRIDS

Eupatorium fistulosum.

E. coelestinum (see-less-*tye*-num). Mist flower, hardy ageratum. Eastern North America. Grows 2 feet tall and as wide. Roundly triangular, coarsely toothed leaves to 3 inches long. Most branches bear 1- to 3-inch wide, fluffy-looking clusters of pale blue-violet flowers in late summer or early fall. These resemble the annual ageratum, hence one common name. White and dwarf forms are available. Can rapidly spread. Zones 6 to 10.

E. fistulosum (fis-tew-*loh*-sum). Joe pye weed. Eastern North America. Grows up to 10 feet tall and 3 to 4 feet wide. Thin, narrow, lance-shaped leaves up to 12 inches long on clump-forming plants with stout, sometimes speckled, stems. Large, rounded or flat heads of reddish purple flowers in late summer and early fall. Much confusion exists among several species, confounded by natural hybridization, so plants may also be listed as *E. maculatum* or *E. purpureum*. Several selections are offered, with either white flowers, purple foliage or shorter growth. Zones 3 to 8.

Euphorbia
(yew-*for*-bee-uh)
Spurge
Euphorbiaceae—spurge family

A diverse genus with over 1,800 species, including the Christmas poinsettia and sharp-spined crown-of-thorns, the euphorbias offer fewer than 18 perennials for the temperate garden. Of these, only four are widely adapted. Most spurges are noted for having colorful bracts and minuscule true flowers.

GROWING GUIDE Full sun. Average to poor, well-drained soil.

PROPAGATION Division, using care not to damage the fleshy roots. Seed.

USES Bed, borders or edging, depending on the species.

SPECIES, VARIETIES, CULTIVARS AND HYBRIDS

E. corollata (kor-oh-*lah*-tah). Flowering spurge. North America.

Euphorbia myrsinites.

Grows 3 feet tall and 18 inches wide. Open, loose growth with jade-green leaves on wiry stems. Airy, open clusters of tiny white flowers resembling baby's breath in summer. Good for cut flowers. Zones 3 to 9.

E. griffithii (gri-*fith*-ee-eye). Griffith spurge. Asia. Grows 2 to 3 feet tall and 2 feet wide. Spreading plant with thick stems and spear-shaped leaves with pink midribs. Coppery to orange bracts 2- to 4-inches long in early summer. Best known cultivar is 'Fire Glow', with red-orange bracts and red midveins. Zones 4 to 8.

E. myrsinites (mur-sin-*ee*-teez). Myrtle euphorbia. Europe. Grows 6 inches tall and 12 inches wide. Trailing plant with pointed, blue-green, evergreen leaves spiraling on woody stems. Bright yellow bracts in spring and early summer. Cut back faded flower stems. Zones 5 to 9.

Euphorbia polychroma.

E. polychroma (pol-luh-*kroh*-muh). Also listed as *E. epithymoides*. Cushion spurge. Europe. Grows 18 inches tall and as wide. Forms evenly rounded mounds of bright green, egg-shaped leaves topped with golden yellow to chartreuse bracts in spring. Does best with partial shade. Zones 4 to 8.

Other species to consider in Zones 7 to 9 include *E. amygdaloides*, *E. characias*, *E. palustris*, and *E. wallichii*.

Filipendula

(fil-eh-*pen*-dew-luh)
Meadowsweet, false spiraea
Rosaceae—rose family

With plumy clusters of tiny pink or white flowers and lush, dark green, divided leaves, filipendula are large, yet graceful plants found growing naturally along streams and in marshy areas. When picked before they are fully open, the flowers are good for cutting, with meadowsweet being hauntingly fragrant. The source of the genus name is the Latin words for "hanging threads," in reference to the thin, threadlike tubers hanging on the fibrous roots of *F. vulgaris*.

GROWING GUIDE Partial to light shade, with more sun tolerated in areas with cool summers. Humus-rich, moist but well-drained, neutral to alkaline soil. Plants are susceptible to mildew and leaf scorch if grown in full sun and dry soil.

Filipendula palmata 'Elegans'.

PROPAGATION Division.

USES Middle to back of beds and borders. Among shrubs, beside streams and pools, wet meadows, bog gardens.

SPECIES, VARIETIES, CULTIVARS AND HYBRIDS

F. palmata (pal-*may*-tuh). Siberian meadowsweet. Siberia. Grows 3 to 4 feet tall and 2 to 3 feet wide. Clump-

Filipendula rubra.

forming plants with dark green, 5- to 9-lobed leaves to 8 inches wide and white hairy beneath. Flat, 6-inch plumes of pale pink flowers in midsummer, ultimately fading to white. 'Nana' grows only 10 inches tall. The species *F. purpurea* , the Japanese meadowsweet, is similar, but with deeper pink flowers and red stems. Zones 3 to 8.

Filipendula ulmaria 'Variegata'.

F. rubra (*rue*-bruh). Queen of the prairie. Eastern United States. Grows 6 to 8 feet tall and 4 feet wide. Clump-forming plants with jagged-edged, 5- to 9-lobed leaves to 8 inches wide on sturdy stems. Branching stems bear frothy pink flower clusters to 9 inches wide in summer, with some repeat flowering in fall. Impressive accent plant. 'Venusta', also listed as 'Magifica', has deeper pink flowers and is considered more vigorous. Zones 3 to 8.

Filipendula vulgaris 'Flora Plena'.

F. ulmaria (ul-*mah*-ree-uh). Queen of the meadow. Europe, Asia. Grows 3 to 6 feet tall and 3 feet wide. Spreading plant with dark green, 3- to 5-lobed leaves, hairy white underneath. Flat, 4- to 6-inch wide clusters of sweetly fragrant white flowers in midsummer. Best grown in masses in wet soil. 'Aurea' has golden foliage, with the flowers removed to increase foliage vigor. 'Flore Pleno' has double white flowers. Zones 3 to 9.

F. vulgaris (vul-*gah*-ris). Also listed as *F. hexapetala*. Dropwort. Europe, Asia. Grows 2 to 3 feet tall and 18 inches to 2 feet wide. Delicate-looking, with fern-like leaves to 10 inches long in ground-hugging clumps. Flat heads to 6-inches across of fragrant, creamy white flowers in summer. Tolerates drier soil than other species. Readily self-sows. Use at the front of the border or in a woodland garden. Zones 3 to 8.

Foeniculum
(fee-*nik*-yew-lum)
Fennel
Umbelliferae—carrot family

Wispy threads of bronze-purple weave magic among the perennials when bronze fennel is used in the garden. Usually thought of for the kitchen or herb garden, fennel's delicately textured foliage has advantages beyond its anise-tinged flavor. Use the smoky appearance to soften and blend colors and forms.

GROWING GUIDE Full sun. Any well-drained soil, preferably enriched with humus. Remove the faded flower heads before the seeds ripen if self-sowing is not desired. Swallowtail butterfly larvae are partial to fennel foliage so grow enough for you and them.

Foeniculum vulgare var. *purpureum*.

PROPAGATION Easily from seed.

USES Middle to back of beds and borders.

SPECIES, VARIETIES, CULTIVARS AND HYBRIDS

F. vulgare var. *purpureum* (vul-*gah*-ree pur-pur-*ee*-um). Also listed as *F. vulgare* var. *consanguineum*. Bronze fennel. Grows 3 to 5 feet tall and 2 feet wide. Thick, celery-like, angular stems. Airy sprays of threadlike, bronze-purple leaves. Flat heads of dull yellow flowers in summer. Zones 5 to 9.

Fragaria
(fra-*gah*-ree-uh)
Strawberry
Rosaceae—rose family

Runnerless alpine strawberries have long been used as edging or groundcover plants in ornamental gardens, but with the advent of the Pink Panda strawberry, gardeners have had a new plant with a new look. The Pink Panda is a cross between *Fragaria grandiflora* and *Potentilla palustris* by English plant-breeder Dr. Jack Ellis in 1966; subsequent backcrosses led to this pink-flowered plant. Readily produced runners quickly carpet an area.

Fragaria 'Pink Panda'.

GROWING GUIDE Full sun to partial shade. Humus-rich, moist but well-drained, slightly acid soil.

PROPAGATION Division, runners.

USES Groundcover, edging.

SPECIES, VARIETIES, CULTIVARS AND HYBRIDS

F. frel (fral). Pink Panda strawberry. Hybrid origin. Grows 8 to 12 inches tall and as wide. Clumps of bright green, 3-part leaves with toothed edges. Spreads by runners; use as groundcover. Deep pink flowers, 1½ inches across, with yellow centers produced in spring and early summer, with some in bloom all season. Occasional small edible berries. Zones 5 to 9.

F. vesca (*ves*-kuh). Woodland strawberry, fraises des bois. Europe. Grows 8 inches tall and as wide. Clumps of dark green, 3-part leaves with toothed edges. White flowers, ½ inch across, produced intermittently throughout the growing season, with small edible berries. Use as an edging. A number of cultivars available, with red, yellow or white berries. Zones 5 to 9.

g

Gaillardia
(gah-*lar*-dee-uh)
Blanket flower
Compositae—daisy family

A favorite perennial for use in warm-color combinations, blanket flower has daisy-like, multicolored blooms that are good for cutting. It is popular because it is easy to grow, tolerates heat and blooms for a long period. The genus is named after the French botanist, Gaillard.

GROWING GUIDE Full sun. Poor to average, very well-drained soil.

Gaillardia x *grandiflora*.

Gaillardia x *grandiflora* 'Goblin'.

Gaillardia are short-lived in fertile, moist soils. Deadhead plants, then trim back in late summer for fall bloom. Stake taller cultivars.

PROPAGATION Divison or root cuttings for named cultivars.

USES Beds and borders, meadow gardens, cut flowers. Excellent mixed with black-eyed Susans and perennial sunflowers.

SPECIES, VARIETIES, CULTIVARS AND HYBRIDS

G. x *grandiflora* (gran-di-*floh*-ruh). Blanket flower. Hybrid origin. A cross between annual and perennial species. Grows 2 to 3 feet tall and 2 feet wide. Sprawling plants with gray-green, toothed, hairy leaves 4 to 6 inches long. Daisy-like, 3-inch flowers borne one to a stalk for a long period during summer. Flowers are usually combinations of yellow, gold, orange, scarlet, crimson or wine-red, often with purple centers. Noted cultivars include 'Baby Cole' and 'Goblin', growing 8 to 10 inches tall; 'Burgundy', with wine-red flowers; 'Yellow Queen', with yellow flowers; and 'Dazzler', with crimson tips and yellow centers. 'Monarch Strain' is a seed-propagated color mix. Zones 3 to 10.

Galium
(*gal*-lee-um)
Sweet woodruff
Rubiaceae—madder family

Providing an easy-to-grow groundcover for shaded areas, sweet woodruff is best known to herb gardeners, who use the vanilla-scented leaves to flavor May wine and make insect-repelling potpourri. Spreads, but not invasively. Woodruff's whorls of rich green leaves are crowned with tiny white flowers in spring.

Galium oderatum.

GROWING GUIDE Partial to light shade. Humus-rich, moist but well-drained soil. Tolerant of acid soils.

PROPAGATION Division.

USES Groundcover under trees and shrubs, woodland gardens. Interplants well with lily-of-the-valley, spring-blooming anemones, ferns and spring-blooming bulbs, such as *Leucojum* and *Galanthus*.

SPECIES, VARIETIES, CULTIVARS AND HYBRIDS

G. odoratum (oh-doe-*rah*-tum). Sweet woodruff. Europe. Grows 6 to 9 inches tall and 12 inches wide. Spreading plant with whorls of 6 to 8 narrow, 1-inch leaves on wiry stems. Fragrant white flowers, ¼-inch across, in spring. Zones 4 to 8.

Gaura
(*gaw*-ruh)
Gaura
Onagraceae—evening primrose family

Now here's a plant for hot summers with water at a premium. No also-ran either, what with its large clumps of willowy leaves and quantities of tall, airy flower spikes with white flowers tinged with pink produced for much of summer.

GROWING GUIDE Full sun. Average to humus-rich, well-drained soil. Deadhead to prolong flowering. Takes several years to become established before it flowers best.

PROPAGATION Seed. Division is difficult because of the long taproot.

USES Sunny beds and borders, slopes. Pale flowers and airy appearance act as a blending agent among other perennials.

Gaura lindheimeri.

SPECIES, VARIETIES, CULTIVARS AND HYBRIDS

G. lindheimeri (lind-*hay*-mer-eye). White gaura. Texas, Louisiana. Grows 3 to 4 feet tall and 2 to 3 feet wide. Clumps of narrow leaves to 3 inches long. Spikes of 1-inch white flowers tinged with pink. Blooms progressively up the spike like gladiolus. Zones 5 to 9.

Geranium

(jeh-*ray*-nee-um)
Cranesbill
Geraniaceae—geranium family

Among the "must have" perennials for English gardeners, geraniums are making inroads stateside. A widely adaptable genus with over 400 species and many cultivars, geraniums offer mounding forms and long-blooming pastel flowers for sunny and partially shaded gardens. These perennial plants are not related to the annual geraniums, which are the genus *Pelargonium*.

GROWING GUIDE Bloom is best in full sun, but in hotter climates, geranium grows better with partial shade. Humus-rich, moist but well-drained soil. Do not overfertilize, as this encourages lanky growth. Deadhead to prolong flowering.

PROPAGATION Division, stem cuttings.

USES Front of beds and borders, edgings.

SPECIES, VARIETIES, CULTIVARS AND HYBRIDS

G. cinereum (si-*ner*-ee-um). Grayleaf cranesbill. Balkans. Grows 6 to 12 inches tall and 12 inches wide. Mounds of gray-green leaves finely divided into lobes. Cup-shaped, 1-inch, pale pink flowers with dark veins in spring, then off and on. A number of selections have vibrantly colored pink, rose or deep red flowers. Less adaptable than other species. Zones 5 to 8.

Geranium dalmaticum.

G. clarkei (*klar*-kee-eye). Clarke's Cranesbill. Nepal. Grows 15 to 20 inches tall and 18 inches wide. Loose, open mounds of deeply cut leaves 4 to 6 inches wide. Great quantities of 1-inch blue flowers with pink veins in spring and early summer. Deep blue or white forms. Zones 4 to 8.

G. dalmaticum (dal-*mah*-ti-cum). Dalmation cranesbill. Balkans. Grows 6 inches tall and 10 inches wide. Rapidly spreading, dense cushions of glossy, rounded, deeply divided leaves to 2 inches wide. Foliage turns red or orange in the fall. Clear pink, 1-inch flowers in clusters of 3, mainly in spring, then off and on during summer. White-flowered form. This is one parent of the hybrid *G.* x *cantabrigiense*, a trailing plant 12 inches tall and 18 inches wide with bright pink or white flowers. Zones 4 to 8.

Geranium himalayense.

G. endressii (en-*dress*-ee-eye). Endress's cranesbill. Pyrenees. Grows 12 to 18 inches tall and 18 inches wide. Mounds of evergreen leaves, deeply divided into 5 segments. Light pink, 1-inch flowers in early summer, with some repeat. 'Wargrave Pink' is the most popular cultivar among many. Zones 4 to 8.

G. himalayense (him-ay-*lay*-ense). Also listed as *G. grandiflorum* or *G. meeboldii*. Lilac cranesbill. Asia. Grows 12 inches tall and 18 inches wide. Spreading mounds of long-stalked, deeply divided leaves to 8 inches wide. Saucer-shaped, 2-inch flowers borne on long stalks are deep blue with dark purple veins. Early summer flowering for 4 to 6 weeks, with some repeat.

Geranium himalayesnse 'Johnson's Blue'.

A number of selections. A parent of the popular hybrid 'Johnson's Blue', growing to 18 inches tall with clear blue flowers for many weeks. Zones 4 to 8.

Geranium macrorrhizum.

G. macrorrhizum (mak-ro-*rise*-um). Bigroot cranesbill. Southern Europe. Grows 15 inches tall and 18 inches wide. Mounds of shallowly lobed leaves to 8 inches wide, and aromatic when crushed. Clusters of

Geranium maculatum.

Helianthemum nummularium
'Buttercup'.

PROPAGATION Division, cuttings.

USES Front of borders, edging, rock
gardens.

**SPECIES, VARIETIES, CULTIVARS AND
HYBRIDS**

  H. nummularium (num-yew-*lay*-
ree-um). Sunrose. Mediterranean.
Grows 1 to 2 feet tall and as wide.
Sprawling plants with woody stems
and 1- to 2-inch, narrow, grayish, evergreen leaves. Loose clusters of 1- to
2-inch, yellow flowers with five petals.
Many cultivars, mainly differing in
flower color; some flowers are double.
Zones 5 to 7.

Helianthus
(hee-lee-*an*-thus)
Sunflower
Compositae—daisy family

Besides the annual sunflowers grown
for their seeds, oil and ornamental
flowers, and the Jerusalem artichoke
(*H. tuberosum*), grown for its edible
roots, there are perennial species that
can be used to good effect in the
garden, even in hot areas. Blooming
for a long period in the fall with
yellow, daisy-like flowers good for
cutting. Sunflowers' generic name is
derived from the Greek *helios*, for sun,
and *anthos*, flower.

GROWING GUIDE Full sun. Most well-
drained soils. Extra watering and fertilizing is beneficial. Staking may be
necessary. Can spread rapidly.

PROPAGATION Division, seed, stem
cuttings.

USES Back of borders. Meadow
gardens. Especially good combined
with large ornamental grasses. Cut
flowers.

**SPECIES, VARIETIES, CULTIVARS AND
HYBRIDS**

Helianthus x *multiflorus* 'Loddon Gold'.

  H. angustifolis (an-gus-ti-*foh*-lee-
us). Swamp sunflower. Grows 5 to 7
feet tall and 4 feet wide. Rough, hairy,
well-branched stems with untoothed,
narrow, lance-shaped leaves to 8 inches
long. Clusters of 3-inch wide, yellow,
daisy-like flowers with dark brown
centers in fall. *H. salicifolius*, willowleaf
sunflower, is similar but hardy to Zone
4, while *H. angustifolius* is hardy in
Zones 6 to 9. *H. maximilliani*,
Maximillian sunflower, is another
desirable variety; it grows to 10 feet tall
and is hardy in Zones 4 to 9.

  H. x multiflorus (mul-ti-*floh*-rus).
Also listed as *H. decapetalus
multiflorus*. Sunflower. Hybrid origin.
Grows 4 to 6 feet tall and 2 feet wide.

Hairy, egg-shaped leaves to 10 inches
long and 6 inches wide. Single or
double, yellow to yellow-orange, 5-
inch flowers for at least a month in the
fall. Several cultivars are available.
Zones 4 to 9.

Heliopsis
(hee-lee-*op*-sis)
Sunflower heliopsis
Compositae—daisy family

Heliopsis is a sunflower lookalike,
albeit smaller, with the translation of
its generic name meaning "sun-like."
Plants are noted for their long
blooming period in summer, ability
to grow in hot, dry climates and
excellence as cut flowers. Cultivars are
preferred over the species for their
more refined growth and appearance.

GROWING GUIDE Full sun. Average to
humus-rich, moist but well-drained
soil. Deadhead regularly to prolong
blooming. Staking may be necessary.
May be short-lived.

PROPAGATION Division, seed. May self-
sow.

USES Back of beds. Meadow garden.
Cut flowers.

**SPECIES, VARIETIES, CULTIVARS AND
HYBRIDS**

Heliopsis helianthoides 'Sommesonne' *or*
'Summer Sun'.

  H. helianthoides (hee-lee-an-*thoy*-
deez). False sunflower. North America.
Grows 4 to 5 feet tall and 2 to 3 feet
wide. Vigorous, erect, freely branching

plant with toothed, egg-shaped leaves to 5 inches long. Abundant clusters of 2- to 4-inch, yellow, daisy-like flowers in summer and early fall. The subspecies *scabra*, often listed as *H. scabra*, is better than the species for the garden, and the cultivars are even better, with most growing to 3 feet tall. Two in particular to look for include 'Golden Greenheart', with double yellow flowers with a green center, and 'Summer Sun', which tolerates heat particularly well and blooms for 10 to 12 weeks. Zones 4 to 9.

Helleborus
(hel-luh-*bor*-us)
Hellebore, Christmas rose, Lenten rose
Ranunculaceae—buttercup family

Helleborus argutifolius.

Like the spring-flowering bulbs, the hellebores renew the spirit of gardeners just when it seems winter will never end. Depending on the climate, hellebores may start blooming as early as midwinter, with the nodding flowers blooming for a month or more, withstanding freezing temperatures and snow. Common names notwithstanding, hellebores are not related to roses. The cup-shaped flowers, in shades of green, white, pinks and dusty red-purples, have five petals centered with golden stamens. If the stem ends are seared in a flame immediately, the flowers are good for cutting.

GROWING GUIDE Does best with sun in the winter and shade in the summer, such as under shade trees or among deciduous shrubs or other perennials. Humus-rich, neutral to slightly alkaline, moist but well-drained soil. Provide a summer mulch to keep soil moist, and a winter mulch for protection. Plants need several years to become established. Where foliage becomes tattered during the winter, it may be removed before flowering.

PROPAGATION Division, but plants do not respond well to disturbance. Seed, sown outdoors. Self-sows.

USES Woodlands with dappled shade, deciduous shrub borders, or among large-leaved perennials. Wonderful when grown in masses. Cut flowers.

SPECIES, VARIETIES, CULTIVARS AND HYBRIDS

H. argutifolius (ar-gew-ti-*foh*-lee-us). Also listed as *H. corsicus* or *H. lividus corsicus*. Corsican hellebore. Corsica. Grows 2 feet tall and 18 inches wide. Prized for clumps of foliage with gray-green, three-parted, spiny-toothed leaves. Clusters of 15 to 30 pale green, 1-inch flowers in late winter or early spring. Tolerates drier soil than most hellebores. Best with cool summers. Zones 6 to 8.

H. foetidus (*feh*-ti-dus). Bearsfoot hellebore, stinking hellebore. Western Europe. Grows 18 inches tall and as wide. Vigorous clumps of dark green leaves deeply divided into four to nine segments. Branching stems bear many pale green, 1-inch, unpleasant-smelling flowers in late winter or early spring. Zones 4 to 9.

H. niger (*nye*-jer). Christmas rose. Southern Europe. Grows 12 inches tall and as wide. Clumps of dark green leaves divided into seven to nine egg-shaped segments. Red-spotted stems bear 2- to 3-inch wide white flowers in late winter or early spring. Most plants offered for sale are seed grown and highly variable. A few vegetatively propagated cultivars can sometimes be found. More difficult to grow than other hellebores. Zones 4 to 8.

Helleborus orientalis.

H. orientalis (or-ee-en-*tay*-lis). Lenten rose. Greece, Asia Minor. Grows 18 inches tall and as wide. Clumps of leathery, dark green leaves divided into seven to nine finely toothed segments; leaves may be over a foot wide. Nodding, cup-shaped flowers, 2- to 4-inches wide in late winter to early spring for up to 10 weeks. Colors range from white to deep plum, sometimes blotched or speckled with darker spots. The easiest hellebore to grow and does even better with fertilization in early spring. Many cultivars and hybrids becoming available. Zones 4 to 9.

Other hellebores to consider include *H. atrorubens*, bearing dark purple flowers in midwinter and *H. viridis*, green hellebore, a deciduous species with green flowers. Both are hardy in Zones 6 to 8.

Hemerocallis
(hem-er-oh-kal-is)
Daylily
Liliaceae—lily family

What's there to say about the most

Hemerocallis 'Treasure Shores'.

ubiquitous perennial in the American landscape today? Obviously, daylilies are easy to grow and widely tolerant. Witness the stories of people who left them uprooted in a garbage bag in a garage or bare root on a bench

Hemerocallis 'Quaker Aspen'.

outdoors overwinter, only to have them bloom the following summer. Or where to begin on the 30,000-plus cultivars, with hundreds more added

Hemerocallis 'Chicago Scintillation'.

Hemerocallis.

every year? The size of these range from 12 inches to over 6 feet, with flowers 2 to 8 inches across borne on leafless stalks, blooming anywhere from late spring to fall. Flower colors run the gamut from ivory to deep red, although most are in the yellow range; there may also be contrasting stripes, edges or throats, single or double forms, with petal edges plain, frilled or ruffled. Growth, somewhat mercifully, remains as grassy clumps, and flowers still last only a day, remaining true to the Greek derivation of *hemero*, day, and *kallos*, beauty. If you can't bear the sight of one more 'Stella D' Oro', why not go back to simpler times, and consider some of the original species.

GROWING GUIDE Full sun to partial shade. A wide range of soils are

Hemerocallis 'Stella D' Oro'.

tolerated, but best growth is with humus-rich, moist but well-drained soil. Extra watering during the growing season is recommended, but not extra fertilizer.

PROPAGATION Division.

USES Anywhere in the landscape with enough sun. Depending on the height, the front, middle or back of beds and borders, edgings, among shrubs or massed.

SPECIES, VARIETIES, CULTIVARS AND HYBRIDS
H. citrina (kih-tree-nah). China. Grows to 40 inches tall and 24 inches wide. Clumps of coarse, dark green, semievergreen leaves to 10 inches long. Fragrant, pale yellow, 6-inch wide flowers. Zones 3 to 9.

Hemerocallis 'Dragon's Mouth'.

H. dumortieri (dew-mor-tee-yew-ree). Japan. Grows 2 feet tall and 18 inches wide. Mounds of arching leaves 18 inches long and ½ inch wide. Flower stems are shorter than the leaves, with each bearing two to four red-brown buds opening to fragrant, golden orange flowers in late spring or early summer. Zones 3 to 9.

H. fulva (ful-va). Tawny daylily. Asia. Grows to 4 feet tall and 3 feet wide. Naturalizing through many parts of the world, this is the daylily seen growing along roadsides, spreading rapidly. Bright green, arching leaves to 2 feet long. Erect stems bear up to 12 tawny orange flowers to 7 inches across in summer. 'Kwanso' has double flowers. Use for mass plantings. Zones 3 to 9.

A large field of mixed Hemerocallis.

H. lilio-asphodelus (lil-ee-oh-ass-foh-del-us). Lemon daylily. Siberia, China, Japan. Grows to 3 feet tall and 2 feet wide. Arching, dark green leaves to 2 feet long and ¾-inch wide. Branched, curving stems bear five to nine fragrant, lemon-yellow flowers in early summer. Slower to become established than other daylilies. Good for mass plantings. Zones 3 to 9.

H. middendorfii (mid-an-dorf-ee-eye). Middendorf daylily. Siberia, Japan. Grows 2 feet tall and as wide. Similar to *H. dumortieri*, but with longer flower stems and tightly clustered 2- to 3-inch long, yellow-orange, fragrant flowers in late spring and early summer. More tolerant of shade and moisture than other daylilies. Zones 3 to 9.

H. minor (mye-nor). Dwarf daylily. Siberia, Japan. Grows to 2 feet tall and 18 inches wide. Arching leaves to 18 inches long. Bell-shaped, light yellow, fragrant flowers lasting two days. Zones 3 to 9.

Hesperis
(*hes*-per-is)
Dame's rocket
Cruciferae—mustard family

Among the quintessential cottage-garden plants, dame's rocket may be short-lived but it scatters itself about the garden with welcome abandon. Resembling phlox, the clusters of lavender, purple, mauve or white flowers bloom from late spring to midsummer, gracing gardens and bouquets. The generic name is an allusion to its way

Hesperis matronalis.

of perfuming the air at dusk, when Hesperus, the evening star, is in the sky.

GROWING GUIDE Full sun to partial shade. Moist but well-drained, neutral to alkaline soil. Deadhead regularly to prolong blooming.

PROPAGATION Seed. Self-sows.

USES Massed at woodland edges, informal gardens, cottage gardens, meadow gardens. White forms particularly glow in late afternoon sun. Cut flowers.

SPECIES, VARIETIES, CULTIVARS AND HYBRIDS

H. matronalis (mah-tro-*nah*-lis). Dame's rocket. Europe, Asia. Grows 2 to 3 feet tall and 2 feet wide. Branching plant with toothed, lance-shaped leaves to 4 inches long. Elongated clusters of four-petaled, ½-inch wide, fragrant flowers late spring and early summer. Double forms exist, and must be propagated by division or stem cuttings. Zones 4 to 8.

Heuchera
(*hew*-ker-uh)
Coral bells, alumroot
Saxifragaceae—saxifrage family

Even though there are almost 70 species of heuchera native to North America, only coral bells played much of a role in gardens for many years. With the advent of 'Palace Purple', with its wrinkled purple leaves, heucheramania is spreading. What heucheras offer are low-growing plants for shade with marbled, sometimes evergreen leaves and wiry, graceful spikes of tiny flowers from late spring to late summer. The airiness of the flowers provides texture to the garden and bouquets. The genus is named after the German botanist Johann von Heucher (1677–1747).

GROWING GUIDE Partial to half shade in most areas, with full sun only in cool-summer areas. Humus-rich, moist but well-drained soil. Good winter drainage is essential. Deadhead regularly to prolong blooming. Use a protective winter mulch to prevent heaving of roots.

PROPAGATION Division of species or cultivars; seed of species.

Heuchera x brizoides 'Northern Fire'.

USES Front of beds and borders, edging, groundcover. Cut flowers.

SPECIES, VARIETIES, CULTIVARS AND HYBRIDS

H. americana (ah-mer-i-*kay*-nuh). Alumroot. Eastern North America. Grows 2 to 3 feet tall and 18 inches wide. Clump-forming plants with 6-inch, rounded, heart-shaped, evergreen leaves with toothed lobes. Young foliage is a mottled purple that disappears with maturity; there is almost continuous new growth. Spikes of tiny, greenish-white flowers on stalks to 20 inches long in early summer. Tough, sturdy, reliable, even in hot regions. Used in breeding hybrid coral bells. 'Sunset', with purple foliage, is the best cultivar. Zones 4 to 9.

Heuchera micrantha 'Palace Purple'.

H. x brizoides (brih-*zoi*-deez). Hybrid coral bells. Hybrid origin. Grows 12 to 30 inches tall and 12 to 18 inches wide, depending on the cultivar. Mounding plants with dark green, rounded leaves with scalloped leaves.

Heuchera sanguinea 'Coral Bells'.

Large, open clusters of red, pink or white flowers in late spring and early summer. Many cultivars of various sizes and flower colors. From crosses of certain of these hybrids with *Tiarella cordifolia*, foam flower, the genus x *Heucherella* was created; the resulting cultivars are noted for mottled, evergreen foliage, and flowers similar to hybrid coral bells with plants spreading by stolons. Zones 4 to 8.

Heuchera sanguinea.

H. micrantha (my-*kran*-thuh). Western alumroot. Western North America. Grows to 24 inches tall and 18 inches wide. Mounding plants with rounded, heart-shaped, gray-green leaves to 4-inches long with toothed, rounded lobes. Loose, open clusters of ivory, ⅛-inch flowers. Important in the development of garden cultivars, including *H. microntha* and 'Palace Purple'. Zones 4 to 8.

H. sanguinea (san-*gwin*-nee-uh). Coral bells. Southwestern North America. Grows 12 to 18 inches tall and 12 inches wide. Low, rounded mats of rounded, heart-shaped leaves to 2 inches long with toothed, rounded lobes. Branched flower stalks to 20 inches tall with ½-inch, bright red, bell-shaped flowers for many weeks in late spring. Must have good drainage in neutral to alkaline soil. Contributes the color to the many cultivars of *H.* x *brizoides*. Zones 4 to 8.

H. villosa (vil-*loh*-suh). Hairy alumroot. Southeastern United States. Grows 1 to 3 feet tall and 18 inches wide. Hairy, rounded, heart-shaped, deeply lobed leaves to 6 inches long, marked with light and dark green. Large, open, airy clusters of ¼-inch, white flowers from late summer to fall. Naturally adapted to hot weather. Zones 6 to 9.

Hosta
(hoss-*tuh*)
Plantain lily, hosta
Liliaceae—lily family

What daylilies are to the sunny perennial garden, hostas are to the shade garden, with their adaptability, few maintenance requirements, long life and neat, symmetrical mounds of leaves with varying textures and colors. Although there are fewer than 20 species, thousands of cultivars have been developed, ranging in size from 6 inches to over 3 feet across and with foliage dark green, blue green or yellow green, plain or variegated with yellow,

Hosta albo-picta.

Hosta 'Golden Tiara'.

cream or white, surfaces varying from shiny to waxen and distinctly veined, wavy-edged or puckered. Mainly grown as foliage plants, hostas bear spikes of white, purple or lavender, lily-like flowers, sometimes fragrant, in summer or fall.

GROWING GUIDE Partial to full shade. Humus-rich, moist but well-drained soil. Good drainage is particularly important in winter. Slugs and snails can be a major pest. May take several years for a plant to get fully established.

PROPAGATION Division.

USES Specimens or small groups in bed or borders, edging or massed as a groundcover. Cut flowers, especially *H. plantaginea* and related cultivars.

SPECIES, VARIETIES, CULTIVARS AND HYBRIDS

H. crispula (*krisp*-yew-lah). Curled-leaf hosta. Japan. Grows to 3 feet tall and 2 feet wide. Very dark green with white edge, wavy and twisted leaves to 5 inches wide and 8 inches long. Large quantities of 2-inch, pale lavender flowers on stalks 2- to 3-feet tall in early summer. Zones 3 to 8.

Hosta sieboldiana elegans.

H. fortunei (for-*tune*-ee-cye). Fortune's hosta. Japan. Grows 2 feet tall and as wide. Slightly gray-green leaves to 12 inches long and 4- to 8-inches wide. Distinctive wings on leaf stems. Pale lilac, 1½-inch flowers on stems held well above foliage. The species and its cultivars are adapted to a variety of growing conditions with little care. Among the related cultivars, several are particularly notable, include 'Francee', 'Gold Standard', 'Hyacintha' and 'Golden Haze'. Zones 3 to 8.

H. lancifolia (lan-si-*foh*-lee-ah). Lance-leaf hosta. Japan. Grows 2 feet tall and 18 inches wide. Glossy, lance-shaped leaves to 7 inches long and 1 inch wide. Long-lasting, trumpet-shaped, 1½-inch, lavender flowers on stiff green stalks to 18 inches tall in late summer. The oldest known hosta in cultivation, with drawings dating to 1690. A parent of many modern hybrids. Somewhat tolerant of dry soil. Zones 3 to 8.

H. plantaginea (plan-*tage*-ih-nee-ah). Fragrant hosta. China. Grows to 30 inches tall and 3 feet wide. Large mounds of long-stemmed, heart-shaped leaves to 10 inches long. Waxy, fragrant, trumpet-shaped flowers to 4-inches long on strong stalks.

Grown in gardens since the late 1800s. The species and related cultivars tolerate more sun and heat than other hostas. 'Royal Standard' is a favored cultivar with white flowers, as is 'August Moon', with its golden leaves and white flowers, while 'Honeybells' and 'Sweet Susan' have lilac flowers, all with fragrance. Zones 3 to 9.

H. sieboldiana (see-bold-ee-*ah*-nah). Siebold's hosta. Japan. Grows 2½ to 3 feet tall and 4 feet wide. Thick, waxy, puckered, almost round, blue green leaves to 15 inches long and 12 inches wide. Stems bearing tight clusters of pale lilac flowers barely rise above foliage in early to midsummer; some gardeners remove them before blooming. Among the cultivars, the variety 'Elegans' has been popular since the early 1900s, but 'Frances

Williams', with its gold-rimmed edges, is considered the most popular hosta of all today. Many other cultivars with blue-green leaves are available, including hybrids with *H. tardiflora*, a small dark green species, and *H. tokudama*, another small plant, as well as with *H. fortunei* and others. Some of the better known blue-leaved cultivars include 'Hadspen Blue', 'Halcyon' and 'Krossa Regal'.

Hosta sieboldiana 'Frances Williams'.

H. sieboldii (see-*bold*-ee-eye). Also listed as *H. albomarginata*. Japan. Grows to 20 inches tall and as wide. Lance-shaped, dark green leaves to 6 inches long and 2½ inches wide, with white margins and undulating edges. Plants spread quickly by creeping root-stock. Bell-shaped, lavender, 2-inch flowers in late summer, with up to 30 per stalk. Zones 3 to 8.

H. undulata (un-dew-*lah*-tah). Wavy hosta. Japan. Grows 18 inches tall and as wide. Strongly undulating and twisting, shiny, leaves to 6 inches long, with white interior and green edges and red-dotted, winged stems.

These are the most common hostas; may also be listed as 'Variegata' or 'Medio-picta'. Flower stems to 3 feet tall bear 2-inch pale lilac flowers in summer. 'Albo-mariginata' has white-margined leaves.

H. ventricosa (ven-trih-*koh*-sah). Blue hosta. China. Grows 2 to 3 feet tall and 3 feet wide. Broad, glossy, heart-shaped, dark green leaves to 7 inches long and 5 inches wide with distinctive veining. Flower stems to 3 feet tall with flaring, bell-shaped, dark purple flowers in summer. Several variegated forms. Very sturdy plant. Zones 3 to 9.

H. venusta (ven-*yews*-tah). Dwarf hosta. Japan. Grows 4 inches tall and 8 inches wide. Pointed, oval leaves to 2 inches long and ¾-inch wide. The 8- to 12-inch flower stems bear 4 to 8 lilac flowers in early summer. Plants spread well by stolons. Variegated and gold-leaved cultivars. Best when grown in groups of at least five plants. Other good small hosta cultivars include 'Ginko Craig', 'Gold Edger' and 'Lime Mound'. Zones 3 to 9.

A variety of different hostas, including Hosta undulata 'Thomas Hogg'.

Iberis sempervirens 'Little Gem'.

i

Iberis
(eye-*beer*-is)
Candytuft
Cruciferae—mustard family

Among the staples of the spring-blooming garden, candytuft provides dense mounds and luxurious cascades of small, long-lasting, fragrant white flowers as the days warm up. A dependable plant, candytuft is attractive the rest of the year because of its fine-textured, evergreen foliage. Many of the 40 or so species of iberis are from Spain, also known as Iberia, hence the generic name. As to the common name, Candie is an old English name for Crete, where other forms were found.

GROWING GUIDE Full sun. Humus-rich, neutral to alkaline, moist but well-drained soil. Prune stems back halfway after flowering to keep the plant bushy and possibly get some reblooming.

PROPAGATION Division, but best left undisturbed; seed, stem cuttings. Provide winter mulch in cold areas with little snow cover.

USES Front of borders, edging, rock walls and gardens.

SPECIES, VARIETIES, CULTIVARS AND HYBRIDS

I. sempervirens (sem-per-*vye*-renz). Candytuft. Southern Europe. Grows to 1 foot tall and 2 feet wide. Mounding, woody-stemmed plant with dark, ever-green leaves to 2 inches long and ¾-inch wide. Two-inch wide clusters of white flowers for up to 10 weeks in spring to early summer. A number of cultivars, with variations in height, flower production and purity of color are available. 'Autumn Snow' and 'October Glory' are noted for their ability to rebloom. Zones 3 to 9.

Iris
(*eye*-ris)
Iris
Iridaceae—iris family

Grown for centuries and the emblem of many kings, irises offer a wide range of blooming times, colors and sizes for the garden and cut flowers for the home. Named for the Greek goddess

Purple bearded iris.

Mixed bearded iris.

Iris, who traversed between heaven and earth on a rainbow, irises do bloom in every color except true red. The intricately formed flowers consist of three upright petals called standards and three drooping petals called falls, which may have a crest or beard on them. Flowers may be bicolored, with the petal edges frilled, ruffled or a different color. Iris blooms may peep through the snow, only inches tall, or stand 3 feet tall, with flowers glowing in autumn's golden light, with most blooming in late spring and summer. Foliage is generally narrow, stiff and sword-shaped, usually growing from spreading, fleshy, rhizomatous roots. With the thousands of species, varieties, cultivars and hybrids, there are irises for every part of the sunny landscape.

GROWING GUIDE Full sun, with partial shade tolerated. Humus-rich, moist but well-drained soil. Deadhead. Pests include iris borer, bacterial soft rot, aphids and thrips. To reduce problems with borers, remove and destroy infected rhizomes at any time and old foliage and litter in the fall to prevent overwintering borer eggs.

Bearded iris.

PROPAGATION Division.

USES Beds and borders. Certain varieties best suited for specific situations, such as rock gardens or bog gardens. Cut flowers.

SPECIES, VARIETIES, CULTIVARS AND HYBRIDS

I. **"Bearded hybrids."** Bearded iris. Hybrid origin. Grows 8 to 36 inches tall and 10 to 24 inches wide. Complex hybrids with thousands of different named plants, with every possible iris color, but all have the typical sword-like leaves. The flowers have both large standards and falls. They have been divided into categories based on the size of the plants. **Dwarf Bearded** types are further divided into miniature dwarfs and standard dwarfs. The miniature dwarfs are 4 to 10 inches tall and are the earliest to flower in early to midspring, with blooms 2 to 3 inches wide and spotted falls. They must have excellent drainage. The standard dwarfs are more vigorous than the miniatures, with flowers about a week later and 3 to 4 inches wide. **Intermediate Bearded** types bloom between the times of the dwarf and tall types. They grow 1 to 2 feet tall with flowers 3 to 4 inches across.

Iris 'Skyfire'.

Tall Bearded types are the ones most people equate with irises. They are the last of the hybrid bearded types to bloom in late spring and early summer, with flowers to 6 inches wide. Tall bearded irises are more susceptible to pests than others, but this can be greatly prevented by growing them in loose soil with excellent drainage and by destroying foliage in the fall. Zones 3 to 10.

I. bucharica (buh-*kar*-ih-kah). Bokhara iris. Bokhara. Grows 12 to 18 inches tall and 1 foot wide. Tuberous roots planted 4 inches deep give rise to arching, 2-inch-wide leaves produced on either side of a central stem. Yellow and

Iris cristata.

white flowers in spring. Zones 6 to 9.

I. cristata (kris-*tah*-tah). Crested iris. Eastern North America. Grows 6 to 9 inches tall and 12 inches wide. Fans of ribbed, light green leaves to 1 inch wide. Shallow rhizomes multiple the clump rapidly. Fragrant, 2-inch flowers in spring are lilac-blue, with the standards shorter and narrower than the fall, yellow crests and a white center spotted purple. There is a white-flowered variety and 'Shenandoah Sky' has light blue flowers and 'Summer Storm' has deeper blue flowers. Native to woodlands. Protect from slugs. Zones 4 to 9.

I. danfordiae (dan-*ford*-ee-eye). Danford iris. Eastern Turkey. Grows 4 to 6 inches tall and 3 inches wide. Belongs to the group known as reticulated iris. Grows from a bulb. Square, hollow leaves develop after the bright yellow flowers in early spring. Standards are ¾-inch long and the falls have dark spots. Zones 5 to 9.

I. douglasiana (doug-las-ee-*an*-ah). Pacific Coast iris. Oregon, California. Grows 1 to 2 feet tall and 2 feet wide. Arching, evergreen, 1-inch-wide, dark green leaves with a red base. Branched stalks bear many beardless flowers in spring and early summer. Colors range from reddish-purple to pale blue, with dark blue veins and a yellow center. A parent of the 'Pacific Coast Hybrids', which are superior. Many hybrids. Zones 8 to 10.

I. ensata (en-*sah*-tah). Also listed as *I. kaempferi*. Japanese iris. Eastern Asia. Grows 2 to 3 feet tall and 18 to 24 inches wide. Stiffly arching, 1-inch-wide, bright green leaves with a prominent midrib. Flower stalks bear three to four flat flowers to 6 inches wide in early to midsummer. Flower colors include deep violet, blue, red-purple and white, often with yellow-tinged falls. Many cultivars and hybrids. Crowns are planted 2 to 3 inches deep in humus-rich, acid, moisture-retaining but not necessarily boggy soil. *I. laevigata* is similar, but without the prominent midrib on the blue-

Iris ensata 'Velvety Queen'.

green leaves. It is more tolerant of wet soil and lime. Several cultivars. Zones 5 to 9.

I. foetidissima (foi-tih-*dis*-ih-mah). Stinking iris, gladwyn iris. Europe, North Africa. Grows 2 feet tall and 18 inches wide. Dark, evergreen leaves to 1 inch wide. The odor of these when crushed is the source of the common name. Flattened, branching stalk bears one to three 2½-inch flowers in late spring and early summer. Flowers are gray-lilac with dark violet veins and a tinge of yellow. Mainly grown for the seeds, which are bright red and remain on the plant for a long time in winter; these may be dried for arrangements. Needs partial shade. Several varieties with yellow flowers and one with variegated leaves. Zones 6 to 9.

I. fulva (*ful*-vah). Copper iris. Southern and Central United States. Grows 2 to 3 feet tall and 2 feet wide. Leaves are 1-inch wide, with drooping tips. Spring-blooming flowers have drooping petals of copper-red to orange-pink. Excellent for the bog garden. Notable for being a parent with *I. brevicaulis* of the 'Louisiana Hybrids', with many fine named cultivars. Zones 7 to 10.

I. x germanica (jer-*man*-ih-cah). German iris. Hybrid origin. Grows 2 to 4 feet tall and 2 feet wide. Gray-green leaves and yellow-bearded flowers of violet-blue in late spring and early summer. Of historical value for its contributions to "Bearded Hybrids." 'Florentina', orris root, with bluish-white flowers, is grown for the perfume industry because of the fixative quality of its roots. Zones 4 to 9.

I. pallida (*pah*-lih-dah). Dalmatian iris, sweet iris. Southern Europe. Grows 2 to 4 feet tall and 2 feet wide.

Silvery-gray leaves to 1½ inches wide and 2 feet long. Branched stalks bear fragrant, lilac-blue flowers with a yellow beard. 'Argentea Variegata' has leaves variegated with white; 'Variegata' has leaves variegated with yellow; 'Dalmatica' has larger, more silvery leaves All are excellent in the garden. Zones 5 to 8.

I. pseudacorus (sood-*ah*-koh-rus). Yellow flag. Europe, North Africa. Grows 2 to 4 feet tall and 2 feet wide. Stiffly upright, deep green leaves to 1 inch wide. Branched stalks bear bright yellow, 2-inch flowers with brown veins in late spring and early summer. 'Flore Pleno' has double flowers; 'Variegata' has leaves variegated with chartreuse. Widely naturalized in wet sites, but tolerates dry soil. Self-sows. Has been used as a medicinal herb for centuries. Seed capsules are dried and used in arrangements. Zones 5 to 9. *I. versicolor*, blue flag, is similar, but hardier (Zones 3 to 9) and with blue-purple flowers.

I. pumila (*pew*-mih-lah). Dwarf iris. Grows 4 to 6 inches tall and 12 inches wide. Gray-green leaves and unbranched flower stalks bearing

Iris pumila 'Sapphire Jewel'.

Iris pumila.

fragrant yellow, purple or blue flowers, with yellow beards, in spring. Notable for its use in producing hybrid dwarf bearded irises. Zones 4 to 9.

I. reticulata (reh-tik-*yew*-lah-tah). Reticulated iris. Grows 4 to 6 inches tall and 4 inches wide. Netted-veined bulbs produce four-angled, pointed leaves and fragrant, purple flowers in early spring. Leaves go dormant by summer. Grows best with dry soil. Several cultivars, with flowers in various shades of blue or reddish-purple. Zones 5 to 9.

I. sibirica (sih-*bih*-rih-kah). Siberian iris. Central Europe, Russia. Grows 2 to 4 feet tall and 2 to 3 feet wide. Erect to slightly arching, bright green leaves to ¾-inch wide. Stalks bear one or three violet-blue, 2-inch, flat flowers in late spring or early summer. May take several years to become established. Not susceptible to pests. Does best with even moisture. Elegant, excellent plants for the garden, with many cultivars, many with larger flowers, and more being offered every year. Related

Iris sibirica.

Iris sibirica.

species include *I. chrysographes*, with dark maroon flowers marked with gold on the falls, and *I. orientalis*, with white flowers. Zones 4 to 9.

I. tectorum (tek-*tor*-um). Roof iris. China, Japan. Grows 1 to 1½ feet tall and 12 to 18 inches wide. Thick rhizomes with fans of light, evergreen, ribbed leaves to 2 inches wide. Branched stalks bear 3-inch, flat, dark-veined, lilac flowers with a white crest in early summer. Grown on thatched roofs in Japan. Prone to slug damage. White-flowered form and variegated-leaf form. Zones 5 to 9.

I. "Xiphium hybrids" (izih-fee-um). English, Spanish, Dutch iris. Grows 12 to 18 inches tall and 12 inches wide. Closely related plants offered as hybrid bulbs which should be planted 4 to 6 inches deep. Rush-like, blue-green leaves. Blooms in early to midsummer, with a broad range of colors, including bronze tones. Zones 6 to 9.

k

Kirengeshoma
(kih-reng-geh-*show*-mah)
Yellow waxbells, kirengeshoma
Saxifragaceae—saxifrage family

Relatively new to American gardens, yellow waxbells is a large, shrubby plant for the moist, shaded garden. Mainly grown for the form and foliage, the shrubby plants contribute a somewhat exotic but graceful look with large, maple-like leaves. The nodding, yellow flowers in late summer and early autumn, followed by horned seed capsules, are a bonus.

GROWING GUIDE Partial to full shade. Fertile, humus-rich, acid, moist but well-drained soil. Protect from strong winds.

PROPAGATION Division, but best left undisturbed for at least three to five years.

USES Back of shaded borders, woodland walks.

SPECIES, VARIETIES, CULTIVARS AND HYBRIDS

Kirengeshoma palmata.

K. palmata (pahl-*may*-tah). Yellow waxbells. Japan. Grows 4 feet tall and as wide. Upright to arching, purplish stems with hairy, maple-like leaves to 6 inches wide. Waxy, 1½ inch, pale yellow, bell-shaped flowers borne near the top of the plant in late summer and early fall. Brownish-green seed capsules with three pointed horns. The speceis *koreana* is similar but slightly taller and hardier, with wider-opening flowers. Zones 5 to 7.

Knautia
(naw-tee-ah)
Pincushion flower, knautia
Dipsacaceae—teasel family

Resembling scabiosas, to which they're closely related, knautias contribute an airy effect to gardens with their summer-blooming flowers.

GROWING GUIDE Full sun. Average to humus-rich, moist but well-drained soil. Deadhead to prolong blooming. Staking may be necessary.

Knautia macedonica.

PROPAGATION Division, seed, stem cuttings.

USES Front to middle of beds and borders. Particularly effective with ornamental grasses and silver-foliaged plants.

SPECIES, VARIETIES, CULTIVARS AND HYBRIDS

K. macedonica (mah-ze-don-ih-kuh). Also listed as *Scabiosa rulmelica.* Crimson pincushion flower. Europe. Grows 2 feet tall and as wide. Sprawling plants with lyre-shaped to feathery leaves. Masses of 2-inch, rounded, crimson flowers on twisting stems in summer. Zones 5 to 8.

Kniphofia
(nee-*fof*-ee-ah, nip-*hoh*-fee-ah)
Red hot poker, torch lily
Liliaceae—lily family

Invaluable for their long blooming season and architectural presence in warm-color gardens, kniphofias are best known for their orange-red flowers, but there are cultivars with ivory, yellow, red, scarlet, coral or even green blooms. Flowering proceeds from the base to the top of the narrow flower spike arising from the clumps of sword-like leaves.

GROWING GUIDE Full sun. Humus-rich, moist but well-drained soil. Winter moisture is particularly deleterious; some gardeners resort to bending the foliage over the plant crown, then tying it down to exclude water. Deadhead to prolong blooming. When flowering is finished, cut foliage back by half.

PROPAGATION Division, seed.

USES Middle to back or center of beds and borders. Also effective planted in masses.

SPECIES, VARIETIES, CULTIVARS AND HYBRIDS

K. uvaria (yew-*vay*-ree-ah). Common torch lily. South Africa. Grows 4 feet tall and 3 feet wide. Clumps of gray-green, sword-like leaves to 3 feet long and 1 inch wide with abrasive edges. Tall, narrow spikes of small, tubular flowers in summer. Species generally superseded by numerous cultivars and hybrids with other species, varying in plant size, flower color and blooming season. Zones 6 to 9.

Kniphofia uvaria.

I

Lamium
(lay-*mee*-um)
Spotted nettle
Labiatae—mint family

From a group of plants mainly considered as weeds comes an easily grown, attractive groundcover for shaded areas of the garden. Without the pain-inducing hairs of the related stinging dead nettle, *Urtica dioica,*

Lamium maculatum 'White Nancy'.

spotted dead nettle is favored for its frequently variegated forms and small flowers throughout summer. The yellow-flowered form, variously listed under the genus *Lamiastrum, Galeobdolon* or *Lamium* is less well-mannered, often becoming highly invasive.

GROWING GUIDE Partial to half shade. Most soils that are moist but well-drained. Trim plants back after flowering to encourage new growth.

PROPAGATION Division, stem cuttings.

USES Groundcover in shaded areas or under trees and shrubs.

SPECIES, VARIETIES, CULTIVARS AND HYBRIDS

L. maculatum (mak-yew-*lah*-tum). Spotted dead nettle. Europe, Asia. Grows to 12 inches tall and 18 inches wide. Heart-shaped, toothed, prominently veined leaves with central, greenish-white stripe. Whorls of magenta, 1-inch, hooded flowers from late spring well into summer. Species has been superseded by cultivars, especially 'White Nancy', with white flowers and silver leaves edged in green, and 'Beacon Silver', with rose-pink flowers and silver leaves edged in green. Zones 3 to 8.

Lavandula
(lav-*van*-dew-lah)
Lavender
Labiatae—mint family

Lavandula angustifolia.

Besides being a beloved, indispensible herb for its fragrant flowers and foliage, lavender is effective as a specimen plant, edging or low hedge in ornamental gardens. The gray-green, finely textured foliage softly blends other plants, while the flowers bloom for a long period and are useful in fresh or dried arrangements.

GROWING GUIDE Full sun. Best in sandy, alkaline, well-drained soil, but other well-drained soils tolerated. Good winter drainage is essential and a winter mulch may be necessary. Deadhead to encourage a second blooming.

Although spring pruning is almost universally recommended for shaping, it can have a deleterious effect, so proceed with caution.

PROPAGATION Stem cuttings, seed.

USES Beds and borders, edging, low hedge. Fresh or dried cut flowers.

SPECIES, VARIETIES, CULTIVARS AND HYBRIDS

L. angustifolia (an-gust-ih-*foh*-lee-ah). Common lavender, English lavender. Mediterranean. Grows 2 to 3 feet tall and as wide. Mounding to sprawling clumps of woody stems with abundant gray-green leaves to 2½ inches long and ¼ inch wide.

Leafless flower spikes rise 4 to 10 inches above foliage with whorls of tiny lavender, purple, pink or white flowers at the top in summer. For drying, cut flowers when showing color but before fully open. Several cultivars, varying in size and flower color. Zones 5 to 9. Other perennial species are usually grown as annuals, except in Zones 8 to 9.

Liatris
(lye-*ay*-tris, *lye*-ah-tris)
Blazing star, gayfeather
Compositae—daisy family

A most undaisy-like member of the daisy family, liatris instead bears tall wands of small, fluffy, purple flowers.

Liatris spicata.

Very popular as cut flowers, they are unusual in that they start blooming at the top of the spike, working their way downward. The flowers are also very attractive to bees and butterflies. The vigorous, long-lived North American natives lend grace to the garden with their grassy dark green leaves.

GROWING GUIDE Full sun. Sandy to average, moist but well-drained soil. Tolerant of dry soil and must have good winter drainage. Staking may be required. Deadhead to prevent self-sowing.

PROPAGATION Division, seed.

USES Beds and borders, meadow gardens, butterfly gardens, massed. Cut flowers.

SPECIES, VARIETIES, CULTIVARS AND HYBRIDS

L. spicata (spih-*kah*-tah). Also listed as *L. callilepis*. Spike gayfeather. Eastern and Central United States. Grows 2 to 3 feet tall and 2 feet wide. Clumps of leaves to 12 inches long and ½ inch wide. Narrow, 6- to 15-inch spikes of magenta flowers in summer. Several cultivars with white, lavender or blue-purple flowers. Most widely available cultivar is 'Kobold', also sold as 'Gnome', growing 18 to 24 inches tall, with mauve-pink flowers. Zones 3 to 9.

Other species to consider include *L. pychnostachya*, Kansas gayfeather, growing to 5 feet tall with mauve-purple flowers; *L. aspera*, rough gayfeather, and its cultivars, growing 4 to 6 feet tall with lavender-purple or white flowers; *L. scariosa*, tall gayfeather, growing 3 feet tall with larger, more open magenta flowers.

Ligularia
(lig-yew-*lay*-ree-ah)
Golden ray, ligularia
Compositae—daisy family

Bold, dramatic plants, ligularias are best suited for shady sites with moist

Ligularia dentata 'Desdemona'.

or boggy soil and cool summer temperatures. The yellow to orange daisy-like flowers brighten the summer garden and readily attract butterflies.

GROWING GUIDE Partial to half shade, with afternoon shade a must. Humus-rich, moist to boggy soil. A favored food of slugs and snails. Leaves often wilt in the afternoon.

PROPAGATION Division.

USES Shaded beds and borders, near pools and streams. Contrast well with ferns and other fine-textured plants. Butterfly garden.

SPECIES, VARIETIES, CULTIVARS AND HYBRIDS

L. dentata (den-*tah*-tah). Also listed as *L. clivorum*. Bigleaf ligularia. China, Japan. Grows 3 to 4 feet tall and as wide. Clump-forming plants with

Ligularia stenocephala 'The Rocket'.

toothed, heart-shaped, leathery leaves to 20 inches wide. Branched stems of 2- to 5-inch yellow-orange, daisy-like flowers in summer. Flowers often look like they are wilting even when not, so some gardeners cut them off when in bud. Cultivars 'Desdemona' and 'Othello' are similar to each other, with bright red new growth maturing from deep purple to green, and are considered more heat tolerant. Zones 5 to 8.

L. stenocephala (sten-oh-*seph*-ah-lah). Narrow-spiked ligularia. Japan, Northern China. Grows 3 to 5 feet tall and as wide. Dark purple stems with light green, toothed, heart-shaped leaves to 1 foot long. Spikes 12 to 18 inches long with many 1-inch, bright yellow flowers in early summer. Cultivar 'The Rocket' grows 3 to 4 feet tall, with lemon-yellow flowers; it may be listed as a form of *L. przewalskii*, which has deeply cut leaves and flowers with three instead of five ray florets in each flower. Zones 5 to 8.

Limonium
(lye-*mon*-ee-um)
Sea lavender, German statice
Plumbaginaceae—plumbago family

Limonium latifolium.

Like its annual relatives, perennial statice is often grown for its easily dried flowers. In the perennial border, they contribute clouds of flowers that soften and fill in around other plants.

GROWING GUIDE Full sun, with afternoon shade in hotter climates. Any well-drained, neutral soil. May take several years to become established and bloom well. Poor drainage and air circulation may result in crown or root rot.

PROPAGATION Division, but difficult because of the long roots. Seed.

USES Front of beds and borders. Contrasts well with silver-foliaged plants. Cut flowers, fresh or dried.

SPECIES, VARIETIES, CULTIVARS AND HYBRIDS

L. latifolium (lah-tee-*foh*-lee-um). Sea lavender. Bulgaria, Southern Russia. Grows 2 feet tall and as wide. Basal rosettes of leathery, evergreen, spoon-shaped leaves to 10 inches long. Wiry, branching stems bearing masses of tiny, lavender-blue flowers. Cultivars

Limonium tataricum.

available with pink, light blue, violet-blue and dark violet flowers in summer. Tolerant of salt spray. Zones 4 to 9.

L. tataricum (tah-*tah*-rih-kum). German statice. Southeastern Europe. Grows 15 inches tall and as wide. Basal rosettes of leathery, spear-shaped leaves to 6 inches long. Wiry but stiffer, branching stems bearing masses of even tinier, pale blue to white flowers in mid- to late summer. The variety '*Nanum*' grows 9 inches tall, while the variety '*Angustifolium*' has narrower leaves and silvery flowers. Zones 4 to 9.

Linum
(*lye*-num)
Flax
Linaceae—flax family

Besides the annual plant that provides flax fiber for linen and linseed oil, the genus *Linum* also gives us several prolifically flowering perennials for the garden. Forming graceful, upright clumps with small, fine-textured

Linum flavum 'Cloth and Gold'.

leaves, they bloom with delicate-looking, five-petaled flowers of blue, yellow or white for up to six weeks during the summer. Each individual bloom lasts only a day, but many are produced. Plants may not live for many years, but they self-sow well.

GROWING GUIDE Full sun or partial shade in hotter climates. Sandy to average, moist but well-drained soil. Winter protection is beneficial in

Linum perenne.

colder areas. Prune by two-thirds after flowering to keep growth from becoming leggy.

PROPAGATION Division, seed, stem cuttings.

USES Beds and borders, especially dry, sunny spots. Rock gardens. Blue flax in meadow gardens.

SPECIES, VARIETIES, CULTIVARS AND HYBRIDS

L. flavum (*flay*-vum). Golden flax. Europe. Grows 18 inches tall and 12 inches wide. Erect, woody stems with narrow, lance-shaped, blue-green leaves. Masses of 1-inch, golden yellow flowers for a long period in summer. Several superior cultivars, including 'Compactum', which grows to 9 inches tall, and 'Gemmel's Hybrid', growing to 12 inches tall. Both species and cultivars should be grown more. Zones 5 to 8.

L. narbonense (nar-bon-*en*-see). Narbonne flax. Southern Europe. Grows 1 to 2 feet tall and 18 inches wide. Erect stems with stiff, narrow, gray-green leaves to ¾ inch long. Funnel-shaped, 2-inch blue flowers with a white center in late spring and early summer. May require staking. The longest-lived perennial flax. There is a white-flowered form, and the cultivar 'Heavenly Blue', growing to 18 inches tall, with dark blue flowers. Zones 6 to 8, or farther north with winter protection.

L. perenne (peh-*ren*-ee). Blue flax.

Europe. Grows 18 inches tall and 12 inches wide. Blue-green, narrow, 1-inch long leaves. Nearly leafless arching stems bear branched clusters of 1-inch, pale blue flowers for up to 12 weeks in late spring and early summer. Tolerant of heat. Best when planted in groups of five or more. White-flowered forms available, along with several cultivars, mainly with shorter growth and more intensely blue flowers. Zones 5 to 9.

Liriope
(leh-*rye*-oh-pee)
Lilyturf
Liliaceae—lily family

At the turn of the century, liriope was hardly grown. Today, it is the foremost heat-tolerant groundcover. The thickly spreading clumps of evergreen, grass-like leaves are adaptable to a variety of conditions and easily grown. The spikes of tiny lavender flowers bloom in late summer, followed by black fruits. The genus is named after the nymph Liriope.

GROWING GUIDE Full sun to full shade. Almost any soil that is well-drained. Cut plantings to the ground in late winter or early spring to make way for the new year's growth.

PROPAGATION Division.

USES Groundcover, edging or for textural effect at the front of beds and borders.

Liriope muscari.

SPECIES, VARIETIES, CULTIVARS AND HYBRIDS

L. muscari (mus-*kar*-ee). Blue lilyturf. China, Japan. Grows to 18 inches tall and 12 inches wide. Clump-forming plant with arching, evergreen leaves to 1 inch wide. Spikes of densely clustered, tiny lavender flowers in late summer, followed by black berries. Many cultivars, mostly with variegated leaves, but some with white flowers. Zones 6 to 9.

Creeping lilyturf, *L. spicata,* is hardy to Zone 4, has narrower leaves, shorter growth, much more invasive growth.

Lobelia
(loh-*bee*-lee-ah)
Cardinal flower
Campanulaceae—bellflower family

One can be easily smitten by the intensely colored, asymmetrical blooms of cardinal flower, only to have the heart ultimately broken by the short-lived affair. So every three years or so, the relationship must be started anew. This time you promise to

Lobelia cardinalis.

provide just the right amount of shade, plenty of soil moisture and a light winter mulch. The affair won't last any longer, but the pleasure is worth the effort, while the the hummingbirds attracted by the flowers are a bonus.

GROWING GUIDE Full sun in cool-summer climates if the soil is always moist. Otherwise, provide partial to light shade. Moist to wet, humus-rich soil. Summer mulch to keep soil moist, and a very light winter mulch for protection in all climates.

PROPAGATION Division, seeds, stem cuttings. With the right conditions, will self-sow.

Lobelia cardinalis 'Queen Victoria'.

USES Shaded beds and borders. Woodland, pool or streamside or bog gardens.

SPECIES, VARIETIES, CULTIVARS AND HYBRIDS

L. cardinalis (kar-din-*nah*-lis). Cardinal flower. Eastern and Central United States. Grows 3 to 4 feet tall

Lobelia siphilitica.

and 2 feet wide. Basal rosettes of toothed, lance-shaped leaves to 4 inches long. Stout purplish stems bear spiked clusters of deep red, 1½-inch flowers with three-lobed lips, blooming in late summer. Cultivars with white or pink flowers and hybrids with other species, mainly with red flowers and bronze leaves, such as 'Bee's Flame' and 'Queen Victoria'. Zones 3 to 9.

L. x gerardii (jer-ard-*ee*-eye). Also listed as *L.* x *vedrariensis.* Hybrid purple lobelia. Hybrid origin. Grows 3 feet tall and 1 foot wide. Dark green, 6-inch long, lance-shaped leaves. Spikes of two-lipped purple flowers in summer. Somewhat more tolerant of moist but well-drained soil and sun. Zones 5 to 8.

L. siphilitica (si-fih-*lih*-tih-kah). Blue lobelia. Eastern United States. Grows 3 feet tall and 18 inches wide. Clump-forming plants with stiff, unbranched stems and toothed, lance-shaped, light green leaves to 6 inches long. Spikes of 1-inch, light blue flowers in late summer, after *L. cardinalis.* There is a white-flowered form. Zones 4 to 8.

Lunaria
(lew-*nair*-ee-ah)
Perennial honesty
Cruciferae—mustard family

Few gardeners know that there is a perennial form of the plant that enriches them with papery "silver dollars." The perennial's "currency" is oval, 2- to 3-inches long and 1 inch wide; these can be dried and used in flower arrangements just as the biennial money plant. Perennial honesty is easily grown in partially to lightly shaded gardens, naturalizing somewhat, and providing fragrant flowers in late spring and early summer, followed by the silvery seed pods.

GROWING GUIDE Partial shade. Average to humus-rich, moist but well-drained soil.

PROPAGATION Division, seed. Self-sows.

USES Beds and borders. Meadow, woodland or fragrance gardens. Dried arrangements.

Lunaria.

SPECIES, VARIETIES, CULTIVARS AND HYBRIDS

L. rediviva (reh-dih-*veev*-ah). Perennial honesty. Europe. Grows 3 to 4 feet tall and 24 inches wide. Shrubby plants with finely-toothed, heart-shaped, dark green leaves to 5-inches long. Loose, open, branching clusters of pale lavender flowers in late spring and early summer, followed by persistent, silvery-white seed pods. Zones 4 to 8.

Lupines.

Lupinus
(lew-*pye*-nus)
Lupine
Leguminosae—pea family

Perfectly sculpted spikes of intense, brilliant colors are the hallmark of lupines. Their glory is often seen in masses, whether as a hybrid in a cottage garden or Texas bluebonnets carpeting a pasture, but even a single specimen can be stunning. Although there are more than 200 species, many of which are native to the United States, lupine history became inextricably intertwined with the English when gardeners began hybridizing them in the 1890s, culminating in the work of Yorkshire hobbyist George Russell in the early 1900s. Easily grown in the English climate, lupines do best in cool-summer areas of the United States. Gardeners in hotter climates still enjoy their beauty by growing them as short-lived perennials or as annuals planted out in the fall for bloom the following spring.

GROWING GUIDE Full sun to partial shade. Humus-rich, moist but well-drained, acid soil. Deadhead faded flowers to encourage repeat blooming. Use a summer mulch to keep soil moist, and a winter mulch for protection. Slugs and snails can be a problem.

PROPAGATION Stem cuttings or seeds, neither of which is easy. Do not disturb once established. May self-sow.

USES Beds and borders, cottage gardens. As specimen plant or in masses.

SPECIES, VARIETIES, CULTIVARS AND HYBRIDS

Hybrid lupines. Bushy plants with gray- to bright green, fan-like leaves divided into a dozen or so pointed leaflets. Bloom spikes 12 to 24 inches tall, densely packed with pea-like flowers in shades of blue, purple, yellow, red, pink, either solid or bicolored in late spring or early summer. Many cultivars, varying in height and color. Zones 4 to 8.

Lupines.

Lychnis
(*lik*-nis)
Campion, catchfly
Caryophyllaceae—pink family

Although short-lived and diverging greatly in appearance, the various garden campions all have a long blooming season. Flowers are good for cutting, and they are easily grown.

GROWING GUIDE Full sun, with partial shade in hotter climates. Average to humus-rich, moist but well-drained soil.

Lychnis chalcedonica.

PROPAGATION Division, seed.

USES Beds and borders. Cottage gardens. Cut flowers.

SPECIES, VARIETIES, CULTIVARS AND HYBRIDS

L. x *arkwrightii* (ark-*rye*-tee-eye). Arkwright's campion. Hybrid origin. Grows 18 inches tall and 12 inches wide. Bronze green leaves. Clusters of 1½-inch scarlet-orange flowers in summer. Pinch plants in spring to encourage branching. Seed pods add visual interest to the garden. Zones 6 to 8.

L. chalcedonica (chal-see-*don*-ih-kah). Maltese cross. Eastern Russia. Grows 2 to 3 feet tall and 18 inches wide. Clump-forming plant with oval, 4-inch long, dark green leaves. Dense clusters of numerous, 1-inch, cross-shaped scarlet flowers. May need staking. White, pink and double forms available. A favorite "old-fashioned" plant. Zones 4 to 9.

L. coronaria (kor-oh-*nay*-ree-ah). Rose campion. Southern Europe. Grows 2 to 3 feet tall and 18 inches wide. Basal rosettes of gray, woolly, oval leaves to 4 inches long. Branched, woolly stems bear bright magenta, 1-inch flowers profusely in summer. Grows well in dry, poor soils. Short-

Lychnis coronaria 'Alba'.

Lychnis coronaria.

lived but readily self-sows. Varieties with white or carmine-red flowers and cultivars with soft pink flowers. Flower-of-jove (*L. flos-jovis*) is similar, but grows to 18 inches with rose-red flowers and is longer-lived. Zones 4 to 8.

L. x *haageana* (hah-jee-*ay*-nah). Haage campion. Hybrid origin. Grows 18 inches tall and 12 inches wide. Basal clumps of dark green, lance-shaped, 4-inch leaves. Clusters of 2-inch orange-scarlet flowers in summer. Needs full sun and consistent moisture; susceptible to slugs. Zone 4 to 9.

L. viscaria (vis-*kay*-ree-ah). German catchfly. Europe. Grows 12 to 18 inches tall and 12 inches wide. Basal clumps of grassy, dark green leaves to 5 inches long. Strong, sticky stems bear clusters of 1-inch, magenta flowers in early summer. Zones 3 to 8.

Lysimachia

(lye-sim-*ahk*-ee-ah)
Loosestrife
Primulaceae—primrose family

If ever a need arises for calming angry oxen, grab some lysimachia, as the genus is named after King Lysimachus of Thrace, whose legend tells of his using loosestrife to calm a beast pursuing him. Otherwise, loosestrife is useful as a native plant beside streams or in other large, sunny or lightly shaded areas, as the roots tend to spread rapidly.

GROWING GUIDE Full sun to partial shade. Average to humus-rich, moist soil.

PROPAGATION Division, seed.

USES Moist meadow gardens, along streams. Cut flowers.

Lysimachia clethroides.

SPECIES, VARIETIES, CULTIVARS AND HYBRIDS

L. clethroides (kleth-*roi*-deez). Gooseneck loosestrife. China, Japan. Grows 2 to 3 feet tall and 3 feet wide. Spreading, shrubby plants with slightly hairy, oval leaves to 6 inches long. Dense, 12 to 18 inch curving spikes of ½-inch white flowers in late summer. Good for cutting. Zones 3 to 8.

L. ephemerum (ef-*fem*-er-um). Europe. Grows 3 feet tall and 1 foot wide. Noninvasive, upright plants with leathery, lance-shaped, gray-green leaves to 6 inches long. Narrow spikes of small white flowers from mid- to late summer. Zones 6 to 8.

L. nummularia (num-yew-*lah*-ree-ah). Creeping Jenny. Europe. Grows 4 to 8 inches tall and 2 feet wide. Prostrate stems with rounded, 1-inch leaves quickly carpet moist, shady areas. Fragrant yellow, 1-inch flowers in early summer. 'Aurea' has lime-green leaves. Zones 3 to 8.

L. punctata (punk-*tah*-tah). Yellow loosestrife. Central Europe, Asia Minor. Grows 2 feet tall and 1 foot wide. Whorled, spear-shaped leaves to 4 inches long, with each "layer" bearing whorls of 1-inch, yellow flowers with a brown throat throughout summer. Zones 4 to 8.

Lysimachia punctata.

m

Macleya
(mak-*lay*-ah)
Plume poppy
Papaveraceae—poppy family

Macleya cordata.

Sometimes a bold stroke is just what a garden needs to give it some elan. Plume poppy is one dramatically impressive candidate for the job. Both the flowers and seed pods can be used in arrangements.

GROWING GUIDE Full sun, with partial shade in hotter areas. Best if grown in a site sheltered from wind, otherwise staking may be necessary. May spread more than desired.

PROPAGATION Division, seed.

USES Large beds or borders where spreading roots won't cause problems. Cut flowers.

SPECIES, VARIETIES, CULTIVARS AND HYBRIDS
   M. cordata (kor-*dah*-tah). Formerly listed as *Bocconia cordata.* Plume poppy. China, Japan. Grows 5 to 8 feet tall and 4 feet wide. Spreading plant with strong, unbranched stem with deeply lobed, gray-green leaves to 8 inches across; the undersides are felty white. Airy plumes to 1-foot long bear ½-inch, petalless, ivory flowers in summer followed by attractive seed pods. Another species, *M. microcarpa,* is inferior and more invasive. Zones 3 to 8.

Malva
(*mal*-vah)
Mallow
Malvaceae—mallow family

Mallows are part of a large group of related plants that offer upright growth and pink, hibiscus-like flowers. Their form, long blooming period and drought tolerance more than make up for their relatively short life and susceptibility to assorted pests.

GROWING GUIDE Full sun, with partial shade in hotter areas. Average, neutral to alkaline, well-drained soil. Pests such as Japanese beetles, spider mites

Malva moschata.

Malva moschata 'Alba'.

and fungal diseases, are worse in hotter climates.

PROPAGATION Division, seed. Self-sows.

USES Beds and borders.

SPECIES, VARIETIES, CULTIVARS AND HYBRIDS
   M. alcea (ahl-*see*-ah). Hollyhock mallow. Europe. Grows 2 to 4 feet tall and 18 inches wide. Erect, multi-branched stems with slightly hairy, five-lobed, toothed leaves. Pink, lavender, or white 2-inch flowers borne in leaf axils along stems and in terminal clusters from summer into early fall. With very upright growth and rose-pink flowers, the variety 'Fastigiata' is grown most frequently. *M. moschata* is similar but not as showy. Zones 4 to 8.

Marrubium
(mar-*rew*-bee-um)
Horehound
Labiatae—mint family

Because of the softening and blending effect of silver-foliaged plants, gardeners always want to add to the list of possibilities. Silver horehound with

Marrubium vulgare.

its round, wrinkled, woolly leaves, is among the best, as it is one of the few silver-gray perennials that does not rot in hot, humid climates.

GROWING GUIDE Full sun. Sandy to average well-drained soil. Drought tolerant. Tends to sprawl if soil is too fertile. Can be pinched or pruned to encourage bushiness. Can die off if soil is too wet in winter.

PROPAGATION Division, seed. Self-sows.

USES Beds and borders.

SPECIES, VARIETIES, CULTIVARS AND HYBRIDS

M. incanum (in-*kan*-um). Silver horehound. Southern Europe, Asia Minor. 2 to 3 feet tall and 2 feet wide. Shrubby plant with stems near the base becoming woody. The pointed, egg-shaped leaves are up to 2 inches long and covered with gray-white hairs. Whorls of tiny white flowers. The common horehound, *M. vulgare*, is similar but slightly less silver; you can make your own cough drops from it. Zones 3 to 9.

Meconopsis
(mee-koh-*nop*-sis)
Meconopsis
Papaveraceae—poppy family

Meconopsis ranks high on the fantasy-plant list, with gardeners diligently working to create just the right conditions. Why bother? Come across a planting bearing the sky-blue flowers just once …. Of course, gardeners in the Pacific Northwest have the best chance of success, with their cool, damp climate and moist, acid soil, but gardeners elsewhere have been success-

ful. The Welsh version, with golden flowers, is much easier to grow.

GROWING GUIDE Partial shade. Fertile, humus-rich, acid soil that is constantly moist but also well-drained. Provide a summer mulch. Protect from wind or stake taller types.

PROPAGATION Division, fresh seed.

Meconopsis betonicifolia.

USES Woodland gardens. Associates well with other plants with similar requirements, such as rhododendrons, ferns, primulas and rodgersias.

SPECIES, VARIETIES, CULTIVARS AND HYBRIDS

M. betonicifolia (bet-on-iss-ih-*foh*-lee-ah). Himalayan blue poppy. Asia. Grows to 4 feet tall and 18 inches wide. Basal rosettes with toothed, heart-shaped leaves diminishing in size as they progress up the stems. Clusters of outward-facing, blue poppy-like flowers to 3 inches across in late spring and early summer. Zones 6 to 8.

M. cambrica (*kam*-brih-kah). Welsh poppy. Western Europe. Grows

12 inches tall and as wide. Ferny, deeply divided leaves with yellow or orange, 2-inch, poppy-like flowers in summer. The variety 'Flore-pleno' has double flowers. Zones 6 to 8.

M. grandis (*gran*-dis). Blue poppy. Asia. Grows 2 to 4 feet tall and 2 feet wide. Clump-forming plant with toothed, hairy, lance-shaped leaves. Upward-facing, sky-blue to purple, 4- to 5-inch flowers in early summer. Cultivars and hybrids with other species have been developed but are difficult to locate. Zones 6 to 8.

Mertensia
(mer-*ten*-see-ah)
Bluebells
Boraginaceae—borage family

Viewing drifts of Virginia bluebells glorying in the dappled shade at the edge of a woodland in spring can number among life's better moments. They are easily grown and should be added to any shady, moist area where they can be allowed to colonize slowly. As the plants go dormant and disappear by midsummer, some gardeners interplant them with ferns.

Mertensia virginica.

GROWING GUIDE Partial to full shade. Humus-rich, acid, moist but well-drained soil. Best if soil is drier when dormant. Slugs may be a problem.

PROPAGATION Division, fresh seed.

USES Woodland gardens.

SPECIES, VARIETIES, CULTIVARS AND HYBRIDS

M. virginica (vir-*jin*-ih-kuh). Virginia bluebells. Eastern United States. Grows 1 to 2 feet tall and 18 inches wide. Spreading clumps of blue-green, egg-shaped leaves to 6 inches long. Upright stems bear nodding clusters of small pink buds that open to 1-inch-long bluish-purple bells. 'Alba' has white flowers, and 'Rubra' has pink flowers. Zones 3 to 9.

Monarda
(moh-*nar*-dah)
Bee balm, bergamot, Oswego tea
Labiatae—mint family

Long-lived, easily grown, widely adaptable, long blooming season in summer,

Monarda didyma 'Cambridge Scarlet'.

with uniquely shaped flowers that are edible with a minty flavor, good for cutting, attracting hummingbirds and butterflies, and drying, along with the leaves, for potpourri. Sound like the miracle perennial? The monardas, native to North America, certainly have become staples in the garden since their discovery in the seventeenth and eighteenth centuries, but they do have the tragic flaw of susceptibility to mildew. There are several ways to overcome this inconvenience, including keeping the soil evenly moist, growing disease-resistant varieties, and cutting the plants back severely after blooming. Monarda's claim with history is use of the leaves of *M. didyma* as a substitute for black tea during the Revolutionary War.

GROWING GUIDE Full sun to partial shade. Humus-rich, moist but well-drained soil. Deadhead regularly to prolong flowering.

PROPAGATION Division for cultivars; division or seed for species.

USES Beds and borders; naturalized in moist meadows or edges of woodlands; near pools or streams; hummingbird and butterfly gardens. Cut flowers.

SPECIES, VARIETIES, CULTIVARS AND HYBRIDS

M. didyma (*did*-ih-mah). Bee balm, bergamot, Oswego tea. Eastern United States. Grows 2 to 4 feet tall and 2 to 3 feet wide. Spreading plants with upright stems. Dark green, aromatic leaves are pointed, toothed, hairy and egg-shaped, to 6 inches long. Clusters of flowers, each with numerous tubular red flowers surrounding a dense center. Grows naturally along stream banks under overhanging trees, spreading by underground stems. A number of cultivars and hybrids in various shades of red, pink, purple or white. Much effort to create mildew-resistant plants; look for 'Marshall's

Monarda fistulosa.

Delight' and hybrids from breeder Piet Ouldolf, among others. Zones 4 to 9.

M. fistulosa (fiss-tew-*loh*-sah). Wild bergamot. North America. Grows 2 to 4 feet tall and 2 to 3 feet wide. Similar to *M. didyma*, but with leaves slightly more hairy and less toothed. Flowers are lavender to pale pink, with a stem and flower sometimes growing out of previous flower heads. Tolerates drier soil and is less susceptible to mildew. Purple-flowered hybrids, such as 'Violet Queen', are usually listed under *M. didyma*, but usually have this species in the parentage, so drier soil is tolerated and plants have better mildew resistance.

Myosotis
(mye-oh-*soh*-tis)
Forget-me-not
Boraginaceae—borage family

The romantic notion of prolifically blooming forget-me-nots far exceeds their role in the garden, but, nonetheless, they should be considered for the woodland or streamside garden. Although short-lived, they readily self-sow.

GROWING GUIDE Partial to light shade.

Humus-rich, acid, moist but well-drained soil for *M. alpestris*; humus-rich, acid, moist soil for *M. scorpioides*. Thin foliage in summer to reduce leaf rot in *M. alpestris*.

PROPAGATION Division, seed. Self-sows.

USES Woodland gardens or near streams or pools.

SPECIES, VARIETIES, CULTIVARS AND HYBRIDS

M. alpestris (ahl-*pes*-tris). Also listed as *M. sylvestris*. Woodland forget-me-not. Europe. Grows 8 inches tall and as wide. Compact, clump-forming plants with hairy, oval leaves to 3 inches long. Tiny blue flowers with yellow centers open along coiling stems in early spring, with occasional blooming in summer. Several cultivars and hybrids, with flowers of white, pink, or various shades of blue. Zones 3 to 8.

M. scorpioides (skor-pee-*oi*-deez). Also listed as *M. palustris*. Water forget-me-not. Europe. Grows 6 inches tall and 12 inches wide. Prostrate stems with rough, hairy, lance-shaped leaves. Tiny blue flowers with yellow centers open along coiling stems in early spring. Can grow even in shallow water. The variety 'Semperflorens' is more compact and blooms longer. Zones 3 to 8.

---

n

Nepeta
(*nep*-eh-tah)
Nepeta, catnip
Labiatae—mint family

The perennial catnips chosen for their ornamental qualities rather than their appeal to felines are easily grown, can bloom abundantly for a long period and provide fine texture in the garden. The town of Nepet, in Tuscany, is said to be the origin of the genus name.

GROWING GUIDE Full sun, with partial shade recommended for hot, humid climates. Sandy to average well-drained soil. Cut plants back by half after flowering to encourage bushy new growth and repeat flowering. In the spring, prune back dead growth.

PROPAGATION Division for both species; seed for *N. mussinii*, which can self-sow; stem cuttings.

USES Beds and borders, edging, mass plantings.

SPECIES, VARIETIES, CULTIVARS AND HYBRIDS

Nepeta x *faassenii* .

N. x *faassenii* (fah-*sen*-ee-eye). Faaseen's nepeta. Hybrid origin. Cross between *N. mussinii* and *N. nepetella*. Grows 18 to 24 inches tall and 18 inches wide. Vigorous, clump-forming plants with branching stems. Gray-green, toothed, heart-shaped leaves to 1½ inches long. Six-inch spikes of ¼-inch lavender-blue flowers for a long period from early to mid-summer, repeating well in the fall if deadheaded. Sterile, so no seed is produced. Considered superior to *N. mussinii*, but many plants sold as *N.* x *faassenii* are probably *N. mussinii*. Many cultivars, including 'Six Hills Giant', which grows to 3 feet tall with dark violet flowers. Zones 4 to 9.

N. mussinii (muss-*seen*-ee-ye). Persian nepeta. Caucasus. Grows 1 foot tall and as wide. Sprawling stems with hairy, softly toothed, gray-green, heart-

Nepeta mussinii.

shaped leaves to 1 inch long. Spikes of lavender-blue flowers in late spring or early summer, with some repeat if trimmed back. White-flowered form available. Zones 3 to 8.

Nepeta sibirica.

Two other nepetas worth searching out are *N. nervosa* (Zones 6 to 8) and *N. sibirica* (Zones 4 to 8). They grow 2 to 3 feet tall, with larger, brighter green leaves and spikes of pale to bright blue flowers in summer. There are many other species, as well as new cultivars and hybrids of nepeta.

Oenethera tetragona 'Yellow River'.

O

Oenothera

(ee-noh-*thuh*-rah)
Sundrops, evening primrose
Onograceae—evening primrose family

Since they're not related to primroses, and the best types for the garden bloom in the daytime, let's speak of the oenothera as sundrops. Sunny, bright yellow flowers do predominate, but there are also pink-flowered ones. A large genus of many plant types, with several native to North America, the best oenothera for the garden are not necessarily the ones chosen. Still, most are undemanding, easily grown and generous with their flowers.

GROWING GUIDE Full sun. Average, well-drained soil, which should not be overly fertile.

PROPAGATION Division or seed.

USES Many are best allowed to carpet an area by themselves; use more restrained growing forms in beds and borders. Casual growth best for informal designs, cottage gardens and meadow gardens.

Oenothera missouriensis.

SPECIES, VARIETIES, CULTIVARS AND HYBRIDS

O. caespitosa (ses-pih-*toh*-sah). Tufted evening primrose. Western North America. Grows 4 to 8 inches tall and 12 inches across. Stemless plants with clusters of 4-inch, narrow, hairy leaves. Fragrant, 2- to 3-inch flowers are white, aging to pink, and open in the evening. Zones 4 to 7.

O. missouriensis (miz-ur-ee-*en*-sis). Ozark sundrops. Southern and central United States. Grows 12 inches tall and 18 inches wide. Sprawling, spreading plants with red-tinged stems and lance-shaped leaves to 6 inches long. Red-spotted flower buds open on summer afternoons to 5-inch, cup-shaped, yellow blooms. Zones 4 to 8.

O. speciosa (spee-see-*oh*-sah). Evening primrose. Southern United States. Grows 12 to 18 inches tall and 24 inches wide. Rapidly spreading, stoloniferous growth with lobed, lance-shaped leaves to 3 inches long. Cup-shaped, pale pink flowers borne in leaf axils open in evening in early summer. Give plenty of room. Zones 5 to 8.

Hybrid sundrops. A variety of hybrids and cultivars, of both certain and uncertain parentage, mainly with *O. fruticosa* and *O. tetragona,* which suffer taxonomic confusion in the trade. Most grow 1 to 2 feet tall and as wide. Lance-shaped, dark green leaves to 3 inches long. Terminal clusters of yellow, cup-shaped, day-blooming flowers. Look for 'Fireworks', 'Yellow River', 'Highlight', 'Summer Solstice' and 'Youngii', among others. Zones 3 to 8.

Nodding sundrops, *O. perennis,* is widely offered but short-lived and not as showy as the hybrid sundrops.

Ophiopogon

(oh-fee-oh-*poh*-gon)
Mondo grass
Liliaceae—lily family

A strong contender with liriope for most-used edging or groundcover in warmer regions, mondo grass differs in that it is less hardy, with narrower leaves and metallic blue fruits. The introduction of black mondo grass from England added a plant to the gardening repertoire that offers stunning, dark-purple foliage.

GROWING GUIDE Partial to light shade. Moist but well-drained soil. Drought tolerant. May take several years to become established.

PROPAGATION Division, seed.

USES Edging, groundcover, between paving stones.

SPECIES, VARIETIES, CULTIVARS AND HYBRIDS

Ophiopohon var. *nigrescens.*

O. japonicus (jah-*pon*-ih-kus). Mondo grass. Japan. Grows 12 inches tall and as wide. Spreading clumps with dark green, grassy leaves to ¼ inch wide and 12 inches long. Short clusters of pale lilac flowers in summer, often hidden by foliage, followed by metallic blue berries. Several variegated cultivars. Zones 7 to 9.

O. planiscapus var. **'Nigrescens'** (plahn-ih-*skah*-pus nih-*gres*-enz). Black mondo grass. Grows 6 inches tall and 12 inches wide. Slowly spreading clumps of dark purple, grassy leaves. Short clusters of white to pale pink flowers in summer followed by metallic black berries. Contrasts well with Japanese blood grass, blue-leaved grasses, or plants with light green leaves. Zones 6 to 9.

p

Paeonia
(pay-*on*-ee-ah)
Peony
Paeoniaceae—peony family

No garden would be complete without the large, silken blooms of peonies in late spring and early summer. Ubiquitous in gardens but with good reason, peonies are among the longest-lived of perennials, widely adaptable, with flowers readily produced with little effort. Thousands of cultivars and hybrids are available, providing a wide range of flower forms and colors.

GROWING GUIDE Full sun, partial shade in hotter climates. Humus-rich, moist but well-drained soil. Important to set the eyes, or red sprouts, at the proper depth, about 1 inch below the soil line. Taller types may need staking. To prevent botrytis blight, cut off all stems and leaves in the fall. Peonies need a certain number of chilling hours to break dormancy, so in hotter areas select cultivars proven in these areas; also it's better to grow early to mid-season and single or Japanese flower forms in these areas. Use a winter mulch where needed to prevent heaving. Use fertilizer cautiously, as too much results in foliage rather than flowers.

PROPAGATION Best left undisturbed, but can be divided in the fall, cutting roots apart with a knife, with each piece having three eyes.

Paeonia.

Paeonia lactiflora.

USES Beds and borders, in front of shrubs, as a low hedge, or beside a wall or fence. Cut flowers.

SPECIES, VARIETIES, CULTIVARS AND HYBRIDS

P. lactiflora (lak-tih-*floh*-rah). Chinese peony. Most peonies offered for sale and grown in gardens are cultivars or hybrids, rather than the species. Many of the thousands of offerings are most closely related to the common, or Chinese, peony (*P. lactiflora*). These are bushy plants growing 2 to 3 feet tall with with large, divided, dark green, shiny leaves. Plants bloom in late spring, with 3- to 6-inch flowers in shades of white, creamy yellow, pink or red and in one of five forms: single, with eight petals and a prominent clusters of yellow stamens; Japanese, with a carnation-like center and a saucer-shaped petal collar; anemone, similar to Japanese but shaggier; semidouble, with stamens apparent; and double, with stamens missing or hidden. Zones 3 to 8.

P. officinalis (oh-fis-ih-*nay*-lis). Common peony, Memorial Day peony. Similar to the Chinese peony with 4-inch single crimson flowers with yellow stamens. Several cultivars with various shades of red or double flowers. Zones 3 to 8.

Other peonies to consider include *P. veitchii, P. tenuifolia,* and *P. mlokosewitschii.* Tree peonies, *P. suffruticosa,* are woody plants.

Papaver orientale.

Papaver
(pah-*pah*-ver)
Poppy
Papaveraceae—poppy family

Poppies are beloved for their papery translucent petals in pastels or brilliant reds and oranges. The Oriental poppy is the only species among the hundred or so in the genus that is reliably perennial and long-lived. Others, such as the Iceland poppy, are best grown as annuals, along with the other truly annual species. Flowers are good for cutting if picked just as the buds begin to open in early morning and the stem ends are seared in a flame.

GROWING GUIDE Full sun. Average, well-drained soil. Poor drainage in winter is usually fatal. Staking may be necessary with taller types. Both a summer and winter mulch is beneficial. Plants go dormant after flowering, so plant poppies where other plants will fill in around them.

PROPAGATION Division, root cuttings.

USES Beds and borders.

Papaver orientale.

SPECIES, VARIETIES, CULTIVARS AND HYBRIDS

P. orientale (oh-ree-en-*tah*-lee). Oriental poppy. Asia. Grows 2 to 4 feet tall and 2 to 3 feet wide. Silver-green, rough-textured stems and leaves, which are lobed and toothed. Cup-shaped flowers in early summer to 4 inches across, often with a black eye, in shades of scarlet, red, orange, apricot, salmon, pink or white. Zones 2 to 7.

Patrinia
(pah-*tree*-nee-ah)
Patrinia
Valerianaceae—valerian family

The tiny, long-lasting flowers of patrinia are beautiful even when faded, so the airy effect, reminiscent of lady's mantle, benefits the garden for many

Patrinia scabiosifolia.

weeks. The quality of fragrance is questionable, smelling somewhat of dogs. The genus is named after a French naturalist, E. L. Patrin (1724–1815).

GROWING GUIDE Partial to light shade. Humus-rich, acid, moist but well-drained soil.

PROPAGATION Division, seed.

USES Beds and borders, blending other flowers and plants together.

SPECIES, VARIETIES, CULTIVARS AND HYBRIDS

P. gibbosa (gib-*bose*-ah). Japan. Grows to 2 feet tall and 1 foot wide. Slowly spreading, clump-forming plants with shiny, toothed, egg-shaped leaves to 6 inches long. Branched clusters of tiny yellow flowers in summer. Zones 5 to 8.

P. scabiosifolia (scab-ee-oh-sih-*foh*-lee-ah). Eastern Asia. Grows 3 to 5 feet tall and 2 feet wide. Slowly spreading, basal clumps of toothed, egg-shaped leaves, with stem leaves divided. Erect, leafy stems with branched clusters of numerous tiny yellow flowers, followed by attractive seeds. Self-sows. Zones 5 to 8.

Penstemon
(pen-*stay*-mon)
Beard tongue
Scrophulariaceae—figwort family

Many species of penstemon are native to North America, with certain ones having gone to Europe to get "refinement." They returned as cultivars and hybrids, with great variation in flower color and plant size. Upright plants with spiky clusters of pastel to scarlet, snapdragon like flowers, penstemons are not particularly long-lived, but are easily grown. The genus name comes from the Greek, for five stamens.

GROWING GUIDE Full sun. Fertile,

humus-rich, moist but well-drained soil. Cannot survive poorly drained winter conditions. Light winter mulch prevents heaving.

PROPAGATION Seed, stem cuttings.

USES Beds and borders.

SPECIES, VARIETIES, CULTIVARS AND HYBRIDS

P. barbatus (bar-*bay*-tus). Beard tongue. Southwestern United States. Grows 2 to 3 feet tall and 18 inches wide. Basal tufts of egg-shaped leaves to 6 inches long. In summer, erect stems bear spikes of slightly nodding, tubular, 1-inch-long scarlet flowers with a bearded lower lip. Most cultivars grow 12 to 18 inches tall with white, pink, orange or scarlet flowers. Zones 3 to 8.

P. campanulatus (kam-pan-yew-*lay*-tus). Harebell penstemon. Central America. Grows 2 feet tall and as wide. Toothed, lance-shaped leaves to 3 inches long and tubular purple, violet, or white flowers. One parent of a number of good garden plants, including 'Apple Blossom' and 'Evelyn', both with pink flowers. Zones 6 to 8.

Penstemon Barbatus 'Prairie Dusk'.

P. digitalis (dij-ih-*tay*-lis). Foxglove penstemon. Eastern and Central United States. Grows 3 feet tall and 2 feet wide. Clump-forming plants with lance-shaped leaves to 7 inches long, becoming smaller up the erect stems. Spikes of bell-shaped whitish-pink flowers in early summer. 'Husker Red', with purple-red leaves and stems and white-flushed purple flowers, is popular. Better for hot, humid climates than the western North American natives. Zones 3 to 9.

Perovskia
(peh-roff-skee-ah)
Russian sage
Labiatae—mint family

Perovskias provide a feathery haze of fine-textured gray foliage and tiny purple-blue flowers in summer into fall. Native from Iran to northwest India, most of the plants grown in gardens are hybrid seedlings of *P. abrotanoides* and *P. atriplicifolia*. There is great variation among the plants sold as Russian sage, including foliage ranging from undissected to finely divided, plant form being highly branched and shrubby to sparsely stemmed. It is best to buy plants that are known to be vegetatively propagated from exceptional plants, no matter what the name.

GROWING GUIDE Full sun. Average, well-drained soil. Drought tolerant. Must have good winter drainage. Cut back plants in spring to encourage bushy growth.

PROPAGATION Stem cuttings.

USES Beds and borders, especially good paired with daylilies and any plant with daisy-like flowers.

SPECIES, VARIETIES, CULTIVARS AND HYBRIDS
   P. atriplicifolia (ah-trih-plis-ih-f*oh*-lee-ah). Russian sage. Most plants sold under this species name are seedlings

Perovskia atriplicifolia.

of various parentage. Grows 3 to 5 feet tall and 4 feet wide. Shrubby plant with variably cut and toothed leaves to about 2 inches long and 1 inch wide. Branched spikes 12 to 15 inches long with tiny tubular lavender-blue flowers for up to 4 months from midsummer to early fall. Zones 5 to 9.

Phlomis
(*floh*-miss)
Jerusalem sage
Labiatae—mint family

Phlomis fruticosa.

A well-grown plant of Jerusalem sage is rather spectacular, with its rounded, bushy form punctuated with whorls of yellow flowers spaced along the stems from base to top. There are other species in this genus that are more

tender and therefore useful in Zones 7 to 9, including the yellow-flowered *P. russeliana* and the pink-flowered *P. samia*.

GROWING GUIDE Full sun, with partial shade in areas with hot, humid summers. Humus-rich, moist but well-drained soil is best, but dry soil is tolerated.

PROPAGATION Division, seed.

USES Beds and borders.

SPECIES, VARIETIES, CULTIVARS AND HYBRIDS
   P. fruticosa (frew-tih-*koh*-sah). Jerusalem sage. Bushy plants with upright stems. Coarse, wrinkled, and woolly oval leaves to 4 inches long. Plants are evergreen from Zone 7 south. Twenty to 30 flowers surround the stem at each whorl of leaves. Blooming time depends on the locale, with spring bloom in the South, summer bloom in the North, and winter bloom in Southern California. Zones 4 to 8.

Phlox
(flox)
Phlox
Polemoniaceae—phlox family

Among the plants native to Eastern North America, no other genus can compare with that of *Phlox* in contributing such important perennials to the garden. From the bright patches of creeping phlox in

Phlox divaricata.

early spring to the last of the garden phlox blooming in summer, these plants provide gardeners with readily available, easily grown, long-blooming masses of color in both sunny and shaded areas. When choosing phlox for the garden, be sure to consider some of the lesser-known kinds, which are some of the most carefree. All phlox bear the distinctive, five-petaled, flat-faced flowers.

GROWING GUIDE Full sun to light shade, depending on the species. Fertile, humus-rich, moist but well-drained soil. Grow disease-resistant varieties to prevent problems with mildew, and thin out *P. paniculata* cultivars to four to six stems to increase air circulation and keep foliage dry when watering. With soil kept evenly moist, spider mite problems are lessened. Deadhead to maintain vigor and prevent self-sowing.

PROPAGATION Division, seed, stem cuttings.

USES The taller types are best for beds and borders; use the shorter, spreading types in wildflower and woodland gardens; the mat-forming ones are ideal for spilling over walls, the fronts of borders, edging walks or rock gardens. Cut flowers.

Phlox paniculata.

SPECIES, VARIETIES, CULTIVARS AND HYBRIDS

P. divaricata (dih-var-ih-*kah*-tah). Wild blue phlox, woodland phlox. Eastern North America. Grows 1 foot tall and as wide. Plants spread slowly by creeping rhizomes and trailing, non-flowering shoots that root at the nodes. Dark green, 2-inch, oblong leaves. Small, loose clusters of slightly fragrant, 1½-inch, light blue flowers. Several cultivars, most with flowers in various shades of blue or pink, but the best is 'Fuller's White' growing to 8 inches tall. *P. x chattahoochee*, often listed as a cultivar, is thought to be a cross between *P. divaricata laphamii* and *P. pilosa*; the pale blue flowers have a purple eye. Grow in partial shade with humus-rich, moist but well-drained soil. Zones 3 to 9.

Phlox stolonifera.

P. maculata (mak-yew-*lah*-tah). Spotted phlox, wild sweet william. Eastern North America. Grows 2 to 3 feet tall and 2 feet wide. Erect plants with hairy stems often mottled red. Roundly lance-shaped, glossy, dark green leaves to 4 inches long. Cone-shaped clusters of fragrant, pink flowers in early summer. Cultivars often replacing garden phlox because of their mildew resistance. More and more new cultivars, mainly with white or pink flowers, some with a darker eye. Grow in full sun in humus-rich, moist but well-drained soil. Zones 3 to 9.

P. paniculata (pah-nik-*yew*-lah-tah). Garden phlox. Eastern North America. Grows 3 to 4 feet tall and 2 feet wide. Clump-forming plants with stiff, erect, leafy stems. Oblong leaves to 6 inches long. Pyramidal clusters of ¾-inch flowers from midsummer to early fall. Great number of cultivars, with some variation in flowering time and with flowers in many shades of

Phlox stolonifera.

purple, pink, red and white, often with darker-colored eyes. Susceptible to mildew and spider mites. Thin to four to six stems. Full sun with humus-rich, moist but well-drained soil. Provide afternoon shade in hotter climates. Zones 4 to 8.

P. stolonifera (stoh-loh-*nif*-er-ah). Creeping phlox. Eastern North America. Grows 6 to 9 inches tall and 12 inches wide. Spreading plants, with stoloniferous roots and non-flowering shoots rooting at the nodes. Spoon-shaped leaves to 1 to 3 inches long. Clusters of 2 to 3¾-inch, lavender-blue flowers in spring. A number of cultivars, mainly with flowers of white or various shades of pink or blue. 'Sherwood Purple' is noted for its purple-blue, highly fragrant flowers. Excellent ground cover for shade. Zones 2 to 8.

P. subulata (sub-yew-*lah*-tah). Moss phlox, creeping phlox. Eastern North America. Grows 6 to 9 inches tall and 12 inches wide. Creeping mounds with narrow, linear, ½-inch-long leaves. Great numbers of ½- to ¾-inch flowers with notched petals completely cover the plants in early

Phlox subulata.

Polygonatum odoratum 'Variegatum'.

America. Grows 1 to 3 feet tall and 2 feet wide. Arching stems with 4-inch leaves. Pairs of greenish-white flowers beneath the leaves in spring, with dark blue berries in fall. A variant is the giant Solomon's seal, sometimes listed as *P. commutatum, P. canaliculatum* or *P. giganteum*, it grows from 3 to 7 feet tall with 7-inch leaves and white flowers in clusters of three to eight. Hybrids include forms with double flowers or variegated leaves. Zones 3 to 9.

P. odoratum (oh-door-*ah*-tum). Fragrant Solomon's seal. Europe, Asia. Grows 2 feet tall and as wide. Angular to ridged, arching stems with 4-inch leaves. Fragrant, greenish-white, bell-shaped flowers, produced either singly or in pairs. The cultivar *P. odoratum thunbergii* 'Variegatum', with creamy-white leaf edges, is among the most elegant plants for shaded gardens. Zones 3 to 9.

Polygonum
(poh-lig-oh-num)
Fleeceflower, knotweed
Polygonaceae—buckwheat family

Anyone who has ever fought knotweed in the garden may wonder why you'd actually try to grow it, but there are a few civilized members that can make a positive contribution, albeit with plenty of room. The genus *Polygonum* has been redirected to *Persicaria* and *Fallopia*, so both old and new names are given below.

GROWING GUIDE Full sun to partial shade. Humus-rich, moist but well-drained soil. Must have at least afternoon sun in hotter climates to prevent leaf scorching. May be bothered by Japanese beetles. Prune to control spreading growth.

PROPAGATION Division.

Polygonum affine 'Donald Lowndes'.

Polygonum amplexicaule 'Inverleith'.

USES Beds and borders, groundcover.

SPECIES, VARIETIES, CULTIVARS AND HYBRIDS

Polygonum affine (ah-fee-nee). (*Persicaria affinis*). Himalayan fleeceflower. Himalayas. Grows 12 inches tall and as wide. Spreading, mat-forming plants with semiwoody stems. Lance-shaped, glossy, dark green leaves to 4 inches long. Leaves turn bronze in the fall and persist until spring. In summer to early fall, dense, 2- to 3-inch spikes of pinkish-red flowers rise above the foliage. Several cultivars, but 'Donald Lowndes' is among the best. Zones 3 to 7.

P. amplexicaule (am-plex-ih-cawl-luh). (*Persicaria amplexicaulis*). Himalayas. Grows 4 feet tall and as wide. Large, leafy plant with dark green, egg-shaped leaves to 6 inches long. Numerous thin, 6-inch spikes of red flowers from summer into fall. Several cultivars with red, pink, or white flowers. Zones 5 to 8.

P. bistorta 'Superbum' (biss-tor-tah sue-per-bum). (*Persicaria bistorta*). Europe, Asia. Grows 2 to 3 feet tall and 2 feet wide. Vigorous, clump-forming plants with oval leaves to 6 inches long and a prominently white midrib. Dense spikes, 4 to 6 inches long, of pink flowers in early summer, held high above the foliage. May rebloom in late summer if soil remains moist and cool. Zones 3 to 8.

Porteranthus
(por-ter-*an*-thus)
Bowman's root
Rosaceae—rose family

Woodland gardens needn't be limited to spring-blooming plants. Bowman's root brings graceful growth and delightful starry flowers to the woodland garden in summer.

Porteranthus trifoliata.

GROWING GUIDE Partial to half shade. Humus-rich, moist but well-drained soil.

PROPAGATION Division, seed.

USES Beds and borders, woodland gardens.

SPECIES, VARIETIES, CULTIVARS AND HYBRIDS
    P. trifoliata (trih-foh-lee-*ah*-tah). Also listed as *Gillenia trifoliata*. Bowman's root. Eastern North America. Grows 2 to 4 feet tall and 2 feet wide. Bushy, clump-forming plants with reddish stems and dark green, lance-shaped, deeply cut leaves. Masses of star-shaped, white flowers to 2 inches wide in summer. Zones 4 to 8.

Potentilla
(poh-ten-*till*-ah)
Cinquefoil, potentilla
Rosaceae—rose family

Potentillas are mainly thought of as woody shrubs for the garden, but a few of the 500 or so species are worthwhile perennials. Both the leaves and flowers resemble those of strawberries, with flower colors including white, pink, yellow and red. The genus name comes from the Latin *potens*, powerful, a reference to the medicinal properties of some species.

GROWING GUIDE Full sun, with partial shade in hotter climates. Average, well-drained soil. Drought-tolerant.

PROPAGATION Division, seed.

USES Beds and borders, rock gardens.

SPECIES, VARIETIES, CULTIVARS AND HYBRIDS
    P. x menziesii (men-zee-see-eye). Hybrid cinquefoil. Hybrid origin. Grows 12 to 18 inches tall and as wide. Open, clump-forming plants with silver-gray foliage held on long stems. Sprays of 1-inch, single or semidouble flowers in brilliant shades of red, orange or yellow. Zones 5 to 8.
    P. nepalensis (nep-ah-len-sis). Nepal cinquefoil. Nepal. Grows 18 inches tall and 2 feet wide. Open, clump-forming plants with hairy

Potentilla atrosanguinea.

leaves held on long stems. Produces sprays of 1-inch carmine or orange-scarlet flowers for a long period in summer. Zones 5 to 8.

Primula
(*prim*-yew-lah)
Primrose
Primulaceae—primrose family

It's hard to imagine spring without primroses, even if it only means setting out a few plants from the grocery. But with over 400 species and innumerable cultivars, primroses offer a vast array of forms and colors for the garden. Sometimes considered strictly plants for cool-summer climates, many of these spring-blooming plants are easily grown throughout the country with help from the specialist mail-order nurseries and the American Primrose Society.

Primula denticulata.

GROWING GUIDE Growing requirements vary from species to species, but generally primroses are plants for partial shade and humus-rich, moist but well-drained soil. Provide both summer and winter mulch. Plants are susceptible to slugs, snails, black vine weevils, aphids, and rust and leaf spot diseases.

PROPAGATION Division, seed.

USES Varies with species, but basically for woodland gardens, planted under shrubs, near streams or pools, or rock gardens.

Primula japonica.

SPECIES, VARIETIES, CULTIVARS AND HYBRIDS

Primula x *ployantha.*

P. auricula (ow-*rik*-yew-lah). Auricula primrose. European Alps. Grows 6 inches tall and as wide. Thick, oval leaves to 6 inches long. Stems and flowers densely coated with the

Primula x *polyantha.*

powdery substance called farina. Clusters of fragrant yellow flowers in early spring. The variety *ciliata* does not have farina and flowers are not fragrant. Cultivars with red or yellow flowers. Partial shade with alkaline, gritty soil. Zones 3 to 8.

P. denticulata (den-tik-yew-*lah*-tah). Drumstick primrose. Himalayas. Grows 12 inches tall and as wide. Spoon-shaped, finely toothed leaves, 4 inches long at flowering, maturing to 12 inches long. Globular clusters of lavender, white or pink flowers with

Primula sieboldii.

yellow eyes in early spring. One of the easiest to grow. Many cultivars. Zones 5 to 8.

P. japonica (ja-*pon*-ih-kah). Japanese primrose. Japan. Grows 1 to 2 feet tall and 12 to 18 inches wide. Vigorous, spreading species for wet soil. Toothed, lobed, spoon-shaped leaves to 12 inches long. Sturdy flower stems bear successive whorls, called candelabras, of 1-inch purple, magenta, pink or white flowers in late spring. Many cultivars and related species. Zones 5 to 7.

P. x polyantha (pah-lee-*anth*-ah). Polyantha primrose. Hybrid origin. Grows 8 to 12 inches tall and 10 inches wide. Basal rosettes of textured, oval leaves. Clusters of 1½-inch flowers on 4- to 6-inch stems in early spring. Vast number of colors, either single or bicolor. Important plant for potted-plant market; these can be transplanted outdoors. Combines well with bleeding hearts, small hostas, hellebores, bloodroot and other spring-blooming perennials for partial shade with humus-rich, moist but well-drained soil. Zones 3 to 8.

P. sieboldii (see-*bold*-ee-eye). Siebold primrose. Japan. Grows 12 inches tall and as wide. Wrinkled, heart-shaped, scalloped-edged, downy leaves to 4 inches long. Flower stems to 12 inches tall with clusters of 1½-inch flowers of purple, pink or white. Foliage goes dormant in summer. Partial to half shade with humus-rich, moist but well-drained soil. Zones 4 to 8.

P. vulgaris (vul-*gah*-ris). English primrose. Europe. Grows 6 to 8 inches tall and as wide. Toothed, wrinkled, roundly lance-shaped, bright green leaves, 3 inches long when flowering, maturing to 6 inches long. Tubular, 1-inch long, pale yellow flowers in spring.

Primula vulgaris.

Subspecies with white or pink flowers. Naturally grows in woodlands and meadows, so tolerates a wider range of conditions than many primroses. Zones 5 to 8.

Prunella
(pruh-*nell*-ah)
Self-heal
Labiatae—mint family

Prunella x *webbiana.*

The name may imply something that looks like one of Cinderella's sisters, but in fact, self-heal is a rather pretty, though diminutive, spreading plant. Forming dense mats of foliage, the plants bloom profusely in summer. Both the common and botanical names refer to the medicinal uses of certain species, with the genus name derived from the German *brunellen*, for an inflammation thought to be cured by the plant.

GROWING GUIDE Full sun to partial shade. Any moist soil. Deadhead flowers to prevent self-sowing.

PROPAGATION Division, seed.

USES Groundcover, particularly near streams or pools.

SPECIES, VARIETIES, CULTIVARS AND HYBRIDS

P. x webbiana (web-ee-*ah*-nah).

Hybrid self-heal. Hybrid origin. Grows to 8 inches tall and 18 inches wide. Mat-forming plants with dark green, egg-shaped leaves to 2 inches long. Whorled clusters of hooded and lipped ½-inch flowers in summer. Several cultivars with various flower colors, including white, purple-blue, lavender, red and pink, with 'White Loveliness' bearing larger flowers than normal. Zones 5 to 8.

Pulmonaria
(pul-moh-*nar*-ee-ah)
Lungwort
Boraginaceae—borage family

Pulmonaria 'Roy Davidson'.

Generally thought of as a subtle plant, pulmonarias can have a significant impact on the spring garden, particularly if some of the showier cultivars are planted in large drifts. Pulmonarias are characterized by spotted leaves and spring-blooming flowers that are often pink in bud but opening to blue. Both the genus and common names refer to the medicinal use of the plant for lung ailments in the sixteenth and seventeenth centuries, based on the "doctrine of signatures," or that the outward appearance of a plant suggested its medicinal uses.

GROWING GUIDE Partial to full shade. Humus-rich, moist but well-drained soil. Provide a summer mulch to keep soil moist. Plants spread by creeping roots, but are seldom invasive.

PROPAGATION Division.

USES Beds and borders. Among the best of groundcovers for shady areas, particularly under trees and shrubs or massed along a path.

SPECIES, VARIETIES, CULTIVARS AND HYBRIDS

P. angustifolia (an-gus-tih-*foh*-lee-ah). Blue lungwort. Europe. Grows 9 to 12 inches tall and 18 to 24 inches wide. Lance-shaped, unspotted, bristly, dark green leaves 8 to 12 inches long. Little sprays of funnel-shaped, nodding flowers, pink bud, open to deep blue in early spring. Makes a good groundcover under spring-blooming shrubs like forsythia and competes well with trees and shrubs for moisture and nutrients. Several cultivars, all very similar, with dark blue flowers. Zones 2 to 8.

P. longifolia (long-gih-*foh*-lee-ah). Long-leaf lungwort. Europe. Grows 9 to 12 inches tall and 18 to 24 inches wide. Narrow, pointed, spotted leaves 12 to 18 inches long. Dense sprays of vivid, purple-blue, funnel-shaped flowers in mid-spring. Holds up well in hot-summer climates. Zones 3 to 8.

P. rubra (*rew*-brah). Red lungwort. Europe. Grows 12 to 18 inches tall and 24 inches wide. Lance-shaped, velvety, pale green, unspotted leaves that are evergreen in milder areas. Sprays of coral-red, tubular flowers appear before the foliage in very early spring. Several cultivars, with flowers in various shades of red, pink and salmon. Zones 4 to 7.

P. saccharata (sah-kah-*rah*-tah). Bethelem sage. Europe. Grows 12 to 18 inches tall and 2 feet wide. Handsome

Pulmonaria saccharata 'Sissinghurst White'.

leaves three times as long as wide, heavily spotted with silver, gray or white; evergreen in milder climates. Showy flower clusters in early spring, with pink buds opening to funnel-shaped blue flowers. Many excellent cultivars with various leaf markings and flower color, including shades of blue, pink, or white. Zones 3 to 8.

······················

r

······················

Ranunculus
(rah-*nun*-kew-lus)
Buttercup
Ranunculaceae—buttercup family

Ranunculus aconitifolius.

Buttercups are found growing around the world, with many being invasive weeds but a few providing their cheerful flowers in a more restrained manner. The genus name is derived from the Latin *rana*, frog, alluding to the wet soil many species prefer.

GROWING GUIDE Full sun to partial shade. Moist, well-drained soil.

PROPAGATION Division, seed.

USES Beds and borders.

SPECIES, VARIETIES, CULTIVARS AND HYBRIDS

R. aconitifolius (ah-kon-ee-tih-*foh*-lee-us). Aconite buttercup. Europe. Grows 2 to 3 feet tall and as wide. Glossy, dark green, fan-shaped leaves divided into three to five parts. Large, open, branching sprays of

1-inch white flowers in late spring and early summer. The varieties are grown more than the species, including 'Flore Pleno', with double white flowers; 'Platanifolius' ('Pleniflorus'), with large, single flowers; and 'Luteus Plenus', with double yellow flowers. Zones 5 to 8.

R. acris **'Stevenii'** (*ay*-kris steh-*ven*-ee-eye). Steven's buttercup. Grows 3 to 4 feet tall and 2 feet wide. Leaves divided into three to seven sections. Large, open, branching sprays of 1-inch yellow flowers in spring. Not invasive, as the species is. Zones 3 to 7.

Ratibida
(rah-*tih*-bih-dah)
Prairie coneflower, Mexican hat
Compositae—daisy family

From the prairies and plains of the southwestern United States comes this drought-tolerant plant with colorful daisy-like flower with prominent centers. These high-domed centers surrounded by drooping yellow, red-brown or mahogany rays provide the source of the common name.

GROWING GUIDE Full sun. Any well-drained soil.

PROPAGATION Division, seed.

USES Beds and borders, meadow gardens, drought-tolerant gardens.

SPECIES, VARIETIES, CULTIVARS AND HYBRIDS
R. columnifera (col-um-*nif*-er-ah). Mexican hat, prairie coneflower. Central and southwestern North

Ratibida columnifera.

Ratibida pinnata.

America. Grows 2 to 3 feet tall and 18 inches wide. Coarse, hairy, gray-green leaves divided into seven to nine segments. Flowers borne singly on long stalks; yellow ray flowers surrounding 1½ inch-tall gray to tan central cone. The variety *pulcherrima* has mahogany-red and yellow ray flowers. Zones 3 to 9.

Ratibida columnifera.

R. pinnata (pin-*nay*-tah). Gray-head coneflower, green coneflower, drooping coneflower. North America. Grows 4 feet tall and 18 inches wide. Coarse, hairy leaves divided into three to five leaflets. Long stems bear flowers with golden yellow rays and a gray or green ¾-inch-tall central cone. Zones 3 to 9.

Rheum
(*ree*-um)
Rhubarb
Polygonaceae—buckwheat family

Rheum palmatum.

Few temperate plants are as boldly exotic as the rhubarbs, whether you choose a strictly ornamental species or the edible kind. The advantage of edible rhubarb is that it is easy to grow, and you get dessert. Care and attention is the price to pay for the striking ornamental types. Either way, the adventurous spirit brings rewards.

GROWING GUIDE Partial to light shade for ornamental types; edible rhubarb can withstand both full sun to partial shade. Fertile, humus-rich, constantly moist but well-drained soil. Remove flower buds on edible types prior to blooming; remove faded flower spikes on ornamental types. Both summer and winter mulches are beneficial. Takes several years to become established.

PROPAGATION Division, seed.

USES Beds and borders for both types, or near streams and pools or bog gardens for ornamental types.

R. rhabarbarum (rah-bar-*bar*-um). Rhubarb. Manchuria. Grows 3 to 4 feet tall and as wide. Clump-forming plants with celery-like, green or red stems to 2 feet long. Heart-shaped, wavy, dark green leaves to 1½ feet long. 'MacDonald' and 'Cherry' have red stems. Zones 4 to 8.

R. palmatum (pahl-*may*-tum). Ornamental rhubarb. China. Grows 5 to 8 feet tall and 4 to 6 feet wide. Fan-like, deeply cut, toothed, heart-shaped, dark green leaves to 3 feet wide. Branched 2-foot spikes of white, pink or red flowers in early summer. Cultivars offer purple foliage that becomes green by summer, staying purple-red underneath. Zones 5 to 7.

Rodgersia
(rod-*jer*-see-ah)
Rodgersia
Saxifragaceae—saxifrage family

Rodgersia aesculifolia.

Only a few rodgersias are needed to make a strong architectural statement near a stream or other water feature, for they are large, bold plants. With the right site, they are worth the effort needed to meet their requirements. The genus is named after Rear Admiral John Rodgers of the U.S. Navy, who was in charge of the expedition during which rodgersias were first brought to the States from Asia.

GROWING GUIDE Partial to light shade. Humus-rich, moist soil. Can tolerate moist but well-drained soil. Does not do well in areas with hot, humid summers. Subject to leaf scorch if it gets too much sun or soil becomes too dry. May take several years to establish.

PROPAGATION Division, seed.

USES Beds or borders, near woodland streams or pools. Combines well with hostas.

R. aesculifolia (ess-kih-*foh*-lee-ah). Fingerleaf rodgersia. China. Grows 3 to 5 feet tall and 4 feet wide. Clump-forming plants with fan-shaped, bronze-tinged, toothed leaves divided into seven leaflets, each to 10 inches long. Clusters to 2 feet tall of fragrant, ivory to pink flowers in summer. Bronzeleaf rodgersia, *R. podophylla*, is similar, but with five-parted leaves. Zones 5 to 6.

R. pinnata (pin-*nah*-tah). Featherleaf rodgersia. China. Grows 3 to 4 feet tall and as wide. Clump-growing plants with bronze-tinged leaves with five to nine toothed, lance-shaped leaflets to 8 inches long. Branched, dense clusters of rose-red flowers in late spring. Several cultivars with flowers in white or shades of red or pink, with 'Superba' among the best. Zones 5 to 7.

R. tabularis (tab-yew-*lay*-ris). Also listed as *Astilboides tabularis*. Shieldleaf rodgersia. China, Korea. Grows 2 to 3 feet tall and as wide. Leaves are circular, and shallowly lobed, 2 to 3 feet across, with the stem attached to the middle. Plumy spikes of creamy white flowers. Zones 5 to 7.

Rudbeckia
(rud-*bek*-ee-ah)
Black-eyed Susan, orange coneflower
Compositae—daisy family

Black-eyed Susans, brightening fields and roadsides in summer over much of the United States, are matched in tended gardens—private, corporate and governmental—with the cultivar 'Goldsturm', bred in Germany in 1937. Certainly, rudbeckias are easily grown, long-lived, long-blooming plants that deserve the attention. Their ubiquity can be accepted when well-used, particularly in creating warm-color gardens. They also provide cut flowers, and the cones remaining after the flowers have faded provide interest in the winter landscape.

GROWING GUIDE Full sun. Average to moist but well-drained soil.

PROPAGATION Division, seed.

USES Beds and borders, meadow gardens, massed in large drifts. Cut flowers.

Rudbeckia fulgida 'Goldsturm'.

R. fulgida (*full*-jih-dah). Orange coneflower. United States. Grows 2 to 3 feet tall and 18 to 24 inches wide. Erect, clump-forming plants with toothed, lance-shaped, hairy, dark green leaves to 6 inches long. Branching stems bear 2- to 3-inch orange-yellow daisy-like flowers with brown-black centers from summer to fall. The cultivar 'Goldsturm' grows to 2 feet tall with 4-inch flowers; it should come only from vegetatively propagated plants as seed-grown strains are highly variable. Zones 3 to 9.

R. lanciniata (lass-in-ee-*ay*-tah). Cutleaf coneflower. North America. Grows 4 to 6 feet tall and 3 to 4 feet wide. Vigorous, clump-forming plants with hairy stems and lance-shaped, deeply cut, toothed leaves. Branching stems with 3- to 4-inch flowers with drooping yellow rays and green centers in summer. 'Golden Glow' grows 3 to 5 feet tall with double, golden yellow flowers. Zones 3 to 9.

R. nitida (*nit*-ih-dah). Shining coneflower. Southern United States. Grows 3 to 4 feet tall and 2 to 3 feet wide. Clump-forming plants with egg-shaped leaves. Branching stems with 3- to 4-inch flowers with drooping yellow rays and green centers in summer. Cultivars supersede species. 'Gold-quelle' grows 3 feet tall with double yellow flowers; 'Herbstonne' ('Autumn Sun') grows 4 to 6 feet tall with an abundance of green-centered yellow flowers in late summer and fall. Zones 4 to 10.

Rudbeckia laciniata 'Golden Glow'.

R. triloba (try-*loh*-bah). Three-lobed coneflower. United States. Grows 2 to 3 feet tall and 18 inches wide. Leaves have three lobes. Numerous 1½-inch yellow flowers with purple-black centers in summer. 'Nana' grows 2 feet tall and blooms from early to midsummer. Zones 3 to 10.

Ruta
(*rew*-tah)
Rue, herb of grace
Rutaceae—rue family

Rue is among the most ornamental of perennial "herbs." The glaucous blue, finely textured foliage enhances any number of color combinations in the garden. It has been cultivated in gardens for thousands of years (with the Romans bringing it to Britain), and

Ruta graveolens.

utilized for any number of medicinal and magical reasons. The larvae of the black swallowtail butterfly find the foliage particularly to their liking.

GROWING GUIDE Full sun. Any well-drained soil. Cut back to old wood in spring. Some people are allergic to a volatile oil produced by the plant in hot weather.

PROPAGATION Stem cuttings.

USES Beds and borders. Butterfly garden.

SPECIES, VARIETIES, CULTIVARS AND HYBRIDS

R. graveolens (grah-vee-*oh*-lenz). Rue, herb of grace. Southern Europe. Grows 2 to 3 feet tall and 18 inches wide. Shrubby plant with finely divided, rounded, glaucous blue leaves with a pungent odor and bitter taste. Small clusters of yellow-green, four-petalled, ¾-inch flowers in summer. 'Blue Beauty' and 'Blue Mound' grow to an 18-inch mound. 'Jackman's Blue' grows 30 inches tall with waxen, very blue foliage. 'Variegata' has leaves dappled with white, but they revert to blue as they age. Zones 5 to 9.

S

Salvia
(*sal*-vee-ah)
Sage
Labiatae—mint family

Travel to almost any temperate or tropical part of the world, and a salvia will be native there. With about 800 species of annual, perennial and woody plants, salvias rank as one of

the most important contributors to the garden. Their reputation is enhanced by their ease of growth and long flowering period. The genus name is derived from the Latin *salvere*, to save, referring to the healing properties of certain species, especially common sage, *S. officinalis*, which has been used since ancient times. Generally, sages have the typical square stems of the mints, with pointed, egg-shaped, often aromatic leaves. The flowers tend to be tubular, with a hooded upper lip and a protruding lower lip. Often borne in spiked whorls, the flowers come in a great range of colors, but most of the perennial garden types are deep purples and blues.

GROWING GUIDE Full sun. Average to humus-rich, moist but well-drained soil. Good winter drainage is essential. Deadhead and trim plants back after flowering to keep growth compact and encourage reblooming. A loose winter mulch is beneficial.

PROPAGATION Division, seed, stem cuttings.

Salvia argentea.

USES Bed and borders.

SPECIES, VARIETIES, CULTIVARS AND HYBRIDS

S. argentea (ar-*jen*-tee-ah). Silver sage. Europe. Grows 3 feet tall and 2 feet wide. Basal rosettes of thick, silver-woolly, wedge-shaped leaves to 8 inches long. Grown for its foliage rather than its white flowers, which should be removed. Some flowers may be allowed to bloom and go to seed for new plants, as silver sage is short-lived. Foliage will suffer in hot, rainy weather. Zones 5 to 9.

S. azurea (ah-*zoo*-ree-ah). Azure sage. Southeastern United States. Grows 3 to 4 feet tall and 2 to 3 feet wide. Basal growth with erect, branching stems. Lance-shaped leaves to 3 inches long, becoming smaller up the stem. Spikes of azure-blue flowers in whorled clusters from late summer to midfall. Tolerant of high temperatures. The variety *grandiflora* (*S. pitcheri*) has hairy stems and larger flowers of sky blue. Stake or allow to flop and bloom through other plants. Zones 5 to 9.

S. jurisicii (jur-ih-*sik*-ee-eye). Jurisici's sage. Yugoslavia. Grows 12 to 18 inches tall and 18 inches wide. Branching plants with hairy stems and hairless, toothed, oblong leaves; stem leaves are deeply divided. Branching 8-inch spikes of deep lilac, upside-down flowers in early summer. Deserves to be more widely grown. Zones 5 to 8.

S. officinalis (oh-fis-ih-*nah*-lis). Common sage. Europe, Asia Minor.

Salvia officinalis 'Purpurascens'.

Salvia x *superba* 'Blue Queen'.

Grows 2 to 3 feet tall and 2 feet wide. Shrubby to sprawling plants with woody lower stems. Gray-green, oblong leaves. Spikes of purple flowers in summer. White-flowered form, cultivars showing variously-colored foliage, including, 'Purpurascens' with reddish-purple leaves, 'Aurea', with leaves variegated with green and yellow, and 'Tricolor', with leaves variegated with white, purple to pink, and green. There are also forms with extra-large leaves and others with smaller leaves and dwarf growth. Zones 4 to 9.

S. pratensis (prah-*ten*-sis). Also listed as *S. haematodes*. Meadow sage. Europe. Grows 2 to 3 feet tall and 2 feet wide. Basal growth with long-stemmed, hairy, wrinkled, oblong leaves 3 to 6 inches long. Branching, flowering stems with lavender-blue flowers in early summer, with repeat bloom if deadheaded. Self-sows. Subject to much taxonomic debate. A number of cultivars, including a white-flowered form and a variegated form, and others with flowers of dark violet, light violet, rich blue, rose-purple or rose-red. Zones 5 to 9.

S. x *superba* (soo-*per*-bah). May be sold as *S. nemerosa* or *S. sylvestris*. Hybrid sage. Hybrid origin. Grows 18 to 36 inches tall and 3 feet wide. Clump-forming plant with woody stems at the base; leafy stems bear gray-green, toothed, rough, oblong leaves to 3 inches long. Numerous spikes of densely packed violet-blue flowers in early to midsummer. If cut back hard after blooming, flowering is repeated in late summer or fall. Does best with cool nights and moist soil, but tolerates drier soil. Choose shorter cultivars for hot, humid summers. Many cultivars, with most varying in height. The best known are 'Blue Queen', 'East Friesland', 'Lubecca' and 'May Night'. There are also pink-flowered forms. Try to find vegetatively propagated rather than seed-grown plants. Zones 4 to 8.

Sanguinaria
(san-gwi-*nar*-ee-ah)
Bloodroot
Papaveraceae—poppy family

Most often used in woodland wildflower gardens, patches of bloodroot are being seen with greater frequency in more formal shaded settings. And deservedly so, as the

Sanguinaria canadensis.

foliage and flowers both provide inspiration with their spring appearance. The yet-to-fully-open, folded leaves encircle the white flowers, which resemble miniature water lilies. Both genus and common names refer to the reddish-yellow sap found in the fleshy roots, which was used as a dye by Native Americans.

GROWING GUIDE Full sun in early spring, such as under deciduous trees and shrubs, followed by light to half-shade. Humus-rich, moist but well-drained soil. Foliage goes dormant by mid- to late summer.

PROPAGATION Division, seed. When buying, be sure the plants are nursery-propagated, not gathered from the wild.

USES Woodland gardens, beds and borders.

SPECIES, VARIETIES, CULTIVARS AND HYBRIDS

S. canadensis (kan-ah-*den*-sis). Bloodroot. Eastern North America. Grows 6 to 9 inches tall and 12 inches wide. Gray- to blue-green, wavy, lobed, kidney-shaped leaves. Single white flowers to 3 inches across in early spring. Flowers remain closed on cloudy days. Each flower lasts only a few days, but a number are produced over several weeks. 'Multiplex' has double flowers with up to 50 petals and are longer lasting; it must be propagated by division. Zones 4 to 9.

Sanguisorba
(san-gwi-*sor*-bah)
Burnet
Rosaceae—rose family

Herb gardeners enjoy burnet (*S. officinalis*) for its fine-textured appearance as well as the cucumber flavor it adds to food. For perennial gardeners, several other species in the genera offer handsome foliage and flowers in summer and early fall. The genus name comes the Latin *sanguis*, blood, and *sorbere*, to staunch or soak up, referring to its styptic ability.

GROWING GUIDE Full sun, with partial shade in hot-summer areas. Humus-rich, acid, moist soil. Deadhead to prolong flowering. Summer mulch is beneficial.

PROPAGATION Division, seed.

USES Beds and borders, bog gardens, near streams or pools. Cut flowers.

SPECIES, VARIETIES, CULTIVARS AND HYBRIDS

S. canadensis (kan-ah-*den*-sis). Also listed as *Poterium canadense*. Canadian burnet. Eastern North America. Grows 4 to 6 feet tall and 4 feet wide. Vigorous, clump-forming plants. Compound leaves to 12 inches long, divided into 10 to 15, toothed, oblong, 3-inch segments. Spikes of white

Sanguisorba canadensis.

flowers resembling bottle brushes, to 6 inches long, in summer. Zones 3 to 8.

S. obtusa (ob-*tew*-sah). Japanese burnet. Japan. Grows 2 to 4 feet tall and 2 to 3 feet wide. Graceful, clump-forming plants with compound leaves to 18 inches long, divided into 7 to 13 segments with blue- to gray-green undersides. Nodding, bottle-brush spikes, 3 to 4 inches long of bright pink flowers in midsummer. White-flowered form available. Zones 4 to 8.

Santolina
(san-toh-*lee*-nah)
Lavender cotton
Compositae—daisy family

Santolina chamaecyparissus.

Among the possibilities for gray-foliaged plants, santolina offers finely textured, low-growing, mounding plants for the front of the border. Able to withstand shearing and shaping, santolinas are often used in knot gardens or as low hedges for borders. The foliage is aromatic and easily dried, traits much appreciated by those making winter arrangements.

GROWING GUIDE Full sun. Sandy to average, well-drained soil. Prune after flowering to encourage fresh new growth. Does best in dry climates. Winter mulch is beneficial.

PROPAGATION Stem cuttings.

USES Beds and borders, rock gardens, low hedges.

SPECIES, VARIETIES, CULTIVARS AND HYBRIDS

S. chamaecyparissus (ka-mee-sip-pah-*ris*-is). Lavender cotton. Mediterranean. Grows 1 to 2 feet tall and 2 feet wide. Shrubby, many-branching, rounded plants with woody lower stems. Numerous narrow, toothed, aromatic gray leaves to 1½ inches long. Summer-blooming, globular yellow flowers to ½-inch across. Cut them off if they're not to your liking. Green lavender cotton, *S. virens*, is similar but with bright green leaves. Zones 6 to 8.

Saponaria
(sap-oh-*nah*-ree-ah)
Soapwort
Caryophyllaceae—pink family

Saponaria ocymoides.

Soap manufacturers don't have to fear competition from soapwort, although the plant sap certainly does have a soapy quality. Better to focus on the great splash of pink flowers tumbling among other flowers or over walls, rocks, or banks in midsummer.

GROWING GUIDE Full sun. Poor to average, well-drained soil. Cut back hard after flowering to encourage new growth and repeat bloom. Does not do well in hot-summer areas.

PROPAGATION Seed.

USES Edges of raised beds or walls, rock gardens.

SPECIES, VARIETIES, CULTIVARS AND HYBRIDS
S. ocymoides (oh-kim-*oye*-deez). Rock soapwort. Alps. Grows 6 to 8 inches tall and 12 inches wide. Trailing plants forming loose mats of many-branched stems with hairy, oval, olive green leaves ½ to 1 inch long. Airy sprays of small pink to rose flowers

in early summer. Several varieties, including 'Rubra Compacta', forming compact mounds, and 'Splendens', with large, intensely rose-pink flowers, and 'Alba' with white flowers. Zones 3 to 7.

Saponaria officinalis.

S. officinalis (oh-fis-ih-*nah*-lis). Soapwort, bouncing bet. Southern Europe; naturalized in Eastern and Mid-western United States. Grows 1 to 3 feet tall and 18 inches wide. Erect, unbranched stems arising from spreading, stoloniferous roots. Egg-shaped, prominently veined, dark green leaves to 4 inches long. Summer-blooming, fragrant pink flowers are 1 to 1½ inches across, with five notched petals. Pinching growth or staking necessary to keep plants from straggling. The double-flowered forms, in white, rose-pink or crimson, are best for the garden, blooming for many weeks. They are good cut flowers. Zones 4 to 8.

Scabiosa
(skab-ee-*oh*-sah)
Pincushion flower, scabious
Dipsacaceae—teasel family

Scabiosa caucasica 'Fama'.

Blooming for weeks on end, mainly in shades of soft blue, scabiosas are

deserving of the popularity as flowers for both the garden and in bouquets. The pincushion moniker relates most strongly to the annual *S. atropurpurea*, with its tufted flowers resembling a velvet pincushion. The genus name has a more prosaic origin, coming from the Latin *scabies*, itch, referring both to the rough leaves and problems early herbalists sought to relieve with it.

GROWING GUIDE Full sun, with partial shade in hot-summer areas. Sandy to average, neutral to alkaline, well-drained soil. Deadhead to prolong blooming. May be slow to establish.

PROPAGATION Division, seed.

USES Beds and borders. Cut flowers.

Scabiosa columbaria ochroleuca.

SPECIES, VARIETIES, CULTIVARS AND HYBRIDS
S. caucasica (kau-*kah*-si-kuh). Pincushion flower. Caucasus. Grows 18 to 24 inches tall and 2 feet wide. Basal leaves are lance-shaped, with a whitish surface covering. Stem leaves are lobed and divided into narrow sections.

Slender stems bear flat, pale blue flowers to 3 inches across in summer. A number of cultivars, with blue or white flowers. 'Fama' is popular for its strongly blue, silver-centered flowers on 18-inch stems. 'Butterfly Blue' grows 12 inches tall and blooms from spring until fall. Zones 3 to 7.

S. graminifolia (gram-mih-nih-*foh*-lee-ah). Grassleaf pincushion flower. Southern Europe. Grows 18 inches tall and as wide. Grassy mats of silvery-green leaves. Stiff flower stems bear 2-inch, lilac-blue to pale pink flowers in summer. Must have well-drained soil. Zones 5 to 8.

S. ochroleuca (ok-roh-*lew*-kah). Yellow pincushion flower. Southeastern Europe. Hairy stems and leaves. Lobed to dissected leaves. Wiry mass of stems bearing 1-inch, lemon-yellow flowers in late summer. Short-lived. Zones 5 to 7.

Sedum
(*see*-dum)
Stonecrop
Crassulaceae —orpine family

Sedum aizoon.

Sedums offer gardeners handsome succulent growth, showy flowers that are both long-lasting and attractive to butterflies, easy-care toughness, wide adaptability and drought tolerance. There are hundreds of plants from which to choose, with many creeping forms good for rock gardens, draping over walls or steps, or as edging plants. Taller, upright types are staples of beds and borders. The genus name is from the Latin *sedeo*, to sit, in reference to the low-growing habit of many species.

GROWING GUIDE Full sun. Any well-drained soil.

PROPAGATION Division, stem cuttings.

USES Beds and borders, edgings, rock walls, walks and rock gardens.

SPECIES, VARIETIES, CULTIVARS AND HYBRIDS

S. acre (*ah*-ker). Gold moss stonecrop. Europe, North Africa, Asia. Grows 2 inches tall and 12 to 18 inches wide. Spreading, mat-forming plant with fleshy, light green, overlapping, evergreen leaves ¼ inch long. Small clusters of bright yellow flowers from late spring into summer. Several varieties and cultivars, including 'Elegans', with silver-tipped leaves. Zones 3 to 8.

S. aizoon (*aye*-zoon). Aizoon stonecrop. Siberia, China, Japan. Grows 12 inches tall and 18 inches wide. Clump-forming plant with upright, unbranched stems and fleshy, shiny, toothed, lance-shaped, light green leaves to 2 inches long and

Sedum sieboldii.

Sedum x 'Autumn Joy'.

½ inch wide. Flat, 3- to 4-inch clusters of ½-inch yellow flowers in summer. 'Aurantiacum' has red stems, dark green leaves, yellow-orange flowers, and red fruits. Zones 4 to 9.

S. x 'Autumn Joy'. Autumn Joy sedum. Hybrid origin. Grows 1 to 2 feet tall and 2 feet wide. Hybrid between *S. spectabile* and *S. telephium*. Clump-forming plant with fleshy, oval, toothed, gray-green leaves to 3 inches long. Dense, rounded, 4- to 6-inch clusters of starry flowers changing from pale pink in early summer to red-pink in late summer and to rust-red in fall. Staking may be necessary. Most widely grown sedum. Zones 3 to 10.

Sedum kamtschaticum.

S. kamtschaticum (kamt-*shah*-ti-cum). Kamschatka stonecrop. Eastern Asia. Grows 6 to 8 inches tall and 12 to 15 inches wide. Spreading, sprawling plant with fleshy, lance-shaped, toothed leaves 1½ inches long and ½ inch wide. Yellow, ½-inch flowers in summer. The variety *'Floriferum'* produces many more flowers. 'Weihen-stephaner Gold' has rust-red buds and golden yellow flowers. Zones 3 to 8.

S. sieboldii (see-*bold*-ee-eye). Also listed as *Hylotelephium sieboldii*. Siebold stonecrop. Japan. Grows 6 inches tall and 12 inches wide. Open-centered, spreading plant with whorls

Sedum spurium.

of three fleshy, rounded, finely toothed, blue-green, evergreen leaves to 1 inch long and edged in red. Clusters of star-shaped, bright pink flower in late summer and fall. Several variegated cultivars are available. Zones 5 to 8.

S. spectabile (spek-tah-*bil*-ee). Showy stonecrop. Eastern Asia. Grows 18 to 24 inches tall and 18 inches wide. Clump-forming plant with upright stem and fleshy, oval, finely toothed, pale green leaves to 3 inches long. Dense, flat, 3- to 5-inch clusters of pale pink flowers in late summer. Several widely available cultivars, including 'Carmine', with soft salmon-pink flowers; 'Brilliant', with rose-pink flowers; 'Star Dust', with pink-tinged white flowers; and 'Variegatum', with variegated leaves. Zones 4 to 10.

S. spurium (*spur*-ee-um). Two row stonecrop. Caucasus. Grows 2 to 6 inches tall and 12 to 18 inches wide. Spreading, mat-forming plant with red, hairy stems and fleshy, oval, toothed, red-edged semi-evergreen leaves to 1 inch long, appear in two rows. Clusters of ¾-inch magenta flowers with orange centers in summer. Several rather colorful cultivars, including 'Dragon's Blood', with purplish bronze leaves and brilliant red flowers; 'Red Carpet', with bronze foliage and red flowers; and 'Ruby

Sedum x 'Vera Jameson'.

Mantle', with purplish-red foliage and deep pink flowers; also cultivars with variegated foliage. Zones 3 to 8.

S. x 'Vera Jameson'. Vera Jameson stonecrop. Hybrid origin. Grows 9 to 12 inches tall and 12 inches wide. Sprawling, clump-forming plant with fleshy, rounded, deep purples leaves to 1 inch long. Clusters, 1- to 4-inches wide, of pink flowers in early fall. Very beautiful for the front of the border. Zones 5 to 9.

Sempervivum
(sem-per-*veev*-um)
Hen and chicks, houseleek, liveforever
Crassulaceae—orpine family

Sempervivum tectorum.

Looking like some rare, exotic, desert plant, sempervivums instead are widely and easily grown plants from the Alps, Apennines and Pyrenees of Europe. The perfectly formed, ground-hugging rosettes of fleshy, red-tipped leaves have been grown in gardens since the time of ancient Romans, who used them as medicinal plants. Much folklore surrounds sempervivums, including Charlemagne's decree that they were to be grown on every roof to ward off lightning. The same use is said to keep witches away. The genus name comes from the Latin *semper*, always, and *vivo*, live, while the common name, houseleek, is from the Anglo-Saxon *leac*, or plant. Hen and chicks comes from the way young plants form around the central "mother" plant. After sending up a long, arching flower stem, the hen goes on to greener pastures.

GROWING GUIDE Full sun. Sandy to average, well-drained soil.

PROPAGATION Detach and replant young plants. Seed.

USES Creeping over raised beds, rocks, walls, among stone walks.

SPECIES, VARIETIES, CULTIVARS AND HYBRIDS

S. tectorum. (tek-*toh*-rum). Hen and chicks, houseleek. Europe. Grows 8 to 12 inches tall and as wide. Dense, 3- to 4-inch rosettes of 50 to 60 evergreen, fleshy, red-tipped leaves. Stoloniferous offsets readily produced. Blooms infrequently with clusters of 1-inch magenta flowers on branching, leafy, hairy stems to 12 inches tall in summer. Over 30 other species, with one of the more interesting being *S. arachnoideum*, cobweb houseleek, with its dense cobweb-like hairs. Hundreds of hybrids and cultivars, many with red leaves. Zones 4 to 8.

Sidalcea
(see-*dahl*-see-ah)
Prairie mallow, false mallow, checkerbloom
Malvaceae—mallow family

Sidalcea malviflora 'Party Girl'.

Looks somewhat like a miniature hollyhock, to which it is closely related. Sidalcea has been the subject of much selection and breeding resulting in a number of more widely adapted, long-blooming cultivars with mallow-like flowers of rich pinks and reds.

GROWING GUIDE Full sun, with partial shade in hot, humid climates. Sandy, humus-rich, acid, well-drained soil. Must have good winter drainage. Particularly susceptible to Japanese beetles. Cut back faded flower stems for repeat bloom. Staking may be necessary. Does best in cool, dry climates.

PROPAGATION Division, seed.

USES Beds and borders. Good in combination with perennials with blue flowers or silver foliage.

SPECIES, VARIETIES, CULTIVARS AND HYBRIDS

S. malviflora (mal-vah-*floh*-rah). Checkerbloom. Western North America. Grows 2 to 4 feet tall and 2 feet wide. Clump-forming, upright plant with deeply lobed, blue-green leaves. Leafy spikes of 2- to 3-inch, five-petaled pink or rose-red flowers in summer. Among the cultivars, 'Elsie Heugh', with pale pink, fringed flowers, is the most widely available. Dwarf varieties, such as 'Oberon' and 'Puck', grow 2 feet tall and don't need staking. Zones 5 to 7.

Silene
(sye-*lee*-nee)
Campion, catchfly
Caryophyllaceae—pink family

Campions are widespread throughout the temperate regions of the world; they are often disregarded as roadside weeds, but several species consistently find their well-mannered, long-blooming way into the fronts of borders, rock gardens, or woodland gardens. The sticky stems of some species provide

Silene vulgaris ssp. *maritima*.

the source of one common name, catchfly.

GROWING GUIDE Full sun to partial shade. Average, well-drained soil.

PROPAGATION Division, seed, stem cuttings.

USES Beds and borders, rock gardens, woodland gardens.

SPECIES, VARIETIES, CULTIVARS AND HYBRIDS

S. schafta (*shaf*-tah). Schafta campion. Caucasus. Grows 6 inches tall and 12 inches wide. Mat-forming plant with rosettes of narrow, oval, light green leaves. Magenta-pink, ¾-inch flowers with notched petals bloom from mid- to late summer. Must have well-drained soil. Zones 5 to 8.

S. vulgaris (vul-*gah*-ris). Also listed as *S. uniflora*. Bladder campion. Europe, Asia, Africa. Erect, branching stems with oval, gray-green leaves to 2 inches long. Deeply notched, pinkish-white flowers in summer, with a bladder-like base. Several varieties and cultivars, including a trailing form, double-white form and nodding, tubular-flowered form. Zones 4 to 8.

Sisyrinchium
(sih-suh-*ring*-kee-um)
Blue-eyed grass
Iridaceae—iris family

Growing wild in meadows and prairies of the Western Hemisphere, syrinchiums are grassy, tufted plants with star-shaped flowers of blue, white, yellow or purple. The common name comes from the species widely found in the eastern half of North America, *S. angustifolium*. For the garden, a South American native with iris-like leaves provides a vertical effect with its foliage and spikes of small yellow flowers.

GROWING GUIDE Full sun. Moist, well-drained soil. Deadhead to prevent self-sowing and to keep the plants vigorous and attractive. Fertilize after flowering.

PROPAGATION Division, seed.

USES Beds and borders.

SPECIES, VARIETIES, CULTIVARS AND HYBRIDS

Smilacina racemosa.

S. striatum (stree-*ah*-tum). Argentine blue-eyed grass. Grows 1 to 2 feet tall and 1 foot wide. Clump-forming plants with lance-shaped, gray-green leaves to 1 inch wide and to 18 inches long. Unbranched, winged stems bear 1-inch, creamy yellow flowers with purple veins on the outside and dark yellow throats. Creeping root-stocks form large clumps, but plants are not invasive. Variegated-leaf form is particularly attractive. Zones 5 to 8.

Smilacina
(smy-lah-*see*-nah)
False Solomon's seal
Liliaceae—lily family

False Solomon's seal does actually resemble the "genuine" Solomon's seal, *Polygonatum biflorum*, with its arching stems of pointed, oval leaves. The two are also often found growing side by side at the edges of North American woodlands. It differs in flowering, with fluffy ivory clusters of flowers at the tips of the stems, rather than the hidden bells of *Polygonatum*, and the berries are red instead of black. The genus name denotes another resemblance, this time with *Smilax*, a genus of woody vines.

GROWING GUIDE Partial to half shade. Humus-rich, acid, moist but well-drained soil. May take several years to establish well.

PROPAGATION Division, seed.

USES Beds and borders, woodland gardens, fragrant gardens, near streams or pools.

SPECIES, VARIETIES, CULTIVARS AND HYBRIDS
   S. racemosa (ray-seh-*moh*-sah). False Solomon's seal. North America. Grows 2 to 3 feet tall and 2 feet wide. Clumps of arching stems bear 10 to 15 pointed, oval, light green, prominently veined leaves 5 to 9 inches long. Feathery, pyramid-shaped clusters of tiny, fragrant, ivory flowers are borne at the ends of stems in spring. Red berries with purple spots, favored by animals. *S. stellata* is similar but grows 1 to 2 feet tall and has star-shaped white flowers in smaller, more open clusters in spring. Zones 3 to 8.

Solidago
(soh-lih-*day*-goh)
Goldenrod
Compositae—daisy family

Solidago canadensis 'Baby Gold'.

Perhaps if goldenrod wasn't so widespread in the wild, we would consider it a glorious, fall-blooming perennial for the garden as Europeans do. Then, too, there's the negative press about goldenrod causing hay fever, when ragweed is the actual culprit. Anyway, it's time to re-think goldenrod, whether in traditional borders or in *nouveau* plantings with other North American natives. There are about 130 species, with most native to North America, but the best ones are the shorter hybrids, with the heritage generally a hopeless jumble. There is even a goldenrod-aster cross. The genus name is probably from the Latin *solidus* and *ago*, to make whole, referring to its use as a herb for healing wounds.

GROWING GUIDE Full sun. Almost any well-drained soil, from sandy to humus-rich. Staking may be necessary with taller types.

PROPAGATION Division or stem cuttings of named hybrids and cultivars.

Spigelia marilandica.

USES Beds and borders, meadow gardens. Cut flowers.

SPECIES, VARIETIES, CULTIVARS AND HYBRIDS
   Hybrids and cultivars. Clump-forming plants with upright stems with narrow, pointed, serrated leaves to 6 inches long. Flowers usually borne in somewhat one-sided, branching clusters of tiny, golden yellow flowers in late summer and fall. Spread by rhizomatous roots, but are not invasive. Among the many hybrids and cultivars, two of the shorter ones are 'Golden Thumb', growing 1 foot tall, and 'Cloth of Gold', growing 18 inches tall. Many other excellent choices grow 2 to 3 feet tall. A cultivar of *S. sphacelata* called 'Golden Fleece' is also very good for the garden. Zones 4 to 9.

Spigelia
(spy-*jee*-lee-ah)
Spigelia, pinkroot, Indian pink
Loganiaceae—logania family

A mass of spigelia, planted along a garden path, is a wondrous sight in early summer. With striking red-and-yellow flowers, it is also a good addition to perennial beds and borders with a warm color scheme. The genus is named after Adrian von der Spigel (1578–1625), a professor of botany at Padua University.

GROWING GUIDE Full sun to partial shade, with protection from hot afternoon sun important. Humus-rich, moist but well-drained soil.

PROPAGATION Division, seed.

USES Beds and borders. The edges of woodlands.

SPECIES, VARIETIES, CULTIVARS AND HYBRIDS

S. marilandica (mare-ih-*lan*-dih-kah). Spigelia, pinkroot, Indian pink. Southeastern United States. Grows 1 to 2 feet tall and as wide. Upright stems with oval, dark green leaves to 4 inches long. Borne at the tips of the stems in early summer, the 2-inch, trumpet-shaped flowers have a five-petaled, yellow "inner" flower. Zones 6 to 9.

Stachys
(*stah*-kis)
Betony, lamb's ears
Labiatae—mint family

Seldom are two members of one genus as dissimilar as betony and lamb's ears. The former is appreciated as much or more for its flowers as for the wrinkled, dark green leaves, while the latter is chosen specifically for its thickly woolly leaves, with plant breeders even going so far as to develop a non-flowering form. Both are long-lived, easy to grow, and attractive to

Stachys byzantina 'Countess Helene von Stein'.

butterflies. The genus name is derived from the Greek word for spikes, referring to the flowers, while the common name originates from the Celtic words for head and good, referring to its ancient herbal use.

GROWING GUIDE Full sun to partial shade for betony; full sun for lamb's ears. Poor to average, well-drained soil. Betony may be deadheaded to prevent self-sowing. Extended rainy summer weather may cause the foliage of lamb's ears to rot or disfigure, but plants often recover by summer's end.

PROPAGATION Division of species and cultivars; seed of species.

USES Beds and borders, groundcover. Also use lamb's ears trailing over raised beds and along paths. Butterfly gardens.

Stachys byzantina.

SPECIES, VARIETIES, CULTIVARS AND HYBRIDS

S. byzantina (bih-zan-*teen*-ah). Also listed as *S. lanata* and *S. olympica*. Lamb's ears. Turkey, southwestern Asia. Grows 12 to 18 inches tall and 12 inches wide. Spreading, mat-forming plants with gray-green, very white-woolly, oval leaves 4 to 6 inches long. Woolly spikes of magenta flowers borne in whorls in summer. Some gardeners remove them just as they begin forming. 'Silver Carpet' does not bloom. Both 'Sheila McQueen' and 'Countess Helene von Stein' have larger, less woolly leaves, and 'Primrose Heron' has chartreuse leaves in spring, slowly mellowing to yellow-green. Zones 4 to 8.

S. macrantha (mah-*kranth*-ah). Also listed as *S. grandiflora*. Betony. Asia Minor. Grows 1 to 2 feet tall and 18 inches wide. Mat-forming with upright stems of elongated, heart-shaped, coarsely serrated, wrinkled, hairy, dark green leaves. Several distinct whorls of 10 to 20 tubular, 1-inch, magenta flowers are held on spikes to 8 inches long above the foliage in late spring. Several varieties, including *robusta*, with 4 to 5 whorls of rose-pink flowers; *rosea* with rose-red flowers; and *superba* and *violacea*, both with deep violet flowers. Wood betony, *S. officinalis*, is similar but with larger leaves and smaller flowers. Zones 4 to 8.

Stokesia
(stoh-*kee*-zee-ah)
Stokes' aster
Compositae—daisy family

Stokesia laevis.

Stokes' aster is a Cinderella plant, having been transformed by the magic of plant breeding from a nice but unassuming wildflower into one of the belles of the perennial garden. Plants are long-lived, long-blooming, and widely adaptable. Excellent for cutting, the blue or white flowers have a lacy, fringed look reminiscent of cornflowers. The genus is named after Jonathan Stokes, an English botanist.

GROWING GUIDE Full sun. Average to fertile, humus-rich, well-drained soil. Benefits from winter mulching in colder climates, but must have good drainage. Best planted in groups of at least three.

PROPAGATION Division of species or cultivars; seed of species.

USES Beds and borders.

SPECIES, VARIETIES, CULTIVARS AND HYBRIDS

S. laevis (*lay*-vis). Also listed as *S. cyanea*. Stokes' aster. Southeastern United States. Grows 1 to 2 feet tall and 18 inches wide. Stiff, branching stems with lanced-shaped, dark green leaves to 8 inches long with a prominent white midrib. Foliage is evergreen in milder climates. Several 4-inch, lavender-blue flowers are borne on single stalks in summer. Each flower consists of both tubular inner florets and long, flat, five-lobed outer florets. Cultivars vary in flower color from lavender-blue to several shades of light to dark blue, pink, yellow and white. Zones 5 to 9.

Stylophorum
(sty-*lah*-for-um)
Celandine poppy, lesser celandine poppy, wood poppy
Papaveraceae—poppy family

Stylophorum diphyllum.

The celandine poppy has a way of drawing attention. Perhaps it is in the nature of any poppy, with so many family members having simple but striking flowers with ethereally translucent petals. Or, maybe it's the way it naturally carpets a woodland floor. Whatever the reason, celandine poppies capture hearts and adapt well to shaded gardens. The term celandine was originally applied to the greater celandine poppy, *Chelidonium majus*, from the Latin word *chelidonia*, swallow, for the correlation of appearance between the bird and flower in the spring.

GROWING GUIDE Partial to half shade. Humus-rich, moist but well-drained soil.

PROPAGATION Division, but difficult. Seed, self-sows.

USES Beds and borders, woodland gardens.

SPECIES, VARIETIES, CULTIVARS AND HYBRIDS

S. diphyllum (dih-*fill*-um). Celandine poppy, lesser celandine poppy, wood poppy. Eastern North America. Grows 12 to 18 inches tall and 12 inches wide. Clump-forming plants with light green, hairy leaves 10 to 15 inches long, deeply lobed into five to seven segments. Stems bear clusters of three to five four-petaled, 2-inch, bright yellow, poppy-like flowers in spring, followed by silvery pods. Foliage goes dormant unless soil remains moist. Cut stems exude a yellow sap used as a dye by Native Americans. Zones 4 to 9.

Symphytum
(*sim*-fih-tum)
Comfrey
Boraginaceae—borage family

Anyone who has battled the rapacious common comfrey, *S. officinale*, will be questioning the presence of comfrey here, but other species, particularly in their variegated form, are somewhat less invasive and complement other perennials quite well, both with the foliage and sky-blue, red or yellow flowers. Both the common and genus names refer to comfrey's ancient herbal use of setting bones, with the Latin *con forma*, meaning to join together, and the Greek *symphyo* translating to unite. A more current use is on the compost pile, where it speeds decomposition.

GROWING GUIDE Full sun to partial shade. Humus-rich, moist but well-drained soil.

PROPAGATION Division.

USES Beds and borders, groundcover, sunny to partially shaded meadow gardens.

SPECIES, VARIETIES, CULTIVARS AND HYBRIDS

S. caucasicum (kaw-*kah*-sih-kum). Caucasian comfrey. Caucasus. Grows 18 to 24 inches tall and 2 feet wide. Clump-forming plants with rough, lance-shaped, pale gray-green leaves to 8 inches long. Spring-blooming clusters of nodding, ¾-inch, bell-shaped flowers opening pink then turning azure blue. Best in partial shade. Zones 3 to 8.

S. grandiflorum (gran-dih-*floh*-rum). Large-flowered comfrey. Caucasus. Grows 10 to 15 inches tall and and 12 to 18 inches wide. Basal clumps with sterile stems lying on the ground and pointing upward. Fertile

Symphytum x *uplandicum.*

stems bear tubular, red-tipped yellow flowers in spring. Oval leaves are wrinkled, shiny dark green, and 4 to 7 inches long. Tolerates shade and drought, but does best in moist soil. Spreads rapidly, so use as a ground cover. The cultivar 'Variegatum' has light green leaves with creamy white margins; other cultivars have pink or pale blue flowers. Zones 3 to 8.

S. x rubrum (*rew*-brum). Red-flowered comfrey. Hybrid origin. Grows 18 inches tall and 2 feet wide. Similar to *S. grandiflorum*, but spreads more slowly. Drooping, tubular, dark red flowers in spring. Use as a groundcover. Zones 3 to 8.

S. x uplandicum (up-*land*-dih-kum). Also listed as *S. peregrinum* or *S. asperrimum*. Russian comfrey. Hybrid origin. Grows 3 to 4 feet tall and 3 feet wide. Clump-forming plant with upright stems bearing lance-shaped, hairy, gray-green leaves to 10 inches long. Clusters of nodding, tubular, 1-inch flowers are pink in bud and open to blue in late spring and early summer. The much-prized cultivar 'Variegatum' has broad, creamy yellow leaf margins and pale lilac-blue flowers. Remove plants that revert to solid green foliage. Zones 4 to 8.

t

Teucrium
(*tewk*-ree-um)
Germander
Labiatae—mint family

Most often thought of for its use as a clipped low hedge, germander may be better served by capitalizing on its fine-textured, aromatic foliage and rosy-purple flowers. Most gardeners overlook other species that can contribute to wildflower and rock gardens. The genus name is from King Teucer, the first king of Troy, who supposedly used teucrium medicinally. The common name is from the Greek word for ground oak.

Teucrium.

GROWING GUIDE Full sun. Poor to average, well-drained soil.

PROPAGATION Divison, stem cuttings.

USES Beds and borders, wildflower gardens, rock gardens and rock walls.

SPECIES, VARIETIES, CULTIVARS AND HYBRIDS

T. canadense (kan-ah-*dense*). Canadian germander. North America. Grows 3 feet tall and 1 foot wide. Upright stems with oval to lance-shaped, serrated leaves to 3 inches long and hairy underneath. Spikes of pale, purplish-pink, hooded, tubular flowers in summer. Grows naturally in humus-rich moist soil at the edges of woodlands. Zones 4 to 8.

T. chamaedrys (kah-*mee*-drees). Wall germander. Europe, Southcentral Russia, North Africa, Asia Minor. Grows to 1 foot tall and as wide. Shrubby plant with woody stems. Scalloped-edged, oval, dark evergreen leaves to 1 inch long. Spikes to 6 inches long of whorled, rose-purple, hooded flowers, ½- to ¾-inch-long, in summer. The cultivar 'Prostratum' or 'Nanum' is a spreading, carpet-forming plant to 8 inches tall.

'Variegatum' has leaves marked with white. Plants sold as *T. chamaedrys* may actually be *T. massiliense* or a hybrid with *T. lucidum*. Must have good drainage. Foliage is attractive to cats. Zones 4 to 9.

T. pyrenaicum (pih-ray-*nah*-ih-kum). Pyrenees germander. Spain, France. Grows 3 inches tall and 10 inches wide. Spreading plant with woody, trailing stem and toothed, round, gray-green leaves to 1 inch long. Loose clusters of white and purple flowers in summer. For rock gardens and rock walls. Zones 6 to 9.

T. scorodinia (skor-oh-*din*-ee-ah). Wood germander. Europe. Grows 1 to 2 feet tall and as wide. Shrubby plants with woody, branched stems. Toothed, heart-shaped to oval, rough leaves. Loose clusters of tiny, pale greenish-yellow flowers in late summer. Native to moors, so does best on humus-rich, acid, moist but well-drained soil. Zones 6 to 9.

Thalictrum
(tha-*lik*-trum)
Meadow rue
Ranunculaceae—buttercup family

Thalictrum delavayi.

Diaphanous flowers of lavender, pink or yellow and graceful, delicate foliage grant the meadow rues status among the elite perennials. Easily grown with the right conditions, they bring much-needed texture and depth to shaded gardens. Good for cutting, the flowers are unusual in that there are no petals, only colorful stamens and sepals. The common name is derived from the similarity of the foliage to that of *Ruta*, rue.

GROWING GUIDE Partial to half shade; more sun is tolerated in areas with cool summers. Fertile, humus-rich, moist but well-drained soil. Does not do well in areas with hot, humid summers. Taller types may need staking.

PROPAGATION Division for species and cultivars; seed for species.

USES Beds and borders, near streams or pools, wildflower gardens. Cut flowers.

SPECIES, VARIETIES, CULTIVARS AND HYBRIDS

T. aquilegifolium (ah-kwi-*leeg*-ih-foh-lee-um). Columbine meadow rue. Europe, northern Asia. Grows 3 feet tall and 1 foot wide. Upright, hollow stems. Leaves form at the base and along the stems, resembling those of columbine, with many rounded, lobed, blue-green leaflets to 1½ inches wide. Somewhat flat-topped clusters to 8 inches wide of fluffy, lilac-purple flowers in spring and early summer, followed by drooping, winged seeds. Best meadow rue for hot climates. A number of cultivars, including some with white, dark purple or pink flowers. With 'Atropurpureum', stems and flowers are dark purple. Zones 5 to 8.

T. delavayi (deh-lah-*vay*-ee). Yunnan meadow rue. Western China. Grows 2 to 4 feet tall and 2 feet wide. Clump-forming, upright stems. Leaves divided several times, with each three-lobed leaflet ½-inch wide. Airy, branching clusters of nodding yellow and lilac flowers in summer. 'Hewitt's Double',

with longer-lasting, double lilac flowers, is most often grown. Also a white form. Plants sold as *T. dipterocarpum* are usually *T. delavayi*. Lavender mist, *T. rochebrunnianum*, is similar but with purplish stems, blue-green leaves and lavender-pink flowers with yellow stamens, blooming from mid- to late summer. Zones 4 to 7.

T. flavum (*flay*-vum). Yellow meadow rue. Europe, Siberia, Caucasus. Grows 4 feet tall and 2 feet wide. Clump-forming plants with sturdy stems. Multiple-divided leaves, with rounded, three-lobed leaflets. Rounded clusters of yellow and white, fragrant flowers in early to mid-summer. More adaptable than other species. More often grown is the dusty meadow rue, *T. f. glaucum*, also known as *T. speciosissimum* or *T. glaucum*, with blue-green leaves and sulfur-yellow flowers. The cultivar 'Illuminator' grows 3 feet tall, with lemon-yellow flowers. Zones 5 to 8.

T. minus (*my*-nus). Lesser meadow rue. Europe, Asia, Africa. Grows 1 to 2 feet tall and as wide. A highly variable species, often given other names, with three-lobed leaflets resembling the maidenhair fern, *Adiantum pedatum*. Grown mainly for foliage; greenish-yellow flowers fade quickly. Plants offered as 'Adiantifolium' usually have the best appearance. Stoloniferous roots, but not invasive. Zones 3 to 7.

Thermopsis
(ther-*mop*-sis)
False lupine
Leguminosae—pea family

With both flowers and foliage resembling those of the lupine, *Lupinus*, the false lupine has a most appropriate genus name taken from the Greek *thermos*, lupine, and *opsis*, like. Attractive, easily grown, and long-lived, thermopsis has deep, drought-resistant roots. Slowly spreading clumps of foliage are crowned with tall spikes of pea-like, yellow flowers in spring, which are good for cutting.

GROWING GUIDE Full sun, with partial shade preferred in hotter climates. Poor to average, well-drained soil. Staking may be necessary with a windy site or when grown in shade.

PROPIGATION Division, but difficult because of the deep roots; seed, if fresh; stem cuttings.

USES Beds and borders, meadow gardens. Cut flowers.

SPECIES, VARIETIES, CULTIVARS AND HYBRIDS

Thermopsis caroliniana.

T. caroliniana (kar-oh-lin-ee-*ay*-nah). Also listed as *T. villosa.* Southern lupine. Eastern United States. Grows 3 to 4 feet tall and as wide. Clump-forming plants with three-parted, oval, blue-green leaves, each 2 to 3 inches long and softly hairy beneath. Erect stems, 6 to 12 inches long, of densely spaced, bright yellow, pea-like flowers in spring, lasting up to a month. The cultivar 'Album' has shorter growth and white flowers. Zones 3 to 9.

T. lupinoides (lew-pih-*noi*-deez). Also listed as *T. lanceolata.* Lanceleaf thermopsis. Alaska, Siberia. Grows 1 foot tall and 18 inches wide. Clump-forming plants with lance-shaped, blue-green leaves, each 1½ inches long and covered with silky hairs. Blooms in summer with whorled spikes of bright yellow, pea-like flowers, followed by curved seed pods. Best for cool-summer climates. Zones 2 to 7.

T. montana (mon-*tan*-ah). Mountain thermopsis. Western United States. Grows 2 to 3 feet tall and 18 inches wide. Similar to southern lupine, but with slightly shorter flower spikes and more linear leaves to 4 inches long. Zones 3 to 7.

Tiarella
(tee-ah-*rel*-ah)
Foamflower, false mitrewort
Saxifragaceae—saxifrage family

Tiarella cordifolia.

Gardeners seem always on the lookout for new plants for shady areas, and recent breeding with native foamflowers are certainly satisfying this need. Five of the six species of tiarella are native to North America and have evergreen leaves, often with burgundy variegation and turning bronze in winter. Short, foamy spikes of white flowers rise above the foliage for about six weeks in spring. These tiny flowers are the source of the genus name from the Latin, translating as little tiara.

GROWING GUIDE Partial to half shade.

Fertile, humus-rich, moist but well-drained soil.

PROPAGATION Division of cultivars and species; seed of species.

USES Beds and borders, particularly with the less spreading cultivars and hybrids; groundcover.

SPECIES, VARIETIES, CULTIVARS AND HYBRIDS

T. cordifolia (kor-dih-*foe*-lee-ah). Allegheny foamflower. Eastern North America. Grows 12 inches tall and 18 inches wide. Spreading plants with hairy, heart-shaped leaves to 4 inches wide. Flower spikes, 3 to 4 inches tall, bear ¼-inch fluffy white flowers in spring. The variety *collinia*, also listed as *T. wherryi*, is slightly taller and more clump-forming with triangular leaves. A number of cultivars and hybrids have been developed, varying mainly in leaf shape and color, but some also having pinkish flowers. Zones 3 to 8.

Tradescantia
(trah-des-*kant*-ee-ah)
Spiderwort
Commelinaceae—spiderwort family

Although there are a hundred or so species of tradescantia, only one has securely taken its place in the perennial pantheon. Certainly deserving, spiderworts are plants of graceful, grass-like foliage and unique, three-petaled flowers with prominent stamens and pistils. Each individual flower lasts only a day, but plants are prolific producers for eight weeks in summer. Easily grown and long-lived, spiderworts are widely adaptable. All in all, a suitable tribute to the Tradescant father and son, both English botanists and gardeners to Charles I, with the son also traveling in 1637 to collect plants from the New World.

GROWING GUIDE Full sun to light shade.

Poor to average, moist but well-drained soil.

Trim stems to 8 to 12 inches in mid-summer to encourage new growth and fall blooming. Staking may be necessary, or surround with short, sturdy perennials.

PROPAGATION Division.

USES Beds and borders.

SPECIES, VARIETIES, CULTIVARS AND HYBRIDS

Tradescantia x *andersoniana.*

T. x andersoniana (an-der-soh-nee-*aye*-nah). Spiderwort. Hybrid origin. Grows 1 to 2 feet tall and 2 feet wide. Hybrid between *T. subaspera, T. ohiensis,* and *T. virginiana.* Clump-forming plants with narrow, linear leaves to 18 inches long, clasping the stems. Clusters of flower buds form in the leaf axils, opening to 1- to 3-inch blooms. Many cultivars, with flower colors including shades of blue, maroon, rose-purple, mauve and white. Flowers may also have veining or an eye of a different color. Zones 4 to 9.

Tricyrtis
(try-*sir*-tis)
Toad lily
Liliaceae—lily family

The attraction of toad lilies may not be readily apparent to the casual observer, but ardent gardeners are drawn to them for their small but uniquely shaped and colored fall-blooming flowers. For the rest of the growing season, toad lilies offer gracefully

Trycirtis hirta.

arching stems and foliage. The source of the common name is open to some debate; although probably due to the spotted flowers, the juice of a species from the Phillipines is reported to be a bait for frogs.

GROWING GUIDE Partial shade, with more sun tolerated in cool-summer climates. Humus-rich, moist but well-drained soil. Taller types may need staking. Benefits from both summer and winter mulches.

PROPAGATION Division.

USES Beds and borders; best when planted in groups of at least three. Cut flowers.

SPECIES, VARIETIES, CULTIVARS AND HYBRIDS

T. formosana (for-*moh*-sah-nah). Also listed as *T. stolonifera.* Formosa toad lily. Taiwan. Grows 1 to 2 feet tall and as wide. Slowly spreading plant with arching stems. Shiny, pointed, oval, dark green leaves to 5 inches long, somewhat clasping the stem. Stems end in branching clusters of 1-inch, funnel-shaped flowers of white spotted with purple, blooming

over a long period in autumn. The cultivar 'Amethystina' is taller, with more erect stems and bluish flowers with red spots. Zones 5 to 9.

T. hirta (*hir*-tah). Japanese toad lily. Japan. Grows 2 to 3 feet tall and 2 feet wide. Clump-forming plant with white-hairy, arching stems. Closely set, pointed, oval, hairy, stem-clasping, dark green leaves to 6 inches long. Star-shaped, 1-inch, white flowers with purple spots borne for about a month in autumn. Blooms appear in leaf axils and at the ends of stems, either singly or in small clusters. Many varieties, cultivars and hybrids are beginning to be offered, varying in growth and flower color and size. Zones 4 to 8.

With the burgeoning interest in tricyrtis, more species and cultivars are being offered every year; if intrigued, search them out.

Trillium
(tril-*lee*-um)
Wake robin
Liliaceae—lily family

Trillium grandiflora.

Trilliums are among the most revered and beloved of all native spring-blooming woodland wildflowers. Unfortunately, that has meant much destruction of natural stands, either by individuals or nurseries collecting in the wild. It is imperative that all plants grown in the garden be nursery-propagated. Trilliums are aptly named from the Latin *tri* because leaves, petals and sepals are in threes. Leaves may be mottled with burgundy or plain green, and the solitary white, pink, yellow or red flowers are either borne

stalkless or short-stalked in the center of leaves.

GROWING GUIDE Partial to half shade. Humus-rich, acid, moist but well-drained soil. Plant rhizomes 2 to 4 inches deep. Foliage goes dormant by late summer.

PROPAGATION Division, with difficulty.

USES Woodland gardens.

SPECIES, VARIETIES, CULTIVARS AND HYBRIDS

T. grandiflorum (grand-ih-*flor*-um). Great white trillium, white wake robin. Eastern North America. Grows 18 inches tall and as wide. Each upright stalk bears three pointed, wavy-edged, oval plain green leaves 3 to 6 inches long. Short-stalked, 2- to 3-inch white, maturing to soft pink, flowers in spring. The easiest to grow and showiest of the trilliums. 'Flore-pleno' has double flowers. Zones 4 to 9.

Trollius
(*troh*-lee-us)
Globe flower
Ranunculaceae—buttercup family

Found growing naturally in moist to wet meadows in the cooler parts of the temperate areas of the Northern Hemisphere, globe flowers require similar conditions in the garden. Given these conditions, they reward the

Ramunculus.

gardener with repeated blooming of golden yellow flowers. The many cultivars available offer various shades of yellow, with all lasting well as cut flowers. The genus name comes from the old German word *trollbume*, round flower.

GROWING GUIDE Full sun in cool-summer climates; partial shade in hotter areas. Humus-rich, moist soil. Deadhead for repeat bloom. Cut back fading foliage in late summer. May take several years to become established. Staking may be necessary.

PROPAGATION Division.

USES Wet meadows, partially shaded wild gardens, bog gardens. Cut flowers.

SPECIES, VARIETIES, CULTIVARS AND HYBRIDS

T. x cultorum (kul-*tor*-um). Hybrid globe flower. Hybrid origin. Grows 2 to 3 feet tall and 18 inches wide. Hybrids between *T. asiaticus, T. chinensis,* and *T. europaeus.* Basal clumps of deeply divided or lobed, dark green leaves. Slender stems with a few leaves each bear several globe-shaped, 2- to 3-inch, yellow flowers with many stamens in late spring. Many cultivars, with flower color varying from dark orange to creamy white. Zones 3 to 7.

T. europaeus 'Superbus' (yew-*roh*-pay-us suh-*per*-bus). Common globe flower. Europe. Grows 1 to 2 feet tall and 18 inches wide. Similar to the hybrid globe flower, but more prolifically flowering with 1- to 2-inch, lemon-yellow flowers in early spring. More tolerant of well-drained soil. Zones 4 to 7.

T. chinensis (chi-*nen*-sis). Usually offered as *T. ledebourii.* Siberian globe flower. Siberia. Grows 2 to 3 feet tall and 18 inches wide. Vigorous plants with deeply divided, lobed, and toothed leaves. Globular, 2-inch, deep orange flowers in spring. 'Golden Queen' grows to 4 feet with 3- to 4-inch golden-orange flowers. Zones 3 to 6.

Uvularia

(yew-vew-*lah*-ree-ah)
Merrybells
Liliaceae—lily family

Uvularia grandiflora.

As befitting the name merrybells, these are delightful perennials that grace shaded borders and woodland gardens with their pale yellow, nodding flowers in spring. Widely adaptable, they are easily grown, with the rhizomatous roots slowly spreading to form luminous patches.

GROWING GUIDE Partial to half shade. Humus-rich, moist but well-drained soil.

PROPAGATION Division, seed.

USES Beds and borders, woodland garden.

SPECIES, VARIETIES, CULTIVARS AND HYBRIDS

U. grandiflora (gran-dih-*flor*-ah). Merrybells. Eastern and central North America. Grows 18 to 24 inches tall and 12 inches wide. Clump-forming plants with upright stems. Oblong, pale green leaves to 4 inches long, sometimes drooping and with edges rolled under. Spring blooming, with bell-shaped, 1½-inch long, pale yellow flowers with six twisted petals hanging down singly or in pairs from the tops of the stems. Zones 4 to 9.

Valeriana

(vah-leh-ree-*ahn*-ah)
Common valerian
Valerianaceae—valerian family

Grown and used since ancient times as a medicinal herb, valerian has a beneficial effect on gardens as well. Long, graceful stems bear clusters of delicate white or pink flowers in summer. These are fragrant and good for cutting. Cats find it attractive, too. The genus name is from the Latin, *valere,* to be healthy. Widely adaptable, it has naturalized in many parts of the United States.

Valerlana officinalis.

GROWING GUIDE Full sun to partial shade. Average to humus-rich, moist but well-drained to wet soil. Tolerates drier, alkaline soil.

PROPAGATION Division, seed. May self-sow.

USES Beds and borders, meadow gardens, near streams or pools, bog gardens. Cut flowers.

SPECIES, VARIETIES, CULTIVARS AND HYBRIDS
   V. officinalis (of-fi-shi-*nal*-is). Common valerian, vervain, cat's valerian, all heal. Europe, Asia. Grows 3 to 4 feet tall and 3 feet wide. Basal clumps of egg-shaped, deeply lobed leaves, with stem leaves divided into seven to ten pairs of lance-shaped, toothed leaflets to 3 inches long. Long stems bear rounded heads of tiny fragrant white or pink flowers in summer. Zones 4 to 9.

Verbascum
(ver-*bas*-kum)
Mullein
Scrophulariaceae—figwort family

Verbascum.

Many people may be familiar with the felty-leaved common mullein, *V. thapsis,* found in fields and along roadsides, but there are also a number of biennial and short-lived perennial verbascums more suited to the garden. These provide a strong vertical element with their tall flower spikes in summer. Verbascums readily hybridize among the species, with the resulting named hybrids offering choice, longer-lived selections. The genus name is thought to be derived from the Latin *barbascum*, beard, in reference to the hairy leaves.

GROWING GUIDE Full sun. Average, well-drained soil. Deadhead for repeat bloom. Staking may be necessary. May take several years to establish.

PROPAGATION Division of cultivars, hybrids and species; seed of species.

USES Beds and borders; best when planted in groups of at least three.

SPECIES, VARIETIES, CULTIVARS AND HYBRIDS
   V. x *hybridum* (hih-*bri*-dum). Hybrid mullein. Hybrid origin. Grows to 5 feet tall and 2 feet wide. Basal rosettes of pointed oval leaves to 10 inches long. Leaves are usually thick, white-hairy, but some are wrinkled and dark green. Flower colors include shades of yellow, pink, apricot and white, often with a contrasting eye. Zones 6 to 9.
   Among the species, the best for the perennial garden include *V. chaixii*, growing 2 to 3 feet tall, with yellow or white flowers (Zones 5 to 8); *V. olympicum*, growing 4 to 6 feet tall, with branching spires of yellow flowers (Zones 6 to 8); and *V. phoeniceum*, growing 2 to 4 feet tall with spikes of purple, pink, red, or white flowers (Zones 6 to 8).

Verbena
(Ver-*bee*-nah)
Brazilian verbena
Verbenaceae—verbena family

Verbena bonariensis.

Mainly native to subtropical and tropical North and South America, verbenas are usually thought of as colorful annuals. Several species are hardier, with one being particularly useful for the airy effect it brings to perennial gardens. The species *bonariensis* is named for Buenos Aires, where it was first found.

GROWING GUIDE Full sun. Average, well-drained soil. Winter mulch is beneficial in the northernmost areas of its hardiness range. With pruning, plants become more shrub-like.

PROPAGATION Root cuttings, stem cuttings, seed. Self-sows.

USES Beds and borders, hedges. Use one to three plants as filler or plant in masses.

SPECIES, VARIETIES, CULTIVARS AND HYBRIDS
   V. bonariensis (boh-nah-ree-*en*-sis). South American verbena. South America. Grows 3 to 4 feet tall and 2 feet wide. Basal clumps of toothed, lance-shaped leaves to 4 inches long. Wiry, somewhat branching stems, with few leaves, bear 2-inch clusters of ¼-inch, purplish-red flowers from early summer though fall. Zones 6 to 9.

Vernonia
(ver-non-ee-ah)
Ironweed
Compositae—daisy family

Only the most callous and cynical person could see a meadow filled with ironweed on an early fall morning, with the mist rising, and not fall in love with it. Among the 1000 or so species of

perwinkle. Europe. Grows 18 to 24 inches tall and 24 inches wide. Wiry stems with rounded, pointed, evergreen leaves, 2 to 3 inches long. Nonflowering stems creep on the ground, rooting at the tips where they touch the ground. Upright flowering stems bear flowers in spring that are 1- to 2-inches wide, blue, and funnel-shaped with 5 flaring lobes. Occasional repeat blooming. 'Reticulata' has leaves with netted yellow lines; 'Variegata', also offered as 'Elegantissima', has white-blotched leaves and is often used in container plantings. Zones 7 to 9.

V. minor (*mine*-or). Common periwinkle. Europe. Grows 6 to 12 inches tall. Wiry, spreading stems, rooting at all nodes. Oval, pointed, glossy, evergreen leaves, 1½ inches long. Blooms in spring with flowers that are ¾- to 1-inch wide, blue, and funnel-shaped with 5 flaring lobes. Occasional repeat blooming. Numerous cultivars, with most having more restrained growth and single or double flowers in shades of dark purple, plum, blue or white; some have leaves that are variegated or edged. Zones 4 to 9.

Viola
(*vye*-oh-lah)
Violet
Violaceae—violet family

A genus with thousands of years of history, having been grown by the ancient Greeks and Romans, violas are a prodigious, promiscuous lot, what with some 500 species and untold numbers of readily produced natural hybrids. Some are irritating weeds, while others are rare plants for the col-lector's garden. The large-faced, annual pansies, *V. x wittrockiana*, are staples of cool-season gardens. Native-plant enthusiasts will seek out those from North American shores. For the peren-nial garden, there is a handful of species with those familiar rosettes of heart-shaped leaves and uniquely shaped, spurred, five-petaled flowers, even some with that haunting, elusive

Viola cornuta.

fragrance. An unusual feature of many violets is the production of two types of flowers: the showy, infertile ones and the inconspicuous, fertile ones, borne close to the soil and often with no petals. The name viola is the Latin form of the Greek word, *ione*, from the myth of Zeus providing violas as the food for the white cow he turned his lover into to hide her from his wife.

GROWING GUIDE Partial shade. Humus-rich, moist but well-drained soil. Deadhead for repeat bloom.

PROPAGATION Division, seed.

USES Beds and borders, edging, wildflower gardens.

SPECIES, VARIETIES, CULTIVARS AND HYBRIDS

V. cornuta (kor-*new*-tah). Horned violet, tufted violet. Pyrenees. Grows 4 to 12 inches tall and 12 inches wide. Tufted plants with oval, toothed, pointed, evergreen leaves 1 to 2 inches long. Leaf-like appendages at the leaf nodes. Purple, 1-inch, somewhat star-like, long-spurred, slightly fragrant flowers on 2- to 4-inch stems in spring, with some repeat. Several varieties and cultivars, with flowers in shades of light blue, apricot, yellow, red and white. Zones 6 to 9.

V. labradorica (lab-rah-*doh*-rih-kah). Labrador violet. North America, Greenland. Grows 2 to 4 inches tall and 8 to 12 inches wide. Clump-forming plants with rounded, pointed,

finely toothed, shiny leaves to 1 inch wide. Bluish-lavender, ¾-inch flowers in spring, and occasionally in summer. Self-sows. Combines well with hellebores, pulmonarias and primulas.The variety 'Purpurea', with purplish-green leaves, is seen more than the species. Zones 3 to 8.

Viola obliqua 'Freckles'.

V. obliqua (ob-*lih*-kwa). Also listed as *V. cucullata*. Marsh blue violet. Eastern North America. Grows 3 to 6 inches tall and 12 inches wide. Clump-forming plants with leaves and flower stems arising directly from the roots. Oval to heart-shaped, wavy-edged, toothed, evergreen leaves to 4 inches wide. Violet, ½-inch flowers with purple veins on the lower petal and dense hairs on the lateral petals. Grows best in moist, shady places. Good groundcover. Self sows. Several well-known cultivars, including purple-spotted 'Freckles', rose-red 'Red Giant', deep blue 'Royal Robe', and 'White Czar'. Zones 4 to 9.

V. odorata (oh-doh-*rah*-tah). Sweet violet. Europe, North Africa, Asia. Grows 6 to 8 inches tall and 12 inches wide. Spreading, tufted plants with oval

Viola odorata 'Royal Robe'.

to heart-shaped, toothed, dark green leaves to 2 inches long arising directly from the roots. Violet, fragrant, ¾-inch flowers from fall to spring in mild climates and in spring in colder ones. Prostrate runner root at the tips. Best known for the large, double-flowered, very fragrant, long-stemmed Parma violets, of which there are several named cultivars. Other cultivars include deep-violet 'Czar', dark blue 'Queen Charlotte', rose-pink 'Rosina' and 'White Queen'. Zones 6 to 9.

W

Waldsteinia
(wald-*stein*-ee-ah)
Barren strawberry
Rosaceae—rose family

If you have suffered the agonies of weeding out the pernicious mock strawberry, *Duchnesia indica*, do not fear with the barren strawberry. It is much more civilized, spreading as a dainty, sun-loving evergreen groundcover, but not invasively.

GROWING GUIDE Full sun to partial shade. Average, well-drained soil.

PROPAGATION Division.

USES Groundcover.

SPECIES, VARIETIES, CULTIVARS AND HYBRIDS
   W. fragarioides (frah-gah-ree-*oi*-deez). Barren strawberry. Eastern North America. Grows 4 to 6 inches

Waldsteinia fragarioides.

tall and 12 to 18 inches wide. Creeping, mat-forming plants with lightly hairy to smooth, evergreen leaves divided into three wedge-shaped, toothed parts. Flat, ¾-inch, 5-petaled, bright yellow flowers in spring on horizontal stems. Zones 4 to 7.
   W. ternata (ter-*nat*-ah). Siberian barren strawberry. Europe, Siberia, Japan. Grows 4 to 6 inches tall and 12 to 18 inches wide. Rosettes of leathery, glossy, hairy three-parted, toothed leaves to 1 inch long. Flat, ½-inch, 5-petaled, bright yellow flowers in spring on vertical stems. More compact than *W. fragarioides* and best suited to cool-summer climates. Zones 4 to 7.

Y

Yucca
(*yuk*-ah)
Yucca, Adam's needle
Liliaceae—lily family

Large clumps of sword-like leaves are striking enough, but add tall spikes massed with fragrant 2-inch flowers, and the result is a plant that definitely makes a statement. Used as an architectural feature in a garden or planted in masses, these widely adaptable perennials are easily grown.

GROWING GUIDE Full sun. Sandy to average, well-drained soil. Drought tolerant.

PROPAGATION Separate young plants from the mother plants.

USES Beds and borders. Specimen plant. Meadow gardens. Drought-tolerant gardens.

SPECIES, VARIETIES, CULTIVARS AND HYBRIDS
   Y. filamentosa (fill-ah-men-*toh*-sah). Adam's needle. Southeastern United States. Grows 4 to 6 feet tall and 3 feet wide. Clump-forming plants with bluish to gray-green, leathery,

Yucca filamentosa.

sharply pointed, sword-shaped, evergreen leaves to 15 inches long and 1 inch wide, with curly threads along the edges. Branching, woody-stemmed sprays arising from the center of the plant with nodding, bell-shaped, creamy white, fragrant, 2-inch flowers in summer. Several cultivars, mainly with cream or yellow leaf margins or leaves striped in cream. Zones 5 to 10.
   Y. glauca (glaw-*kah*). Adam's needle. Central and southwestern United States. Grows 3 feet tall and 2 to 3 feet wide. Clump-forming plants with gray-green, white-margined, sharply pointed, sword-shaped leaves to 30 inches long and ½ inch wide, with a few white threads along the edges. Straight or slightly branching woody-stemmed sprays arising from the center of the plant with nodding, bell-shaped, greenish-white with a red-brown tinge, fragrant, 2½-inch flowers in summer. Zones 6 to 10.
   Y. gloriosa (glow-ree-*oh*-sah). Adam's needle. Southeastern United States. Grows 6 to 8 feet tall and 4 feet wide. Very stiff, sharply pointed, sword-shaped, evergreen leaves to 2 feet long and 2½ inches wide, borne on a single stiff stem. Branching, woody-stemmed sprays arising from the center of the plant with nodding, bell-shaped, creamy white, sometimes tinged with red or purple, fragrant, 2-inch flowers in summer. Zone 7.

Ferns

Gardeners interested in perennials should start a fern awareness campaign. As a group, ferns are among the most underutilized of perennials. Often relegated to the more unhospitable spots in a yard, they deserve better as they offer gardeners a wide range of easily grown, long-lived plants with a great variety of sizes, shapes, textures and even colors, albeit, predominantly shades of green. The fronds are superb for use in flower arrangements.

Growing ferns only in the deepest shade does them a disservice, as they do best with partial to medium shade, with some even tolerating full sun. With exceptions, a wide range of soils and climates is tolerated, too, with most ferns thriving in moist, humus-rich soil, much as in their native habitats. Emerging ferns are coiled and called fiddleheads. The leaves are called fronds, with each consisting of two parts, the stipe, or leaf stalk, and the blade, which may be undivided, or simple, or finely cut, with each type of division having a specific term. Most ferns spread by means of rhizomatous roots, which makes division easy. Ferns do not produce seeds, but rather single-celled spores, which are held in small clusters or spore cases called sori (singular, sorus) on the backs of fronds. Growing ferns from spores is a rather challenging process.

There are over a thousand different species of ferns from temperate climates around the world. Many of these are well-suited to gardens but have limited availability. The ones listed below are all easily grown and are available from either local or mail-order nurseries.

GROWING GUIDE Partial to heavy shade. Humus-rich, slightly acid, moist but well-drained soil. Summer mulching helps to keep the soil moist. Ferns tolerating dry soil include *Dennstaedtia, Cheilanthes, Dryopteris affinis* and *Dryopteris filix-mas*. Ferns tolerating the most sun include *Matteuccia, Thelyp-teris palustris, Osmunda, Dryopteris affinis, Dryopteris filix-mas, Athyrium filix-femina,* and *Dennstaedtia punctiloba*

PROPAGATION Division.

USES Beds and borders, groundcover, near pools and streams, woodland gardens, as accents or massed.

SPECIES, VARIETIES, CULTIVARS AND HYBRIDS

Adiantum capillus-veneris (ah-dee-*ahn*-tum ka-*pill*-us veh-*ner*-is). Southern maidenhair. North America. Fronds 10 to 22 inches long, arching, deciduous. Zones 7 to 10.

Adiantum pedatum.

A. pedatum (ped-*ah*-tum). Maiden-hair fern. Eastern North America. Fronds 12 to 30 inches long, erect-arching, deciduous. Several subspecies. Zones 2 to 8.

A. venustum (veh-*nus*-tum). Himalayan maidenhair. Himalayas. Fronds 8 to 12 inches long, arching, semievergreen. Zones 5 to 8.

Asplenium platyneuron (ah-*splay*-nee-um plah-tee-*new*-ron). Ebony spleenwort. Eastern North America. Fronds 8 to 18 inches long, sterile prostrate, fertile erect, evergreen. Several varieties. Zones 4 to 8.

A. trichomanes (tri-*kom*-ah-neez). Maidenhair spleenwort. North America, Europe, Asia. Fronds 4 to 7 inches long, arching, evergreen. Zones 2 to 9.

Asplenosorus ebenoides (ass-plen-oh-*sor*-us eb-eh-*noi*-deez). Scott's spleenwort. Hybrid origin. Fronds 6 to 12 inches long, erect, evergreen. Zones 5 to 8.

Athyrium filix-femina.

Athyrium filix-femina (ah-*thi*-ree-um fih-lix-*fay*-mih-nah). European lady fern. Europe, Asia. Fronds 1 to 2 feet long, erect, deciduous. Many different varieties and cultivars, with crested, dwarf or finely dissected fronds. Zones 4 to 8.

Athyrium niponicum var. *pictum.*

A. niponicum var. ***pictum*** (nip-on-ik-um *pik*-tum). Also listed as *A. goeringianum* 'Pictum' and *A. iseanum* 'Pictum'. Eastern Asia. Japanese painted fern. Fronds 8 to 20 inches long, arching, deciduous, tricolored. Zones 4 to 9.

A. thelypteroides (thuh-lip-ter-oi-deez). Also listed as *Diplazium acrostichoides* and *Deparia arostichoides*. Silvery spleenwort, silvery glade fern. Eastern North America, Eastern Asia. Fronds 1½ to 4 feet long, erect-arching, deciduous. Zones 4 to 9.

Blechnum penna-marina (blek-num *pen*-nah mah-*rin*-ah). Little hard fern. Australia, New Zealand, Chile. Fronds 4 to 8 inches long, erect-arching, evergreen. Zones 5 to 8.

B. spicant (*spee*-kant). Deer fern,

hard fern. Northwestern North America, Europe. Fronds, sterile 8 to 20 inches long, prostrate; fertile, 16 to 30 inches long, erect; evergreen. Many cultivars. Zones 5 to 8.

Cheilanthes lanosa (kye-*lan*-theez lah-*no*-sah). Hairy lip fern. United States. Fronds 6 to 16 inches long, erect, deciduous. Zones 5 to 8.

Cyrtomium caryotideum (sir-*tom*-ee-um kare-eh-oh-*tid*-ee-um). Holly fern. Asia. Fronds 1 to 2½ feet long, arching, evergreen. Zones 6 to 10.

C. falcatum (fal-*kah*-tum). Japanese holly fern. Asia. Fronds 1 to 1½ feet long, arching, semievergreen. Several cultivars. Zones 6 to 10.

C. fortunei (for-*tune*-ee-eye). Holly fern. Asia. Fronds 1½ to 2½ feet long, erect, semievergreen. Zones 5 to 10.

Cystopteris bulbifera (kis-*top*-tah-ris bul-*bif*-er-a). Bulblet bladder fern, berry fern. North America. Fronds 1½ to 3 feet long, arching, deciduous. Zones 3 to 8.

C. fragilis (frah-*jil*-is). Fragile fern, brittle bladder fern. North America, Europe. Fronds 5 to 16 inches long, erect-arching, deciduous. Zones 2 to 9.

Dennstaedtia punctilobula.

Dennstaedtia punctilobula (den-*stet*-ee-ah punk-tee-*lob*-yew-lah). Hay-scented fern, boulder fern. North America. Fronds 15 to 30 inches long, erect-branching, deciduous. Zones 3 to 8.

Diplazium pycnocarpon (dye-*play*-zee-um). Also listed as *Athyrium pycnocarpon*. Narrow-leaved spleenwort, glade fern. Eastern North America. Fronds 1½ to 3½ feet long, sterile erect-arching, fertile erect, deciduous. Zones 4 to 9.

Dryopteris affinis (*dree*-op-teh-ris af-*feen*-is). Also listed as *D. borreri* and *D. pseudomas*. Golden-scaled male fern, scaly male fern. Europe, Asia. Fronds 2 to 3 feet long, erect, semievergreen. Many cultivars. Zones 4 to 8.

D. x bootii (*boot*-ee-eye). Boott's wood fern. Hybrid origin. Fronds 1½ to 3 feet long, erect, deciduous. Zones 3 to 7.

D. carthusiana (kar-*thooz*-ee-an-ah). Also listed as *D. spinulosa*. Spinulose wood fern, toothed wood fern. North America, Europe, Asia. Fronds 1 to 3 feet long, erect-arching, deciduous. Zones 2 to 7.

D. cristata (kris-*tah*-tah). Narrow swamp fern, crested wood fern. North America. Fronds 1 to 3 feet long, erect, evergreen. Needs constantly moist soil. Zones 3 to 7.

D. cycadina (sye-kah-*deen*-ah). Also listed as *D. atrata* and *D. hirtipes*. Black wood fern, shaggy wood fern. Asia. Fronds 1½ to 3 feet long, erect, semievergreen. Zones 5 to 8.

D. dilatata (dil-lah-*tah*-tah). Also listed as *D. austriaca*. Broad wood fern. Europe, Asia. Fronds 2 to 3½ feet long, erect-arching, deciduous. Several cultivars. Zones 4 to 8.

D. erythrosora (ehr-ah-*throw*-soh-rah). Autumn fern. Asia. Fronds 1½ to 2 feet long, arching, evergreen. Zones 5 to 8.

D. filix-mas (*fil*-iks-mas). Male fern. North America, Europe, Asia. Fronds 2 to 4 feet long, erect, deciduous. Many cultivars. Zones 4 to 8.

Dryopteris filix-mas.

D. goldiana (gohl-dee-*an*-ah). Goldie's wood fern, giant wood fern.

Northeastern North America. Fronds 3 to 4 feet long, arching, deciduous. Zones 3 to 8.

D. intermedia (in-ter-*mee*-dee-ah). Also listed as *D. spinulosa* var. *intermedia*. Evergreen wood fern, glandular wood fern, fancy fern. Northeastern North America. Fronds 1½ to 3 feet long, erect-arching, evergreen. Zones 3 to 8.

D. marginalis (mar-jih-*nal*-is). Marginal wood fern, leather wood fern. Northeastern North America. Fronds 1½ to 2½ feet long, erect-arching, evergreen. Zones 2 to 8.

D. purpurella (pur-pur-*el*-lah). Also listed as *D. erythrosora* var. *purpurescens*. Japan. Fronds 3 to 3½ feet long, arching, evergreen. Exceptional. Zones 5 to 9.

Gymnocarpium dryopteris (jim-noh-*kar*-pee-um dree-*op*-ter-is). Also listed as *Dryopteris disjuncta*. North America, Europe, Asia. Fronds 9 to 12 inches long, erect-arching, deciduous. Zones 2 to 7.

Matteucia struthiopteris.

Matteucia struthiopteris (mah-*too*-kee-ah stroo-thee-*op*-ter-is). Also listed as *M. pensylvanica*, *Pteretis nodulosa* and *Struthiopteris filicastrum*. Ostrich

Onoclea sensibilis.

Osmunda regalis.

fern, shuttlecock fern. North America, Europe, Asia. Fronds 2 to 6 feet long, erect, deciduous. Fiddleheads edible. Spreads rapidly. Zones 2 to 6.

Onoclea sensibilis (oh-*nok*-lee-ah sen-*sih*-bil-is). Sensitive fern, bead fern. Eastern North America. Fronds 1 to 3 feet long, erect, deciduous. Fertile frond are pod-like and used in flower arrangements. Spreads rapidly. Zones 2 to 10.

Osmunda cinnamomea (os-*mun*-dah kin-ah-*moh*-mee-ah). Cinnamon fern. North America. Fronds 2½ to 5 feet long, erect, deciduous. Cinnamon-colored fertile fronds. Tolerates sun. Zones 2 to 8.

O. claytoniana (klay-ton-ee-*ah*-nah). Interrupted fern. Eastern North America, Eastern Asia. Fronds 2 to 4 feet long, erect, deciduous. Spores borne in middle of frond. Zones 2 to 8.

Osmunda claytoniana.

O. regalis (ray-*gah*-lis). Royal fern. Eastern North America, Europe. Fronds 2 to 5 feet long, erect, deciduous. Several cultivars. Zones 2 to 10.

Phyllitis scolopendrium (*fill*-ih-tus sko-lo-*pen*-dree-um). Also listed *Asplenium scolopendrium* and *Scolopendrium vulgare*. Europe. Fronds 8 to 16 inches long, erect-arching, evergreen. Need neutral to alkaline, very well-drained soil and a summer mulch. Many cultivars, with crested, crisped, or dissected margins on fronds. Zones 5 to 9.

Polypodium vulgare.

Polypodium vulgare (pol-lee-*pod*-ee-um vul-*gah*-reh). Common polypody. Europe, Asia. Fronds 3 to 10 inches long, erect evergreen. Many cultivars, with crested or dissected fronds. Zones 5 to 8.

Polystichum acrostichoides (pol-*lih*-stih-kum ah-kro-sti-*koi*-deez). Christmas fern.

P. makinoi (*mak*-ih-noi). Makino's holly fern. China, Japan. Fronds 20 to 30 inches long, arching, evergreen. Zones 5 to 9.

P. munitum (muh-*nih*-tum). Western sword fern. Western North

Polystichum acrostichoides.

Polystichum setiferum.

America. Fronds 1½ to 5 feet long, arching, evergreen. Zones 6 to 9.

P. polyblepharum (pol-ee-bleh-*far*-um). Also listed as *P. setosum*. Japan, Korea. Fronds 1 to 2 feet long, arching, evergreen. Zones 5 to 8.

P. setiferum (say-*tih*-feh-rum). Also listed *P. angulare* and *Aspidium angulare*. Southern Europe. Fronds 1½ to 4 feet long, erect-arching, semievergreen. Many cultivars, with crested and finely divided fronds or dwarf growth. Zones 5 to 8.

Rumohra adiantiformis (rue-*moh*-rah ah-dih-an-tih-*for*-mis). Leather fern. South Africa, South America, New Zealand, Australia. Fronds 1½ to 3 feet long, erect-arching, evergreen. Zones 8 to 10.

Thelypteris decursive-pinnata (thuh-*lip*-teh-ris deh-*kur*-sehv pin-*nah*-tah). Also listed as *Phegopteris decursive-pinnata*. Japanese beech fern. Asia. Fronds 1 to 2 feet tall, erect, deciduous. Zones 4 to 10.

T. hexagonoptera (hex-ah-go-*nop*-teh-rah). Also listed as *Dryopteris hexagonoptera* and *Phegopteris hexagonoptera*. Broad beech fern, southern beech fern. Eastern North America. Fronds 15 to 24 inches long, arching, deciduous. Zones 5 to 9.

Thelypteris novaboracensis.

T. novaboracensis (no-vab-ohr-ah-*sen*-sis). Also listed as *Parathelypteris noveboracensis*. New York fern, tapering fern. Eastern North America. Fronds 1 to 2 feet long, erect, deciduous. Rapidly spreading. Zones 4 to 8.

T. palustris (pah-*lews*-tris). Also listed as *Thelypteris thelypteroides, Dryopteris thelypteris* and *Lastrea thelypteris*. Marsh fern. Eastern North America. Fronds 1½ to 2½ feet long, erect, deciduous. Needs wet soil. Zones 2 to 10.

Woodsia obtusa.

T. phegopteris (feh-*gop*-ter-is). Also listed as *Dryopteris phegopteris* and *Phegopteris commectilis*. Narrow beech fern, Northern beech fern. North America, Europe, Asia. Fronds 8 to 18 inches long, arching, deciduous. Zones 2 to 5.

Woodsia ilvensis (*wood*-see-ah il-*ven*-sis). Rusty woodsia. North America, Europe, Asia. Fronds 3 to 8 inches long, erect-arching, deciduous. Good for rock gardens. Zones 2 to 6.

W. obtusa (*wood*-see-ah ob-*tew*-sah). Blunt-lobed woodsia. Eastern North America. Fronds 5 to 16 inches long, erect, deciduous. Zones 3 to 10.

Woodwardia areolata.

Woodwardia areolata (wood-*ward*-ee-ah ah-ree-oh-*lay*-tah). Also listed as *Lorinseria areolata*. Netted chain fern. Eastern North America. Fronds 1 to 2 feet long, erect, deciduous. Zones 3 to 9.

W. fimbriata (fim-bree-*ah*-tah). Also listed as *W. chamissoi*. Giant chain fern. Western North America. Fronds 3 to 5 feet long, arching, evergreen. Zones 8 to 10.

Ornamental grasses

In the not so distant past, grass in the flower beds meant that weeding needed was overdue. Now if you don't have grasses there, at least those designated ornamental, you're hopelessly out of date. What gardeners have discovered is that ornamental grasses are easily grown, widely adapted plants that bring much-needed, graceful, fine texture to the garden. They offer year-round interest with the long-lasting seed heads and foliage that persists during the winter. Both foliage and "flowers" are also quite useful for cutting, either fresh or dried. The possibilities include a wide range of sizes, shapes and colors, with most growing in full sun.

GROWING GUIDE Full sun. Humus-rich, moist but well-drained soil. Average to poor soil and dry conditions are usually tolerated. Trim plants back to ground level before growth begins in the spring. May take several years for plants to become established. Staking may be necessary for taller types.

PROPAGATION Division.

USES Beds and borders, as specimens or massed, groundcover, meadow gardens. Cut flowers.

SPECIES, VARIETIES, CULTIVARS AND HYBRIDS

Andropogon gerardii (an-dro-poh-gon jer-ard-ee-eye). Big bluestem. North America. Grows 5 to 6 feet wide and 2 to 3 feet tall. Clump-forming plant with blue-green stems

Andropogon gerardii.

and gray-green leaves ½ inch wide; turns bronze-purple in fall. Purplish flowers. Drought tolerant. Zones 3 to 9.

Arrhenatherum elatius spp. **bulbosum 'Variegatum'** (ah-ren-ah-ther-um eh-lay-tee-us bul-boh-sum var-ee-ah-gah-tum). Striped oat grass. Grows 12 inches tall and 8 inches wide. Europe. Mounding plant with blue-green leaves striped white. Goes dormant in summer with hot temperatures. Zones 4 to 8.

Anthenatherum elatius spp. *bulbosum* 'Variegatum'.

Arundo donax (ah-run-doe doe-naks). Giant reed. Southern Europe. Grows 14 to 18 feet tall and 6 feet wide. Semievergreen, blue- to gray-green, 1- to 2-feet long, drooping leaves along upright stems. Plumed bronze-to-silver flowers in fall. Variegated form. Zones 7 to 9.

Briza media (bree-zah me-dee-ah). Quaking grass. Europe. Grows 2½ feet tall and 1 foot wide. Tufted clumps with 4-inch, green leaves turning yellow by midsummer. Airy flower clusters in early summer. Cut to 1 foot in summer. Tolerant of dry, poor soil. Zones 4 to 8.

Arundo donax.

Calamagrostis x acutiflora 'Stricta' (kal-ah-mah-gros-tis ah-kew-tih-flor-ah strik-tah). Feather reed grass. Europe. Grows 6 feet tall and 2 feet wide. Very upright clumps of leaves to 3 feet long and ½ inch wide. Feathery, bronze-purple flowers fading to yellow. 'Karl Foerster' is similar. Zones 5 to 9.

Calamagrostis x *acutiflora* 'Stricta'.

Chasmanthium latifolium.

Chasmanthium latifolium (kas-man-thee-um lah-tih-fol-ee-um). Wild oats. Eastern North America. Grows 3 to 4 feet tall and 18 inches wide. Leaves 9 inches long and 1 inch wide; turns bronze in fall and yellow in winter. Drooping green flower clusters turn bronze in fall. Tolerates partial shade. Zones 5 to 8.

Cortaderia selloana.

Cortaderia selloana (kor-tah-deh-ree-uh sel-oh-ah-nah). Pampas grass. South America. Grows 8 to 12 feet tall and 6 feet wide. Clump-forming plants with gray-green, arching leaves. Showy flower plumes mature to silver-white. Many cultivars. Zones 8 to 10.

Deschampsia caespitosa.

Deschampsia caespitosa (deh-schamp-see-ah sess-pih-toh-sah). Tufted hair grass. Europe, Asia, North America. Grows 2 to 3 feet tall and 2 feet wide. Tufted, mounding plant with evergreen, arching leaves to 2 feet long. Airy, branching flower head to 8 inches wide, maturing to pale yellow in summer. Does best with cool summers. Several cultivars. *D. flexuosa*, crinkled hair grass, grows to 20 inches tall and tolerates shade. Zones 4 to 9.

Eragrostis curvula (eh-rah-gros-tis kur-vuh-lah). Weeping love grass. North America. Grows 3 feet tall and 2 feet wide. Tufted, upright plant with arching leaves; yellow in winter. Arching flowers turn pale yellow by fall. Very drought tolerant. Zones 5 to 9.

E. trichodes (trik-oye-deez). Sand love grass. North America. Grows 4

feet tall and 2 feet wide. Clump-forming, upright plant with dark green leaves. Upright to arching flower, bronze maturing to pale yellow. Zones 4 to 9.

Erianthus ravannae (eh-rih-an-this ra-van-eye). Plume grass. Europe. Grows 12 feet tall and 4 feet wide. Clump-forming plant with gray-green, hairy leaves to 30 inches long. Plumes of silver-bronze flowers in fall. Zones 6 to 9.

Erianthus ravannae.

Festuca cinerea (fes-tew-kah sin-er-ee-ah). Europe. Grows 14 inches tall and 8 inches wide. Tufted plant with blue leaves. Does best with cool summers. Many cultivars, which supersede *F. ovina* var. *glauca*. Zones 4 to 9.

Hakonechloa macra 'Aureola' (ho-kon-ee-kloh-ah mak-rah ah-ree-oh-lah). Hakone grass. Japan. Grows 12 to 18 inches tall and 2 feet wide. Arching growth with variegated leaves, pink-tinged in fall. Does well in shade. Zones 6 to 9.

Helictotrichon sempervirens (heh-lik-to-trik-on sem-per-vye-renz). Blue

Hakonechloa macra 'Aureola'.

oat grass. Central Europe. Grows 3 to 4 feet tall and 1 foot wide. Tufted hummocks with stiff, blue- to gray-green leaves 16 inches long and ½ inch wide. Arching beige flowers in early summer. Evergreen in mild climates; may go dormant with hot summers. Zones 4 to 8.

Helictotrichon sempervirens.

Imperata cylindrica 'Red Baron' (im-per-ah-tah sih-lin-drih-kah).

Imperata cylindrica 'Red Baron'.

Japanese blood grass. Japan. Grows 18 inches tall and 12 inches wide. Upright growth with leaves green at the base, but the rest red, intensifying in fall. Zones 5 to 9.

Melica altissima (meh-lik-ah al-tis-ih-mah). Melic grass. Europe. Grows 2 feet tall and 1 foot wide. Evergreen tufts of broad leaves. Arching clusters of beige flowers in summer. 'Atropurpurea' has purple-red flowers. May go dormant by late summer. *Melica ciliata* is similar but with blue-green leaves and white flowers. Zones 5 to 8.

Micanthus sinensis 'Varigatus'.

Micanthus sinensis.

Micanthus sinensis (mis-kanth-us sih-nen-sis). Eulalia grass, Japanese silver grass. Eastern Asia. Grows 6 to 8

Micanthus sinensis 'Silver Feather'.

feet tall and 3 to 4 feet wide. Clump-forming, upright plants with arching leaves. Stiff stems bear clusters of feathery flowers, copper-bronze in summer turning silvery in autumn. Foliage turns pale yellow in fall. may need staking. Most widely grown of ornamental grasses. Many cultivars, varying in size, growth habit, flower color, leaf variegation and hardiness. Generally hardy in Zones 5 or 6 to 9.

Molinia caerulea (mo-leen-ee-ah say-ruh-lee-ah). Moor grass. Europe, Asia. Tufted, mounding plant with

Molina caerulea.

Panicum virgatum 'Heavy Metal'.

blue-green leaves turning yellow in fall. Clusters of delicate, purple flowers in summer. Needs acid soil. Tolerates partial shade. Several varieties and cultivars, including a variegated form. Zones 4 to 8.

Panicum virgatum (pan-ah-kum vir-gah-tum). Switch grass. North to Central America. Grows 4 to 8 feet tall and 2 feet wide. Upright, clump-forming plant. Feathery clusters of green to pink flowers in late summer. Foliage and flowers become yellow in fall. Several cultivars, mainly turning red or burgundy in fall. 'Heavy Metal' has blue-green leaves turning yellow in fall. Zones 5 to 9.

Pennisetum alopecuroides (pen-eh-see-tum ah-lo-pek-yew-roy-deez). Fountain grass. Eastern Asia. Grows 2 to 4 feet tall and 18 to 24 inches wide.

Pennisetum alopecuroides.

Mounding plant with shiny, arching leaves. Bristly flowers in summer or fall. Flowers and foliage turn tan in fall. Exceptional garden plant. Many cultivars. Zones 5 to 9.

Phalaris arundinacea var. *picta.*

Phalaris arundinacea var. picta (fah-lah-ris ah-run-dih-nah-see-ah pik-tah). Variegated ribbon grass. North America, Europe, Asia. Grows 3 to 4 feet tall and 3 feet wide. Rapidly spreading plant with white-striped leaves. In hot-summer areas, cut to ground in midsummer to stimulate new growth. 'Feesey' is more tolerant of heat. Good groundcover. Zones 4 to 9.

Sesleria autumnalis (sess-ler-ee-ah aw-tum-nah-lis). Autumn moor grass. Europe, Asia. Grows 2 feet tall and 1

Sorghastrum nutans 'Ramsey'.

foot wide. Spiky, 16-inch hummocks with light green leaves. Upright flower stems with feathery clusters of silver-white flowers in summer. Evergreen in mild climates. Does well in hot climates. Zones 5 to 8.

S. heufleriana (hew-fler-ee-an-ah). Europe. Grows 20 inches tall and as wide. Hummocks with blue-green leaves. Feathery clusters of dark purple-brown flowers in spring. Drought tolerant. Zones 4 to 8.

Sorghastrum nutans (sor-gas-trum new-tanz). Indian grass. North America. Grows 6 feet tall and 2 feet wide. Upright plant with gray-green leaves ¼ inch wide forms clumps 3 feet tall. Flower stems to 6 feet with reddish-pink plumes in fall. Foliage turns orange and flowers gold in fall. 'Sioux Blue' has blue foliage and is very upright. Zones 3 to 9.

Spartina pectinata.

Spartina pectinata (spar-teen-ah-pek-tih-nah-tah). Prairie cord grass. North America. Grows 6 feet tall and 2 to 3 feet wide. Upright plants with arching, leathery leaves with rough edges. Insignificant flowers. 'Aureo-

marginata' has glossy leaves with gold edges and golden yellow fall color. Native to moist, boggy soils but tolerates dry soil. Spreads rapidly. Zones 5 to 9.

Spodiopogon sibiricus (spoh-dee-oh-poh-gon sye-beer-ih-kus). Europe. Grows 4 to 5 feet tall and 18 inches wide. Stiff, clump-forming plants with short, pointed leaves held at right angles to stems. Feathery clusters of silvery flowers in midsummer. Foliage turns burgundy-red in fall, then brown with frost. Grows in partial to light shade. Zones 4 to 8.

Stipa gigantea.

Stipa gigantea (stee-pah geh-gant-ee-ah). Giant feather grass. Southern Europe. Grows 5 feet tall and 3 feet wide. Mound-forming plant with gray-green, rolled leaves forming 2-foot hummocks. Flowering stems bear airy clusters of silver-yellow flowers in summer. Does best in mild climates with cool summers. Zones 7 to 8.

Chapter 6

ACQUIRING AND PLANTING PERENNIALS

PROCURING PERENNIAL PLANTS

*A*mong the more provident aspects of late-twentieth-century life is the availability of goods, be they exotic cooking ingredients or the newest—or oldest—varieties of perennials. Gone are the days when only a handful of local nurseries offered perennials and the number of mail-order sources was limited. Today, perennials are widely offered for sale, from a basic selection at discount department stores in spring, to vastly stocked local garden centers and a staggering number of mail-order companies. Each of these sources has advantages and disadvantages. The inveterate shoppers among you will revel in the possibilities, making the most of any and all possible sources for procuring perennials to use in every nook and cranny of your yard.

One of the blessings (or banes, if your garden is already overflowing) of today's gardening is the ever-increasing selection of well-grown perennials available at local garden centers.

Local garden centers that specialize in perennials enable gardeners to select from among a wide range of varieties and sizes.

For several months during the spring, hardware stores, home supply stores and discount department stores bring in plants for sale. Annuals are their bread-and-butter, and the perennials they offer are usually limited to the most com-mon—and easily propagated—types growing in 4-inch or 1-gallon pots. If you need to buy in quantity for a mass planting, these places may prove a good source. The key is to get the plants soon after they arrive, before they've set too long in the hot sun with infre-quent watering. The real fun of shopping at these places is the adventure of finding something special. If you're the kind of person who likes to stop at yard sales, hoping to discover a genuine cameo for 50 cents, then this is your milieu.

Depending on their focus, local nurseries and garden centers can range from offering little better than the mass merchandisers to having a wide range of perennials. Do your own personal research and talk with other gardeners in your area for suggestions of the best places. Again, plants are mainly available in 4-inch or 1-gallon pots.

Container-grown plants in this size pot are usually old enough to bloom the first season. Look for plants that are bushy and compact, with healthy green foliage and no signs of insects or disease. Plants that seem over-sized for the con-tainer are most likely rootbound, which can cause them to be slower in getting established in your garden.

Another local source that can be invaluable is gardeners who have gotten bitten by the gardening bug so badly that, as their gardens proliferate, they find it sensible to sell some of their

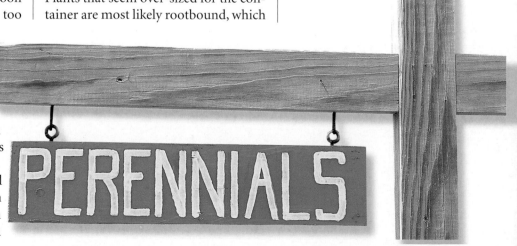

extras. Often, these are people who collect and specialize, so it's a good chance to acquire hard-to-find varieties. To find these people, check the classified ads, roadside signs or local plant societies. The plants may be offered bare-root or growing in containers. A variation on this theme are the plant sales and swaps conducted by local plant societies.

Mail-order sources provide the greatest selection of perennials. These range from mom-and-pop operations to large, long-established corporations. Some companies specialize in certain genera, while others offer the full range of perennials. The plants may be available as seed, dormant bare-root plants, young seedlings or older, larger plants in pots. Make sure you understand what you're getting before ordering. Most of these companies, especially the smaller ones, are run by people who are dedicated plant enthusiasts, and are quite reliable. If you've never ordered plants by mail or have no first-hand information about the quality offered by a particular company, make your first order a small one.

Those who have ever ordered anything by mail that is even vaguely garden related are probably already receiving catalogs from some of the major companies. For the smaller companies, you will have to call or mail a request for a catalog, usually including a nominal fee. The offerings may be a simple list or an elaborate catalog with color photos. The catalogs that contain detailed descriptions about the plants are among the most valuable sources of information about perennials. Gardeners seldom suffer post-Christmas depression because their mailboxes are filled at this time with catalogs for poring over and planning the garden during the long winter nights. Companies ship dormant, bare-root plants in early spring, and container-grown plants are sent at the time of the last expected frost for your area unless requested otherwise.

Both bare-root and container-grown plants are ideally planted as soon as bought or received. Bare-root plants are the most difficult to handle if not planted immediately. They are usually wrapped in moistened packing material and plastic. Left too long in this, the roots will rot. Removed too soon, they will dry out. When planting right away is not possible, unwrap the plants, pot up in containers of potting soil, and put in a protected place outdoors. Small seedlings are also best potted up and cared for until they attain some size before planting into the garden.

Young plants, shipped in 4-inch pots, have been carefully packed to arrive in good condition. Open the box immediately and water well, place in indirect light, then plant or repot as soon as possible.

Carefully remove a plant from the container so as not to pull the top from the roots. If the plant is rootbound, loosen the rootball with your fingers or cut the sides with a knife.

PLANTING PERENNIALS

Preparing the soil before planting is crucial to successfully growing perennials as it's difficult, if not impossible, to improve the soil after perennials are planted. For details on this process, see the sidebar on Advance Soil Preparation.

Once both soil and plants are ready, try to plant on a cool, cloudy day when rain is predicted. Late afternoon is the best time to plant as the cool evening gives the plant time to adjust. Try to avoid hot or windy weather. When unavoidable, keep the plant watered and provide protection for several days, such as placing a cardboard box over the plant during the hottest part of the day.

When planting bare-root perennials, don't let the roots dry out. It's best to soak them for several hours in a weak fertilizer solution. With a trowel or spade, dig a hole large enough for the roots to spread out. Set the plant in the hole so that the point where the roots meets the stem or crown is at ground level. Fill in with soil around the roots, tamping gently, then water thoroughly.

The boons of container-grown plants are that they are already actively growing and, with a caveat, they can be planted any time during the growing season. Planting in spring, near or after the last frost, depending on the hardiness of the plant, is still the best time because the cool spring weather gives the plant time to establish new roots before hot weather, and it probably has not become rootbound yet. When ready to plant a container-grown perennial, dig a hole, grasp the plant at the base near the soil, and gently tug it from the pot. If it doesn't easily come out, turn the pot on its side and tap it several times to jar the root ball loose. Use your fingers to loosen the roots slightly. If there is a mass of roots on the outside of the soil ball, free them up even more or slash the sides of the root ball with a knife. This may seem cruel and unusual punishment, but it stimulates new root growth out into the soil. Place the plant in the hole, setting it at the same depth as it was in the pot. Water thoroughly.

Container-grown plants can be set out anytime during the growing season, but be sure to prepare the soil well before planting, then properly care for the plants afterward.

Advance Soil Preparation — The Key to Success

Nothing...*nothing* is more important to the successful growth of plants than proper advance soil preparation. Skip this all-important first step, and you're asking for trouble. Abide by it, and you've taken a huge step in ensuring a thriving, easy-to-care-for garden.

No matter what type of soil you have, from the lightest sand to the heaviest clay, a liberal addition of organic matter works miracles. Organic matter can be anything from compost to well-rotted leaf mold, fine fir bark, or peat moss. Almost every area of the country lays claims to indigenous, inexpensive organic material, readily available to gardeners.

A good rule-of-thumb is that the amount of organic matter you add should be equal to the depth to which you intend to turn the soil. If you're preparing the soil for raised beds, the minimum depth you should till is six inches; eight or 12 inches or more is that much better. This may contradict some traditional advice, but experience has proved it to be very successful.

If you intend to till the soil to a depth of 8 inches, then you should add 8 inches of organic material on top of the soil before you till to incorporate it to the full depth. This takes some doing, but it helps develop an extensive, healthy root system. This results in a hardy, vigorous, productive garden, able to withstand periods of drought and more resistant to disease and pests.

Depending on what you're planting and the characteristics of your soil, you may want to add fertilizer and lime as you incorporate the organic matter. Explain your situation to your local nursery staff or extension agent to find out if such additions are necessary.

After tilling the organic matter into the soil, rake the area smooth and plant your plants. Keep the area well-watered for the first few weeks after planting. You'll be amazed at the growth the plants put on in such superior soil, even in the first year.

Well-tended seedlings yield many plants.

STARTING PERENNIALS FROM SEED

An idiosyncracy of people new to gardening is the desire to start plants from seed. Indeed, there are few processes as miraculous as watching a seed become leaves and flowers, but let's talk reality here. Starting a tomato is one thing; starting a perovskia is another—for a number of reasons.

First of all, perennials are a diverse group of plants, with many different conditions necessary for successful germination. Second, we're talking delayed gratification. It's usually at least a year before the plants are big enough to set out into the garden, and then they may or may not bloom that year. In the meantime, they must be attended to in a nursery area, including watering them all summer and protecting them during the winter. Third, perennials are often grown as a specific variety that will not come true from seed but only from vegetative propagation, such as division or cuttings. Fourth, many perennials multiply quite handily on their own, readily providing new, blooming-size plants.

But...there are times when starting perennials from seed does make sense. For one, maybe you just want to. This may be simple hardheadedness, a need for a great many plants at a reasonable cost or a desire to grow rare plants that do not readily multiply and/or do come true from seed. And some perennials do quickly germinate, grow and bloom the first year if started early enough. These include certain varieties of English daisy, delphinium, shasta daisy and painted daisy.

The procedure for starting perennial seed is much the same as for any other plant. There's a plethora of seed-starting paraphernalia available, but horticultural-grade vermiculite and a plastic seed-starting tray is simple and easy. Read the instructions on the seed packet to determine whether there are special requirements, such as the need for heat, light, darkness, soaking, cold period or scratching the seed coat. Germination times vary greatly, so keep the growing media moist throughout the waiting period. Once germinated, provide bright, indirect light, either by growing under fluorescent lights, or placing in a greenhouse or lathhouse.

Once several sets of leaves have developed, transplant the seedlings to larger pots or into a nursery bed, if all frost is past. Shelter them with shade cloth or lath or continue growing them in a cool greenhouse or indoors under lights until they start sending out new leaves again. At this point, they can be kept growing in pots or set into a nursery bed outdoors. Water and fertilize regularly during the summer. Mulch the nursery bed in late fall after the ground has frozen or cover with a cold frame. The plants should be ready to set into the garden the following spring.

Chapter 7

❦

BE AWARE, OR THE ART OF GARDEN MAINTENANCE

The best gardeners may never recognize the Buddha on the garden path, but they have attained a state of awareness nonetheless. Or, as my father would put it, "The best fertilizer is the owner's footsteps." In other words, plants are living entities, and, thus, benefit from care and attention. How much is dependent on a variety of factors, such as the climate, the plants chosen and the style of garden. The personality of the one who gardens also comes into play.

First, let's assume that someone who wants to garden at all has at least some willingness to devote time to it. Next, you, and only you, can decide just how much time and effort you want to invest. For some, an hour or so a week is all the time to be committed to the garden. Others will be out there every day for a couple of hours. Fortunately, both extremes, as well as all of us in the middle, are readily accommodated by

Spending time in the garden doing chores can be a relaxing, reflective time that gives you the opportunity to be outdoors, get healthful exercise and enjoy the beauty of the natural world.

perennials—when the garden style and size as well as the varieties of plants are chosen carefully in the beginning. If you're unsure, start out with a small area, using the plants that are the easiest to grow.

Both spring and fall demand that a greater number of hours be set aside for garden care, but by utilizing certain time- and energy-saving techniques, much of the rest of the growing season is spent admiring rather than toiling in the garden. As referred to earlier with my father's comment, spending time in the garden has a number of benefits, both for you and your plants. While being enchanted by the blooms of the phlox, you will notice that the liatris nearby needs to be deadheaded or the leaves of another plant are slightly chlorotic, suggesting a need for extra fertilization.

The following sections on garden care and maintenance provide the basics that have proved successful for most gardeners over the years. Reams more can and have been written, and certain plants or situations may be the exception to the rule. Nevertheless, these guidelines will stand most gardens and gardeners in good stead, requiring some effort but not so much that the garden becomes burdensome. In fact, the results should be so satisfactory that the biggest problem may be that you want to expand your beds or borders, growing ever more perennials.

MULCHING

Used correctly, organic mulches applied during the growing seasoon are as close as it gets to a gardening panacea. The benefits include keeping weeds down, conserving soil moisture, keeping soil cooler in summer and warmer in winter, preventing soil erosion, improving soil structure, attracting earthworms, improving soil fertility and keeping plants clean and attractive.

Yes, there can be a downside to them, but not enough to not use them at all. For instance, in cool climates, the mulch should be pulled aside or applied later in the season to let the soil warm up. With plants that tend to rot with winter mois-

ture, either draw the mulch away in the fall or place between the plants but not right up to the crown. Mulching creates hiding places for slugs and snails, so where these pests are a menace, more aggressive control will be necessary. Non-decomposed mulches, such as shredded hardwood bark, tie up soil nitrogen as they decompose, so adding extra nitrogen (such as a fish emulsion solution) may be necessary. Another problem is likely to occur if you put the mulch on without loosening the soil surface just before applying. A mulch

put on top of a crusted soil surface can result in an impervious layer developing between the two, defeating the goal of having the soil and mulch blend together into one rich layer.

Although any time is a good time to apply mulch, the ideal is in spring just as growth starts. Pull up any weeds, loosen the soil surface lightly, then apply 2 to 4 inches of an organic mulch over the surface of beds and borders, tapering it thinly near the base of the perennials. More can be applied during the growing season, if necessary. Some of the organic

Keeping several inches of organic mulch on the garden has many benefits. Before applying a mulch, be sure to pull up any weeds and loosen the soil surface slightly.

mulches to consider include half-rotted compost, buckwheat hulls, cocoa hulls, shredded hardwood bark, ground corncobs or leaves or composted manure.

WATERING

Making sure plants get the right amount of moisture—neither too much nor too little—is one of the key areas where the observation powers of the gardener come into play. There is no one simple gauge, but rather a number factors are involved. For example, some plants are shallow-rooted, which means they're where the soil dries out quickly, while others have roots reaching down deep into the soil where it seldom dries out. Some plants need lots of moisture, while others are tolerant of drought. New transplants need plenty of water until new roots get established. When plants set their flowers is another time when moisture is crucial. Mulched gardens or areas where plants are closely spaced retain more soil moisture than raised beds. You can't just go by the amount of rainfall received, since other environmental factors affect availability of moisture for plants. These include temperature, intensity of the sun and wind. The soil type affects moisture retention, too, with clay soil or soils rich in organic matter retaining more than sandy soils. So the adage of plants needing 1 inch of water a week is almost so general as to be worthless.

The best way to determine if your plants' moisture needs are being met is to take all of these factors into consideration while keeping a watchful eye on both the plants and the soil. Particularly at the height of summer, walk through the garden at least once a day. The first hint of plants needing water is that the color of the leaves will be duller than normal. The next stage is wilting. While a slight amount of wilting is somewhat normal during the hottest part of the day, don't let plants wilt longer than a few hours, or they may not recover. The easiest way to determine soil moisture levels is by simply digging down a few inches to see if the soil is moist.

Try to limit supplemental watering in order to conserve this natural resource. When conditions require watering the garden, soak the soil thoroughly to encourage deep rooting.

When natural rainfall is not adequate, the easiest, most efficient method of watering is to use a soaker hose, which puts water into the soil, not on the leaves where it can encourage diseases and their spread. Other methods include watering with a hose fitted with a soft-flow nozzle so that the water soaks into rather than splashes off the soil, or using a sprinkler. With either of these methods, water in the morning so the foliage has a chance to dry off before nightfall.

Whatever method you use, be sure to water deeply or not at all. Shallow watering makes for shallow roots that are more readily susceptible to drought. To conserve the valuable resource of water, don't waste it. Water slowly, allowing water to penetrate rather than run off, and apply just as much as necessary to soak the soil. To determine this, first keep in mind that perennial roots go about 1 to 1½ feet deep into the soil and that 1 inch of water penetrates sandy soils about 15 inches and clay soils about 5 inches. When you water, measure the length of time it takes to apply 1 to 3 inches, depending on your soil type. The next day after watering,

dig into the soil to see how far the water has penetrated. This will give you the amount of time it takes to apply a certain amount of water, which you can then adjust accordingly.

WEEDING

The gardener's joke about weeding goes, "The best way to make sure you are removing a weed and not a valuable plant is to pull on it. If it comes out of the ground easily, it is a valuable plant." Hopefully, you have a better one-on-one relationship with your plants than that, but early spring weeding is particularly hazardous until you become familiar with the different perennials. The other keys to weeding are based on common sense. Make weeding a frequent and regular task, pulling the weeds while they are still small. When pulling, try to disturb the roots of the neighboring perennials as little as possible. If a large clump of soil is removed when weeding, bring in additional topsoil or compost to fill in the hole. To keep weeding chores to a minimum, work the soil lightly in spring and apply an organic mulch.

Use a hand- or machine-edger in the spring to retard the growth of grass into the flower beds. For the best plant growth, fertilize in the spring and again in midsummer.

install some type of barrier edging, such as wood, plastic, brick, or stone. The edging can be installed at the same height as the lawn so that mowers can run over them, or it can be placed above, which necessitates some other method of cutting the grass next to it. While some people derive great pleasure from a crisp, defining line, others prefer to grow creeping, sprawling perennials next to it to soften the effect.

FERTILIZING

To manufacture their food by photosynthesis and carry on other life processes, plants utilize a number of mineral elements, which are absorbed mainly in water from the soil. Most soils have some nutrients naturally available, but the combination of nutrients being leached from the soil and used by the plants necessitates adding more in the form of fertilizers in order to get the kind of growth we expect in gardens.

The primary nutrients required by plants are nitrogen, phosphorus and potassium. The three numbers on a bag or box of fertilizer, such as 5–5–5, represent the percentages by weight of these three nutrients, always in the order of nitrogen, phosphorus, potassium. The remainder of the fertilizer is filler material, some of which may be other nutrients that can be utilized by plants. Fertilizers that contain all three elements are called complete fertilizers. When one or two of the primary nutrients are missing, a zero appears in the three numbers, such as 21–0–0.

Gardeners use the ratio between these numbers as an indicator of the type of growth expected. In choosing a fertilizer ratio best for your various perennials, it helps to understand the roles of these nutrients. Nitrogen is important in leaf and stem growth and health. It quickly washes away or is used up by plants. Phosphorus is essential for healthy root growth, the production of fruit and seeds, and disease resistance. Much of the soil in the United States is deficient in phosphorus, and phosphorus is not easily dissolved in the soil,

EDGING

Besides weeds popping up in a bed or border, there is the problem of the surrounding grass creeping into them. Of course, sometimes perennial areas have only paved or mulched paths between them, in which case this won't be a problem. Since the vast majority of beds and

borders are interspersed with lawns, keeping the two apart can be a real headache. One solution is to dig or pull out the grass several times a season. Another is to have a strong back or know someone who does who is willing to dig a space between the lawn and the perennials. The most efficient method is to

but once in the soil it remains there over a long period. Potassium plays a number of roles in plant health and growth. It, too, is usually deficient in soil, except in the West. Although highly soluble in water, potassium clings tightly to soil particles, making an application last for a relatively long time.

When growing plants mainly for foliage, a fertilizer with a higher ratio of nitrogen is usually chosen, such as 6–3–3. For general growth, a balanced fertilizer, such as 5–5–5 is preferred. When flowers or fruit are the goal, such as with most perennials, a ratio like 3–6–6 or 3–6–3 is a good choice. The most accurate and efficient way to determine how much fertilizer to use is look at results from a soil test. If the soil has been well-prepared, including the addition of fertilizer, no further feeding is necessary the first year. A general rule of thumb for succeeding years is to feed once in the spring, using about 3 pounds of fertilizer with a ratio such as 3–6–6 or 3–6–3 per 100 square feet. Apply fertilizer again at the same rate in midsummer. A fertilizer with a different concentration but the same ratio is applied accordingly; for example, one and one-half pounds of 6–12–12 in place of the recommendation above. Always be sure to read the manufacturer's directions.

The choices among fertilizers are many. Some are applied in dry form, be it granules, crystals, powders or pellets. These are sprinkled on the soil and worked in lightly. Depending on the chemical makeup and form, the nutrients may be available for a short or long period. Some fertilizers are made to be dissolved in water before applying to the soil or foliage (plants can also absorb nutrients through their leaves). These are taken up quickly by the plants, but they are also quickly depleted.

Another issue when buying fertilizer is whether it comes from an "organic" or "inorganic" source. Organic fertilizers may be from plant or animal sources, such as manure, fish byproducts, seaweed, alfalfa meal, soybean meal, cottonseed meal or bloodmeal. Also included in this category are fertilizers from natural mineral sources, like rock phosphate or greensand, a mineral deposit found on the ocean floor.

There are environmental and ethical concerns with both inorganic as well as many organic sources. Proponents of inorganic fertilizers stress that the plant doesn't distinguish between organic or inorganic, the cost is less, and the effect faster. Advocates of organic fertilizers look to the larger picture of the negative long-term effects of inorganic fertilizers and the positive effects of organic fertilizers. Now that complete organic fertilizers are readily available (even vegan ones), the argument seems moot. Not only do organic fertilizers provide nutrients over a long period, but they also help to increase the all-important humus in the soil.

Over time, the use of organic mulches will lower the pH somewhat. It's a good idea to test the pH of the soil every spring. The best material to raise the pH is dolomitic limestone, available in powder or granules. Although it is best to follow soil-test recommendations, a basic guide to using it is that 5 to 10 pounds of dolomitic limestone to 100 square feet of garden will raise the pH one point. In lowering the pH, ground sulfur, calcium sulfate, iron sulfate or aluminum sulfate may be used, as may fertilizers designed for acid-loving plants. In lowering the pH, it is best to follow either the soil-test or product recommendations.

Stones or other types of barrier edging retard the growth of grass into flower beds, while an organic mulch slows the growth of weeds and adds nutrients and humus as it decomposes.

STAKING

Supporting perennials is not imperative, but anyone who has had one (usually just coming into bloom) be blown over by wind, break off from its own weight or generally flop over and look untidy, the small amount of effort ahead of time is well worth it. Basically, there are two types of staking needs: one for tall, single-stemmed plants, such as delphinium, digitalis or monkshood, and another for plants with thin, floppy stems, like yarrow, aster, shasta daisy, echinacea or coreopsis. When properly used, supports become almost invisible as the plant grows during summer.

There are a number of different types of supports that can be purchased, including Y-stakes, linking stakes, and grids with legs or simply a ball of twine and bamboo or wooden stakes or poles. Supports can also be improvised from twiggy brush or saplings.

To support tall single stems, choose a sturdy stake or pole that is slightly shorter than the mature height of the plant in bloom, plus 12 inches. Insert the stake or pole 12 inches into ground and 1 inch from the stalk in the spring or early summer. For purchased stakes with a "curl" on the top, "attach" the stem by slipping it into the circle. With a plain stake or pole, use a plant tie or piece of twine to loosely tie the plant stalk to the support. If the tie is too tight, the stem can be injured.

For floppy-stemmed plants, the support is put in place early in the season, or when plants are about 8 to 12 inches tall. Whichever of the following methods is used, be sure to insert the support stakes 6 to 10 inches into the ground. Grid supports are put directly over the plant. Another method is to put thin bamboo or wood stakes around the plant, then connect them with soft green twine. Or insert several twiggy tree or shrub branches, each about 18 to 24 inches long (depending on the mature height of the plant), into the soil around and among the plant stems.

PINCHING, THINNING AND DISBUDDING

Removing or pinching out the growing tip of a plant forces side branches to be more vigorous, making plants bushier and producing more flowers. With your fingertips, scissors or small pruning shears, remove a small amount of the top growth. This can be done once or several times in spring and early summer, as desired, but usually not after the end of June. Chrysanthemums and asters are the two perennials most often pinched.

Sometimes you may want to have

To support tall, single-stemmed flowers, insert a bamboo, metal or wooden stake into the ground an inch from the stem. Use a plant tie or twine to loosely tie the plant to the stake.

Plants with thin, floppy stems or heavy flowers benefit from having the stems supported. Whether homemade or purchased, put the support in place when the plants are about 8 to 12 inches tall, so that the stems can grow up through it.

fewer shoots, particularly if a plant tends to produce too many, causing spindly growth and disease problems because of poor air circulation in the middle of the plant. To prevent this, remove some of the stalks when growth is 4 to 6 inches tall.

In disbudding, some of the flower buds are removed, usually the side buds around a central one. This enables the plant to put all its energy into the remaining bud on each stem. Remove the buds early in their development.

DEADHEADING

Rather than a reference to a rock band's groupies, the term deadheading is a self-explanatory gardening term referring to the removal of the dead or faded flowers. This is not just compulsive behavior to keep everything neat and tidy, although it certainly does serve that purpose. But deadheading also prevents seed development, which can weaken a plant, cause it to stop blooming, or allow it to become a nuisance with a plethora of seedlings. Of course, sometimes the seedlings are desired; the choice is yours.

Removing the faded flowers from perennials not only keeps the garden looking tidy, but can also strengthen the plant, encourage repeat blooming or prevent self-sowing.

INSECT AND DISEASE CONTROL

Most perennial gardeners are seldom bothered by pests. The main exceptions are those people who live in a Japanese beetle zone or those who grow a great number of plants from a single genus. Instituting preventive measures increases your advantage over pests even more. These include:

● selecting plants best adapted to your climate or site;

● keeping plants regularly watered and fertilized so that growth is vigorous and not stressed;

● growing disease-resistant varieties;

● checking plants regularly and treating for any pest at the first sign;

● regularly removing and destroying dead or distressed leaves or flowers;

● cleaning up plant material thoroughly in the fall so pests and winter hiding places are minimized;

Pests in a perennial garden can be kept to a minimum by choosing the right plants for the site, feeding and watering adequately and encouraging natural predators, such as toads.

Ladybugs, as well as other natural predators, should be encouraged to inhabit your garden.

● hand-picking injurious insects and destroying them;

● making your garden a haven for natural predators, such as birds, bats, toads, ladybugs, praying mantis and others;

● laying boards in the garden at night to attract slugs and earwigs, then destroying the pests in the morning.

If a serious insect or disease problem develops, use an organic pest control according to the manufacturer's directions. Some of the safest yet effective organic insect controls include insecticidal soaps, pyrethrum and rotenone. For caterpillar-type pests, use *Bacillus thuringiensis*, or Bt. You will probably have to read the fine print on the container to determine exactly what the active ingredient in the product is. The natural controls for fungal diseases are dusting with sulfur, thinning out growth to improve air circulation, keeping the soil evenly moist and avoiding wetting the foliage when watering. There are no controls for viral diseases; plants must be destroyed. To prevent further occurrences, choose naturally resistant plants and control the aphids or leafhoppers that spread viral diseases.

DIVIDING PERENNIALS

With each passing year, most perennials send out an ever-widening circle of new plants from the roots. As these spread and grow, each perennial not only is competing with others for water, nutrients and space but also with itself. The process of digging up the entire plant, composed of many plantlets, and breaking or cutting these apart is known as division. Dividing perennials is an important part of their upkeep as it serves to rejuvenate an aging plant and to control the size of a plant, and it provides additional plants.

Those perennials that bloom in the spring and summer are usually dug up and divided in late summer or fall, except in areas where winter temperatures are -20° F or colder. In these colder climates, spring division allows plants to have a full growing season to become established. For plants that bloom very early in the spring, wait to divide them until after they finish flowering. Fall-blooming plants are also divided in early spring.

To have the greatest success when dividing, water the plants well several days ahead of time, then try to divide on a cool, cloudy day. When the center of the clump has not died, it is often possible to use a trowel or spade to dig up portions at the outer edges of the plant. Otherwise, dig up the entire clump. Use your hands to divide the clump into smaller sections with two to four buds, sprouts, or stems in each portion. For roots that are tightly bound or thick and carrot-like, use a knife or sharp-edged, heart-shaped Dutch perennial spade to cut the roots apart. When dividing plants in active growth, cut the tops back by half.

Fill in the hole from which the clump was removed with a mixture of top soil, organic matter, and a handful of a fertilizer higher in phosphorous and potassium than nitrogen. If desired, replant one or more of the divisions in this spot, using the others in another part of the garden or sharing them with friends. Keep newly divided plants well watered until established and sending up new growth.

PROPAGATING FROM STEM AND ROOT CUTTINGS

Although far fewer perennials can be propagated from stem cuttings than among trees and shrubs, for the ones can be done by this method (see the Encyclopedia section), it is an efficient way to get additional plants without digging up the parent plant. Spring is usually the best time to take stems cuttings of summer-blooming plants, and early summer is best for plants blooming in the spring and fall.

To take a stem cutting, cut a piece 4 to 8 inches long from the top of the stalk, cutting just below the point where leaves join the stem. Remove the leaves on the lower half of the cutting, moisten this portion, dip in rooting hormone powder, and insert in a pot of moistened soilless seed-starting mix or vermiculite. Insert a label with the name of the plant and date written on it. Cover the pot with a clear plastic bag. Place in a warm spot with bright, indirect light. Mist the cuttings several times a day with water, and keep the potting mix moist. Most cuttings will root in about a month. A good clue that cuttings are rooted is that new growth will start. At that time, transplant to a larger pot or a nursery bed. When plants are large enough, transfer to the garden.

Root cuttings is a method to use when a large number of new plants are wanted from among the perennials that are able to be propagated this way. Best done in early spring, either the entire plant is dug up and all or part of the roots are cut up or a few of the outer roots are cut off without disturbing the rest of the plant.

For plants with fine roots, such as phlox, yarrow, sea holly, spurge, blanketflower, sage and stokesia, cut the roots into pieces 2 inches long. Spread them horizontally over the surface of a tray of moistened potting mix. Cover them with ½ inch more of potting mix. Keep the soil moist until sprouts develop, then transfer the plants to individual pots, caring for them until the plants are large enough to be set into the garden.

For plants with large, fleshy roots, such as bee balm, bleeding heart, baby's breath, poppies and peonies, cut the roots into pieces 2 to 3 inches long, making sure you keep the top ends facing the same direction. Plant these pieces vertically, top ends up, in moistened potting mix with ¼ inch sticking above the soil. Keep the soil moist until sprouts develop, then transfer to individual pots, caring for them until the plants are large enough to be set into the garden.

Digging up and dividing plants in the spring or fall, usually every 3 to 5 years, can rejuvenate them as well as control the amount of space they take up in the garden.

You'll seldom meet an old gardener, at least not in thinking and outlook on life. The anticipation of spring, harbingered by sturdy blooms of hellebores, beckons us into each new year and more adventures in the garden. Maybe this year, we'll finally get that color combination just right. And what about that new poppy we've heard about? Wouldn't it be fun to see what could be done with that no-man's-land on the east side of the house? A garden is never done. Fresh challenges and enticements present themselves around every corner. How could we ask for anything more? Yet we do, over and over, of ourselves and the plants. Sometimes the results are less than the fantasy and our backs ache, but we need only once more to experience the sunshine on our skin, the rain upon parched soil, the scent of Parma violets or lavender, the silken texture of a petal to know that we really wouldn't have it any other way.

Although some perennial foliage or seedheads can add interest to the garden in winter, the rest of the plant debris should be cleaned up in the fall before adding a loose mulch.

FALL CLEANUP AND WINTER PROTECTION

Cleaning up plant debris in the autumn not only makes the garden more pleasant to look at during the winter, it also reduces the places where pests can overwinter. After several frosts have killed plants back to the ground, cut off the dead stems to 2 to 4 inches tall and compost. Woody or evergreen plants are not cut back until the following spring, when winter damage is assessed.

Even when plants are fully hardy in your area, applying a winter mulch is a good insurance policy. This protection is particularly important in keeping shallow-rooted plants from being heaved out of the ground from alternate freezing and thawing of the soil during the winter. For the risk-takers among us, a winter mulch is the main method of keeping marginally hardy plants alive.

Wait to apply the winter mulch until the ground has frozen to a depth of 2 inches and plants are completely dormant. Using a loose, open organic material, such as oak leaves, salt hay, pine boughs, or straw, spread a 3- to 6-inch layer around plants. Use a thicker layer for the more tender perennials. Remove the winter mulch in the spring, gauging both the weather and plant growth carefully, with the mulch around some plants removed earlier than others.

Gardening keeps our hearts young, beckoning us outdoors each day, enticing us with a vast palette of plants and possibilities for beauty and friendship. ❦

ZONE AND FROST MAPS

Zone Map

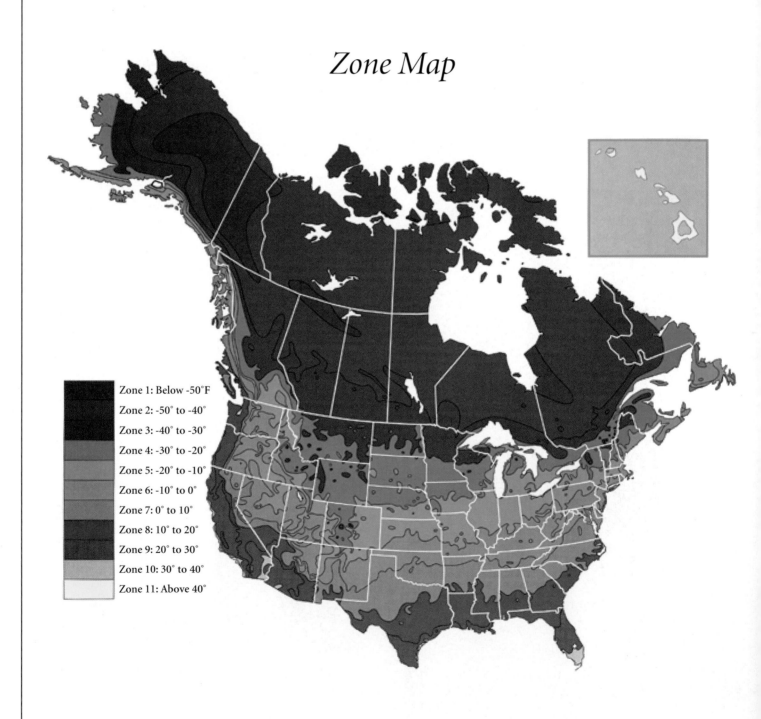

Zone 1: Below -50°F
Zone 2: -50° to -40°
Zone 3: -40° to -30°
Zone 4: -30° to -20°
Zone 5: -20° to -10°
Zone 6: -10° to 0°
Zone 7: 0° to 10°
Zone 8: 10° to 20°
Zone 9: 20° to 30°
Zone 10: 30° to 40°
Zone 11: Above 40°

Average Dates of Last Spring Frost

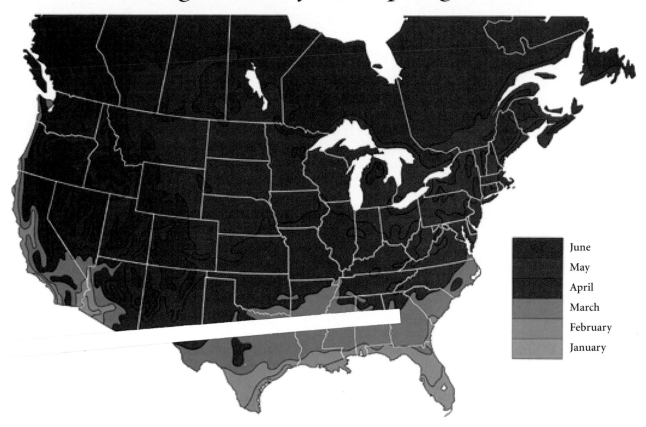

June
May
April
March
February
January

Average Dates of First Fall Frost

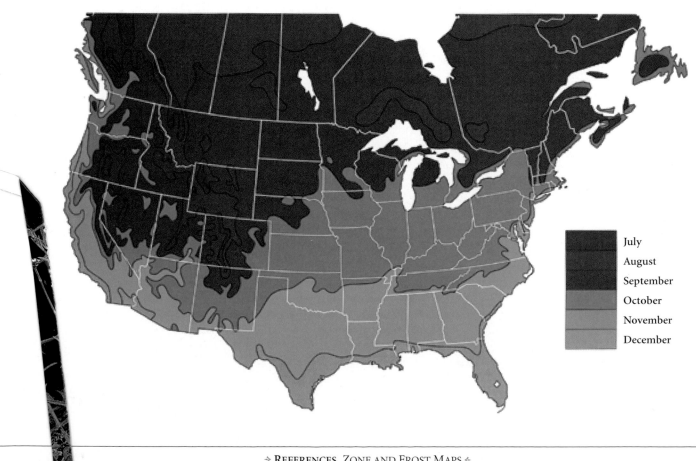

July
August
September
October
November
December

FURTHER READING

GENERAL PERENNIAL REFERENCES

Apps, Darrel, Editor. *Hearst Garden Guides: Perennials.* New York: Hearst Books, 1993.

Armitage, Allan M. *Herbaceous Perennial Plants; A Treatise on Their Identification, Culture, and Garden Attributes.* Athens, Georgia: Varsity Press, 1989.

Clausen, Ruth Rogers and Nicolas H. Ekstrom. *Perennials for American Gardens.* New York: Random House, 1989.

Jellito, Leo and Wilhelm Schacht. *Hardy Herbaceous Perennials, Volumes 1 and 2.* Portland, Oregon: Timber Press, 1990.

Phillips, Roger and Martyn Rix. *Perennials: Volumes 1 and 2.* New York: Random House, 1991.

Thomas, Graham Stuart. *Perennial Garden Plants or The Modern Florilegium.* London & Melbourne: J. M. Dent & Sons Ltd, revised edition 1982.

Woods, Christopher. *Encyclopedia of Perennials; A Gardener's Guide.* New York: Facts On File, 1992.

REFERENCES FOR SPECIFIC PLANTS

Daylilies

Erhardt, Walter. *Hemerocallis Daylilies.* Portland, Oregon: Timber Press: 1992

Hill, Lewis and Nancy. *Daylilies The Perfect Perennial.* Pownal, Vermont; Storey Communications, 1991.

Munson, Jr., R. W. *Hemerocallis The Daylily.* Portland, Oregon: Timber Press, 1989.

Stout, A. B. *Daylilies.* Portland, Oregon: Timber Press, reissued 1986.

Ferns

Foster, F. Gordon. *Ferns to Know and Grow.* Portland, Oregon: Timber Press, 1984.

Jones, David L. *Encyclopedia of Ferns.* Portland, Oregon: Timber Press, 1987.

Mickel, John. *Ferns for American Gardens.* New York: Macmillan Publishing Company, 1994.

Geraniums

Bath, Trevor and Joy Jones. *The Gardener's Guide to Growing Hardy Geraniums.* Portland, Oregon: Timber Press, 1994.

Yeo, Peter F. *Hardy Geraniums.* Portland, Oregon: Timber Press, 1985.

Grasses

Darke, Rick, Consulting Editor. *Manual of Grasses.* Portland, Oregon: Timber Press, 1995.

Greenlee, John. *The Encyclopedia of Ornamental Grasses.* Emmaus, Pennsylvania: Rodale Press, 1992.

Ottesen, Carole. *Ornamental Grasses: The Amber Wave.* New York: McGraw-Hill, 1989.

Hellebores

Rice, Graham and Elizabeth Strangman. *The Gardener's Guide to Growing Hellebores.* Portland, Oregon: Timber Press, 1993.

Hostas

Aden, Paul, Editor. *The Hosta Book.* Portland, Oregon: Timber Press, 1988.

Grenfell, Diana. *The Gardener's Guide to Growing Hostas.* Portland, Oregon: Timber Press, 1996.

Schmid, W. George. *The Genus Hosta.* Portland, Oregon: Timber Press, 1992.

Iris

Glasgow, Karen. *Irises: A Practical Garden Guide.* Portland, Oregon: Timber Press, 1996.

Kohlein, Fritz. *Iris.* Portland, Oregon: Timber Press, 1981.

McEwen, Currier. *The Siberian Irises.* Portland, Oregon: Timber Press, 1996.

Stebbings, Geoff. *The Gardener's Guide to Growing Irises.* Portland, Oregon: Timber Press, 1997.

Peonies

Harding, Alice. *The Peony.* Portland, Oregon: Timber Press, reissued 1993.

Page, Martin. *The Gardener's Guide to Growing Peonies.* Portland, Oregon: Timber Press, 1997.

Rogers, Allan. *Peonies*. Portland, Oregon: Timber Press, 1995.

Pinks

Bird, Richard. *Border Pinks*. Portland, Oregon: Timber Press, 1994.

Galbally, John with Eileen Galbally. *Carnations and Pinks for Garden and Greenhouse:*

Their True History and Complete Cultivation. Portland, Oregon: Timber Press, 1997.

Poppies

Grey-Wilson, Christopher. *Poppies The Poppy Family in the Wild and in Cultivation.*

Portland, Oregon: Timber Press, 1993.

Primroses

Halda, Josef. *The Genus Primula in Cultivation and the Wild.* Englewood, Colorado: Tethys Books, 1992.

Richards, John. *Primula*. Portland, Oregon: Timber Press, 1993.

Swindells, Philip. *A Plantsman's Guide to Primulas.* New York: Sterling Publishing, 1991.

Salvias

Clebsch, Betsy. *A Book of Salvias.* Portland, Oregon: Timber Press, 1997.

Trilliums

Case, Jr., Frederick W. and Roberta B. Case. *Trilliums*. Portland, Oregon: 1997.

REFERENCES FOR SPECIFIC TYPES OR ASPECTS OF PERENNIAL GARDENING

Bog or Wet-Site Gardens

Chatto, Beth. *The Damp Garden.* Portland, Oregon: Timber Press, 1996.

Butterfly and Bird Gardens

Arbuckle, Nancy and Cedric Crocker, Project Editors. *How to Attract Hummingbirds and Butterflies.* San Ramon, California: Ortho Books, 1991.

Ernst, Ruth Shaw. *The Naturalist's Garden: Bring Your Yard to Life with Plants That Attract Wildlife.* Emmaus, Pennsylvania: Rodale Press, 1987.

Lewis, Alcinda, Guest Editor. *Butterfly Gardens: Luring Nature's Loveliest Pollinators to Your Yard.* Brooklyn, New York: Brooklyn Botanic Garden, #143, 1995.

Mahnken, Jan. *Hosting the Birds: How to Attract Birds to Nest In Your Yard.* Pownal, Vermont: Storey Communications, 1989.

Merilees, William. *Attracting Backyard Wildlife.* Stillwater, Minnesota: Voyageur Press, 1989.

Sedenko, Jerry. *The Butterfly Garden: Creating Beautiful Gardens to Attract Butterflies.* New York: Villard Books, 1991.

Smith, Geoffrey. *The Joy of Wildlife Gardening.* North Pomfret, Vermont: Trafalgar Books: 1990.

Stokes, Donald and Lillian and Ernest Williams. *The Butterfly Book: An Easy Guide to Butterfly Gardening, Identification and Behavior.* Boston: Little, Brown, 1991.

The Xerces Society in Association with the Smithsonian Institution. *Butterfly Gardening.* San Francisco: Sierra Club Books, 1990.

Color and the Garden

Brown, Deni. *Alba: The Book of White Flowers.* Portland, Oregon: Timber Press, 1989.

Cox, Jeff and Marilyn. *The Perennial Garden: Color Harmonies Through the Seasons.*
Emmaus, Pennsylvania: Rodale Press, 1985.

Jekyll, Gertude. *Colour in the Flower Garden.* Portland, Oregon: Timber Press, reissued 1994.

Keen, Mary. *Gardening with Color.* New York: Random House, 1991.

Kohlein, Fritz and Peter Menzel. *Color Encyclopedia of Garden Plants and Habitats.* Portland, Oregon: Timber Press, 1994.

Wilder, Louise Beebe. *Color in My Garden: An American Gardener's Palette.* New York: Atlantic Monthly, reissued 1990.

Ziegler, Catherine. *The Harmonious Garden: Color, Form, and Texture.* Portland, Oregon: Timber Press, 1996.

Cottage Gardens

Fish, Margery. *Cottage Garden Flowers.* Winchester, Massachusetts: Faber & Faber, 1980.

Gardner, Jo Ann. *The Heirloom Garden: Selecting and Growing Over 300 Old-fashioned Ornamentals.* Pownal, Vermont: Storey Communications, 1992.

Genders, Roy. *The Cottage Garden and Old-fashioned Flowers.* New York: Viking Penguin, 1987.

Hamilton, Geoff. *Cottage Gardens.* London: BBC Books, 1995.

Haskell, Ruth Rohde, Guest Editor. *American Cottage Gardens.* Brooklyn, New York: Brooklyn Botanic Garden Handbook #123, 1990.

Lloyd, Christopher and Richard Bird. *The Cottage Garden.* New York: Prentice-Hall, 1990.

Phillips, Sue. *Creating A Cottage Garden.* New York: Grove Weidenfeld, 1990.

Swindells, Philip. *Cottage Gardening in Town and Country.* New York: Sterling, 1991.

Drought-Tolerant Gardens

Chatto, Beth. *The Dry Garden.* Portland, Oregon: Timber Press, 1996.

Walters, James E. and Balbir Backhaus. *Shade and Color with Water-Conserving Plants.* Portland, Oregon: Timber Press, 1992.

Fragrant Gardens:

Bonar, Ann. *Gardening for Fragrance.* New York: Sterling, 1991

Genders, Roy. *Scented Flora of the World.* New York: St. Martin's Press, 1977.

Lacey, Stephen. *Scent in Your Garden.* Boston: Little, Brown, 1991.

Reddell, Rayford and Robert Galyean. *Growing Fragrant Plants.* New York: HarperCollins, 1989.

Rohde, Eleanour Sinclair. *The Scented Garden.* London: The Medici Society, reissued 1989.

Sanecki, Kay. *The Fragrant Garden.* London: Trafalgar Square, 1981.

Squire, David and Jane Newdick. *The Scented Garden.* Emmaus, Pennsylvania, 1988.

Taylor, Jane. *Fragrant Gardens: Gardening by Design.* New York: Sterling, 1987.

Verey, Rosemary. *The Scented Garden: Choosing, Growing, Using the Plants That Bring Fragrance to Your Life, Your Home and Your Table.* New York: Van Nostrand Reinhold, 1981.

Wilder, Louise Beebe. *The Fragrant Path: A Book About Sweet-scented Flowers and Leaves.* New York: Macmillan Publishing, reissued 1990.

Wilson, Helen Van Pelt and Leonie Bell. *The Fragrant Year: Scented Plants for Your Garden and Your Home.* New York: Barrows, 1967.

Groundcovers

Thomas, Graham Stuart. *Plants for Ground-Cover.* Portland, Oregon: Timber Press, 1970.

Wyman, Donald. *Ground Cover Plants.* New York: Macmillan, 1970.

Native Plant Gardens

Art, Henry A. *A Garden of Wildflowers: 101 Native Species and How To Grow Them.* Pownal, Vermont: Storey Communications, 1986.

Ferreniea, Viki. *Wildflowers in Your Garden: A Gardener's Guide.* New York: Random House, 1993.

Jones, Jr., Samuel B. and Leonard E. Foote. *Gardening with Native Wild Flowers.* Portland, Oregon: Timber Press, 1991.

Martin, Laura C. *The Wildflower Meadow Book: A Gardener's Guide.* Chester, Connecticut: Globe Pequot, 1986.

Phillips, Harry R. *Growing and Propagating Wildflowers.* Chapel Hill, North Carolina: University of North Carolina Press, 1985.

Rock Gardens

Ferguson, Katherine. *Harrowsmith Gardener's Guide to Rock Gardens.* Charlotte, Vermont: Camden House, 1988.

Foster, H. Lincoln. *Rock Gardening A Guide to Growing Alpine and Other Wildflowers in the American Garden.* Portland, Oregon: Timber Press, 1968.

Foster, H. Lincoln and Laura Louise. *Cuttings from a Rock Garden.* Portland, Oregon: Timber Press, 1997.

Ingwerson, Will. *Alpines.* Portland, Oregon: Timber Press, 1991.

Innes, Clive. *Alpines: The Illustrated Dictionary.* Portland, Oregon: Timber Press, 1995.

Shade Gardens

Druse, Ken. *The Natural Shade Garden.* New York: Clarkson, Potter, 1992.

Fish, Margery. *Gardening in the Shade.* Winchester, Massachusetts: Faber & Faber, 1984.

Morse, Harriet K. *Gardening in the Shade.* Portland, Oregon: Timber Press, reissued 1962.

Schenk, George. *The Complete Shade Gardener.* Boston: Houghton Mifflin, 1984.

Books on Perennial Garden Design and History

Chatto, Beth. *The Green Tapestry: Choosing and Growing the Best Perennial Plants for Your Garden.* New York: Simon & Schuser, 1989.

Elliott, Jack. *The Smaller Perennials: A Comprehensive A-Z.* Portland, Oregon: Timber Press, 1997.

Fish, Margery. *We Made A Garden.* Portland, Oregon: Timber Press, reissued 1995.

Harper, Pamela. *Designing with Perennials.* New York: Macmillan, 1991.

Hill, Lewis and Nancy. *Successful Perennial Gardening: A Practical Guide.* Pownal, Vermont: Storey Communications, 1988.

Hudak, Joseph. *Gardening with Perennials Month by Month.* Portland, Oregon: Timber Press, second edition 1993.

Lovejoy, Ann. *The American Mixed Border: Gardens for All Seasons.* New York: Macmillan, 1993.

McGourty, Frederick. *The Perennial Gardener.* Boston: Houghton Mifflin, 1989.

Rice, Graham. *Hardy Perennials.* Portland, Oregon: Timber Press, 1995.

Rice, Graham. *Plants for Problem Spaces.* Portland, Oregon: Timber Press, 1988.

Robinson, William. *The English Garden.* Portland, Oregon: Timber Press, reissued 1984.

Robinson, William. *The Wild Garden.* Portland, Oregon: Timber Press, reissued 1994.

Smith, Mary Riley. *The Front Garden: New Approaches to Landscape Design.* Boston: Houghton Mifflin, 1991.

Williamson, John. *Perennial Gardens: A Practical Guide to Home Landscaping.* Chester, Connecticut: Globe Pequot, 1992.

Books on Propagation

Hill, Lewis. *Secrets of Plant Propagation.* Pownal, Vermont:

Storey Communications, 1985.
Lloyd, Christopher and Graham Rice. *Garden Flowers from Seed.* Portland, Oregon: Timber Press, 1994.
Thompson, Peter. *Creative Propagation: A Grower's Guide.* Portland, Oregon: Timber Press, 1992.

Botanizing for Perennial Gardeners
Capon, Brian. *Botany for Gardeners.* Portland, Oregon: Timber Press, 1990.
Coombes, Allen J. *Dictionary of Plant Names.* Portland, Oregon: Timber Press, 1985.
Stearn, William T. *Botanical Latin.* Portland, Oregon: Timber Press, fourth edition, 1992.

Books on Organic Gardening
Bradshaw, Fern and Barbara Ellis, Editors. *Rodale's All New Encyclopedia of Organic Gardening: The Indispensable Resource for Every Gardener.* Emmaus, Pennsylvania: Rodale Press, 1992.
Cox, Jeff with the Editors of Rodale Garden Books. *Your Organic Garden.* Emmaus, Pennsylvania: Rodale Press, 1994.
Hamilton, Geoff. *The Organic Garden Book: The Complete Guide to Growing Flowers, Fruits, and Vegetables Naturally.* London, New York: Dorling Kindersley, 1993.

Books You Shouldn't Have To Live Without
Barton, Barbara J. *Gardening by Mail: A Source Book.* Boston: Houghton Mifflin, fourth edition, 1994.
Isaacson, Richard T. *The Andersen Horticultural Library's Source List of Plants and Seeds: A Completely Revised Listing of 1993-96 Catalogues.* Chanhassen, Minnesota: Andersen Horticultural Library, fourth edition, 1996.
Wyman, Donald. *The Gardening Encyclopedia.* New York: Macmillan, updated edition, 1987.

APPENDIX -
PLANT SOCIETIES

Plant and gardening societies offer gardeners an opportunity to learn more about gardening in general and specific plants in detail, both from publications and from spending time with other gardeners.

The American Dianthus Society
Rand B. Lee, President
P. O. Box 22232
Santa Fe, NM 87502-2232
randbear@nets.com
Annual Dues $15

American Fern Society
Dr. Richard Hauk
456 McGill Place
Atlanta, GA 30312
Annual dues $8

American Hemerocallis Society
Elly Launius, Secretary
1454 Rebel Drive
Jackson, MS 39211
Annual dues $18

American Horticultural Society
Alexandria, VA 22308-1300
oliverahs@aol.com
Annual dues $35

American Hosta Society
Robyn Duback
7802 NE 63rd Street
Vancouver, WA 98662
giboshiman@aol.com
Annual dues $19

American Iris Society
Marilyn R. Harlow,
    Membership Secretary
P. O. Box 8455
San Jose, CA 95155-8455
103262.1512@compuserve.com
Annual dues $18
Sections of AIS include:
    Dwarf Iris Society of America
    Historic Iris Preservation Society
    Louisiana Iris Society of America
    The Reblooming Iris Society

The Society for Japanese Irises
Society for Pacific Native Iris
Society for Siberian Irises
Species Iris Group of North America
Spuria Iris Society

American Penstemon Society
Ann W. Bartlett,
    Membership Secretary
1569 South Holland Court
Lakewood, CO 80232
Annual dues $10

American Peony Society
Greta Kessenich
250 Interlachen Road
Hopkins, MN 55343
Annual dues $7.50

American Primrose, Primula &
    Auricula Society
Addaline W. Robinson
9705 SE Spring Crest Drive
Portland, OR 97225
Annual dues $20

American Rock Garden Society
P. O. Box 67
Millwood, NY 10546
Annual dues $25

Cottage Garden Society
5 Nixon Close, Thornhill
Dewsbury, West Yorkshire
England WR12 OJA
Annual dues $20

The Flower and Herb Exchange
Diane Whealy
3076 North Winn Road
Decorah, IA 52101
Annual dues $5

Hardy Fern Foundation
P. O. Box 166
Medina, WA 98039-0166
Annual dues $20

The Hardy Plant Society
Mrs. Pam Adams
Little Orchard, Great Comberton
Pershore, Worcestershire
England WR10 3DP

Hardy Plant Society of Oregon
Julie Maudlin, Membership Chair
2148 Summit Drive
Lake Oswego, OR 97034
Annual dues $20

International Violet Association
Elaine Kudela
8604 Main Road
Berlin Heights, OH 44814-9620
Annual dues $15

Los Angeles International Fern Society
P. O. Box 90943
Pasadena, CA 91109-0943
Annual dues $20

National Chrysanthemum Society
Galen L. Goss
10107 Homar Pond Drive
Fairfax Station, VA 22039-1650
Annual dues $12.50

Northwest Perennial Alliance
Ann Bucher, NPA Chair
P. O. Box 45574, University Station
Seattle, WA 98145
Annual dues $15

INDEX

✿